The Corrs:
Their Music, Their Lives,
Their Legacy

D1385654

Todd R. Nicholls

BLACKHALL
Publishing

This book was typeset by Artwerk Limited for

Blackhall Publishing,
27 Carysfort Avenue, Blackrock,
Co. Dublin,
Ireland.

Email: blackhall@eircom.net
Website: www.blackhallpublishing.com

A catalogue record for this book is available from the British Library

ISBN: 1 842180 31 2

Printed in Ireland by
ColourBooks Ltd

Dedication

This book is dedicated to the Cosgraves — *Mo Chlann Éireannach.*

Contents

Acknowledgements

In writing any book there are numerous people who help and inspire, some without even knowing it. I would first of all like to thank Brian Hallinan for his superb editing and for his unfailing support and enthusiasm back in Wellington, New Zealand. Thank you also to Laura Watson for putting up with his long absences during those crucial weeks.

A big thank you to the Cosgrave family in Dublin, especially Tom, for everything they did in helping with the preparation of this book. Daniel Lindberg in Sweden ably and efficiently provided information throughout the research period and deserves thanks, as do Cormac Fox and Mikko Hanninen for giving their thoughts on The Corrs.

Thank you to David and Matthew McKechnie for putting up with a grumpy flatmate in the last few months.

Thank you to Blackhall Publishing in Dublin for their encouragement and assistance and to Tony Mason as well. Various journalists in Ireland also helped and especially deserving of thanks are Anne Campbell, Michael Ross, Ian Coognan, Margaret Roddy and Kevin Courtney. Thank you to Niall Carson for the great job he did with the photographs.

Thank you also to the countless people who gave of their time to be interviewed, many of whom do not wish to be named. This list — including people in Dundalk, Dublin, Belfast, England, the USA, Australia and New Zealand — is too long to publish, but you know who you are.

Various publications gave their permission to use quotes and illustrations and deserve thanks. They include the *Argus*, *Belfast Telegraph*, *Daily Express*, *Dundalk Democrat*, *Q Magazine*, *Heat*, *Daily Mirror*, *Drum Magazine*, *Highlife*, *Hot Press*, *Irish Echo*, *Sunday Independent*, *Christchurch Press*, *Mojo Magazine*, *Irish Independent*, *Sunday Times*, *Irish News*, *RTÉ Guide*, *The Irish Times*, *The Times*, *Sydney Morning Herald*, *Sun* and *Man Magazine*.

Thank you also to the various authors and publishers who allowed their work to be quoted.

This is a Sumner Ink! Project.

About Sumner Ink!

New Zealander Todd R. Nicholls (30) has been a journalist and writer for seven years. He holds a BA (Hons) and an MA from Canterbury University in politics and journalism and a Diploma in Journalism from that same institution. He also holds a Bachelor of Legal Science from Queen's University in Belfast. He has worked for various newspapers and magazines in New Zealand and as a press secretary in the New Zealand Parliament. In Ireland he has worked for *The Irish Times, Ireland on Sunday* and *The Irish News*. This is his third book. With Brian Hallinan he is the founder of Sumner Ink!, a partnership designed to promote the partners' writing interests.

New Zealander Brian Hallinan has collaborated with Todd R. Nicholls on a number of writing projects since they met while studying political science at the University of Canterbury. He holds a BA (Hons) and an MA from that institution. Brian has worked as an advisor in the New Zealand Department of Labour and Department of Prime Minister and Cabinet, and is presently an analyst with the Treasury. Brian co-founded Sumner Ink! and helped to edit this book.

Todd Nicholls, 2001

CHAPTER 1

A Night of Dreams

Andrea Corr moves like a cat from the back of London's Royal Albert Hall. Having just belted out a passionate rendition of 'Queen of Hollywood', perhaps her own personal theme song, she speaks with girlish innocence to the 5,500 Londoners who have assembled to spend St Patrick's Day 1998 with The Corrs.

In many respects it's a strange place for The Corrs to be on Ireland's national day. Dublin would have been more appropriate, although the smooth pop and Irish melodies of The Corrs had already conquered their home audience and everyone knew that Britain was the *real* market for the band to make an impact. And what better night for The Corrs to try and make a nation-wide splash than St Patrick's Day?

In their constant struggle to be overwhelmingly popular in the British market, the band, their management and their record company certainly thought that this was an ideal opportunity. 'We weren't selling enough albums or getting enough attention in the UK ... so we thought about what we could do to get everyone's attention,' said Andrea in the months after the concert. 'We realised there was only one night a year we could legitimately control the airwaves — St Patrick's night. So we booked out the Albert Hall and managed to get Radio One to broadcast the gig live for an Irish St Patrick's night special. Even VH-1 did a big special series surrounding the build-up to the concert. It was like a masterstroke. It meant that for one night we were the talk of Britain and Ireland, for the first time we were on mainstream radio and performing at one of the world's most prestigious venues.'

The opportunity to strut their stuff on the British stage had arisen for The Corrs.

*   *   *   *

Andrea Corr is striking. Dark, with penetrating but smiling eyes, and a smile that radiates star quality, this evening the 24-year-old wears a black one piece that is tight fitting and in its simplicity highlights her girlishness. Reflecting her Catholic upbringing, she wears a cross around her neck. She appears at home in front of the microphone, as if she had been born to perform.

She speaks to the crowd in a tone that you would wish of the girl next door: mild, wholesome, real. Given the effort she has put into the last song she could be excused for being tired. 'There is something very special we are going to do now,' she says innocently, as if the crowd consisted of just her parents and she was putting on her own individual pantomime. 'There is a Fleetwood Mac revisited album that is coming out later this year and we have been fortunate enough to be able to cover one of their tracks, one of our favourite tracks because there are so many ... we are doing "Dreams" on this album and it's called *Legacy*. So not only is it special that it's St Patrick's night, that we are here, that we are going to play this Fleetwood Mac song, [but] that we have a very special guest on the stage with us tonight ... please welcome Mick Fleetwood.'

Fleetwood, wearing a red and gold waistcoat, white shirt and black trousers, stands from his already set position behind the drums to acknowledge the crowd. The welcome he gets suggests his own band have many fans in the audience tonight, perhaps even more than The Corrs themselves. Before the crowd has the opportunity to become accustomed to the mighty presence of Fleetwood, the beautiful strains of Sharon Corr's violin fill the Royal Albert Hall. Sharon, the classically trained musician in the family, is also classically beautiful and, to the outsider, slightly distanced. Possessing dark, haunting and even mystical Irish eyes, tonight she seems to be working hard. Not only does she play the violin with virtuous gusto, she is also prominent on backing vocals. And like a big sister should, she casts an occasional watchful eye over the antics of her younger sibling on lead vocals.

Distinguishing The Corrs' version of 'Dreams' from Fleetwood Mac's, the strains of the violin echo around the hall and introduce almost perfectly the other instruments, including the booming drums of Fleetwood in behind. The moment's uniqueness is assisted by the crowd's realisation that this great song, with lyrics touching the heart of any true romantic, has now moved from one generation to the next and not dated at all. Stevie Nicks, the song's author, would have been proud:

> *Now here you are again,*
> *you say you want your freedom,*
> *well who am I to keep you down?*
> *It's only right that you should play the way you feel it,*
> *but listen carefully to the sound,*
> *of your loneliness ...*

Andrea stands neatly behind the microphone, giving these meaningful lyrics more respectful attention than she would her own. After all, to be sung properly each word needs to be realised, understood and communicated. Especially when you have one of the founders of Fleetwood Mac starting to pump on the drums behind you. And pumping is what Mick Fleetwood is aiming to do. Slowly building into the song, his head is focused solely on the beat and on the passion of the 1977 classic.

While Fleetwood helps rock the Royal Albert Hall, giving The Corrs impetus, legitimacy and the benefit of his energy and brute strength on the drums, birthday girl Caroline Corr sits between her sister Andrea and brother Jim, adding backing vocals and beats from the traditional Irish instrument, the *bodhrán*. Described by various music journalists as the Corr girl most likely to be comfortable going out for a night with the boys, she too is stunning to look at, if somewhat overshadowed by her two sisters. Tonight she looks slightly awkward, shy even, sitting in front, although the effect closes the gap at the front of the stage and the band appears stronger as a result. The sum is greater than each individual part. Caroline's time in the spotlight will come on the next song, the impressive 'Haste to the Wedding', when she goes head-to-head with Fleetwood, thrashing the drums in spirited fashion.

Right on the edge, and purposefully letting his sisters get the attention, Jim Corr plays guitar with ease and almost a fatalistic spirit. Jim, the oldest and most experienced musician of the family, is also the band member perhaps most aware of the magic being created. It is as if he is somewhat removed from what is being undertaken, taking time to enjoy the thrill of something special after years of struggle on the music circuit. Aged 34, despite not stating it, he is the consummate big brother. Not only does he look out for his sisters to his right, but he also seems to have the future goals of the band written on the back of his hand. This is an important night in fulfilling his and the band's destiny. Talented, he was the first Corr to choose music as a career, playing in various semi-professional and professional bands. Although a fine producer in his own right, tonight he seems to be just enjoying the thrill of being part of an occasion where magic is being created and natural talents are flowing:

> Now here I go again,
> I see the crystal visions,
> I keep my visions to myself ...

Andrea looks seductively away from the audience as she does from time to time on songs, flirting with both the camera and the crowd, realising the power of fantasy and image. The audience, both at the hall and on television, becomes part of her spell. With the energy of Fleetwood on drums, the pace of the song is perfect — Andrea's vocals giving the words special meaning. Fleetwood is giving The Corrs' performance energy and they are responding to his experience and, perhaps subconsciously, looking for approval from one of the greats of British pop culture. For one of the few times in the concert The Corrs really start to rock and the crowd realises something special is happening.

The pace rises as Andrea fingers the tin whistle, Sharon lets the violin almost have a mind of its own, Caroline follows with in-time strums and Fleetwood is almost thumping holes in his drum kit. The tempo rises further still, the bass of Keith Duffy and the backing vocals of Sharon and Caroline giving the band almost perfect musical symmetry. Andrea, responding to the pace and the passion of the song's underlying theme and the committed work of her siblings, Fleetwood and backing musicians, rides the moment. She sings the words 'You will know' with particular passion and feeling. It is a magical moment and something fully appreciated by a crowd with its fair share of British stiff upper lips.

The Corrs and Fleetwood get the recognition they deserve after producing one truly memorable effort, the applause of the audience going on for longer than the norm. It was more than just a show of respect. Something special, something unique has happened. Although both the band and the crowd have appreciated the magic of the music, perhaps even The Corrs themselves don't realise the impact this performance will eventually have. Fleetwood and the big-band atmosphere that he has helped inspire have thrust The Corrs into the spotlight. 'After that, everyone wanted to talk to us and Radio One decided that they would play our new song 'Dreams'. I can honestly say that St Patrick's night was the biggest milestone in our history so far,' said Andrea at the time. 'I wouldn't have minded if we had been given the chance to prove ourselves and then failed, but I was determined that we wouldn't give up without being given a fair go.'

Despite wide acclaim and the eventual release of the remixed 'Dreams', the night was also memorable for the more traditional fan base of The Corrs: the performances of the haunting 'Haste to the Wedding' and the traditional 'Toss the Feathers' being particular highlights. Although the crowd also got to their feet and rocked to the catchy 'So Young' — played as the first song in the encore — it was 'Dreams' that caught the imagination of an unsuspecting British public. Later that night, millions tuned in to the BBC in Britain and saw the concert in its entirety and this new version of 'Dreams'. Where in the past The Corrs had had a solid following — especially in Ireland, Australia and South East Asia — they were now being fully paraded in Britain on this most Irish of nights. As the cliché goes, all Irish eyes were smiling. The concert and the one-night domination of the British airwaves (the concert was also played on Radio One) saw The Corrs eventually win a widespread middle-of-the-road following in Britain.

* * * *

According to some media reports, the careers of Jim, Sharon, Caroline and Andrea Corr are almost fairytale-like. Four siblings from a small Irish town, with a passion for music almost bred into them, decide to form a band to help them win parts in a movie. They all look good and although only one of them is cast in a reasonable part, they meet a man who wants to manage them and shape their careers. He's ambitious, visionary, a dreamer perhaps.

They start to write and produce music that reflects the environment where they grew up. They work night and day to create the sound that they know they are capable of. Although turned down by numerous record companies, they continue to work industriously and get their big break when Jean Kennedy Smith, the United States ambassador to Ireland, sees them play. The good impression helps get them to the USA where they play at the Kennedy Library in Boston. Later they almost force themselves and their music on legendary producer David Foster. He is impressed with their looks and is convinced they can play. They get a record deal straight away.

The band and its management practically sell their first album door to door. It is well received in Ireland and Australia and various other parts of the world but it fails to make a significant impact in Britain or the USA. Their second album is written, produced and marketed with the aim of producing sure-fire hits. It fails to make an initial impact but eventually they get a big break. A cover of 'Dreams' is remixed and is well received. Their second album is re-released with a series of remixes included.

They finally achieve the sort of success they have been looking for in Britain, their second album selling more copies in 1998 than any other. Their first album also shifts vast quantities now that they have broad appeal. They also become part of a renaissance in Irish music and culture that sees Irish acts become accepted in Britain, Europe and further afield. They become amongst the most obvious examples of the supposed Celtic Tiger — Ireland's booming economy — in action.

Their record company suggests that they do an acoustic album of their original works, some new songs and three covers. It is quickly produced, but sells well and further expands their audience base.

Perhaps their biggest goal remains becoming successful in the USA. Their third album is written, produced and marketed with that aim in mind. They step up their publicity campaign there in an effort to make their mark. On the back of the success of their second album, their third original album again sells substantial quantities in Britain, Europe, Asia and Australasia. Despite this, critics suggest The Corrs have placed too much emphasis on becoming commercially successful. That, as a result, their music has lost its essential soul and heart. That they have become better known for their looks and style than for their music. That somewhere in the Pepsi advertisements, the fashion shoots and the magazine layouts they have lost direction in an industry quick to exploit any talent that can make money.

On the face of it the story of The Corrs is a rag to riches tale. They have come from relatively humble origins to be one of the hottest acts in the Western music markets today. Yet, to date, the story of their rise to fame has not been told in any serious fashion. This book is *not* The Corrs' story. The band will write that themselves and it will play a major part in putting their success into context. Although they will undoubtedly be the best placed to write about their careers, they will almost certainly be the least qualified to assess them. In short, to date The Corrs have not received serious analysis. This book seeks to redress that.

CHAPTER 2

Thanks Be To Ireland

I think the music reflects something about the Irish people as a whole. The Irish have a lot of hope, despite all the troubles they've gone through over the years, they've always known how to laugh and have fun. That's where the tradition of up-tempo Irish music and dancing comes from. But there's that mystical, haunting sound as well, which I think reflects the environment. I mean, when you get up first thing in the morning, there is literally a mist surrounding everything. Our music is influenced by our environment, and we play what we feel.

Sharon Corr

Is it remarkable that four siblings from Dundalk, a small town not far from one of the world's most well-publicised divided societies, can sell well over twenty million albums worldwide? Is it remarkable that four siblings with little formal music training can appear on the covers of numerous magazines around the world and have more words written about them than some heads of state? Is it remarkable that four siblings from an unremarkable family have made a bigger splash in the music market than what even *they* thought possible?

On the face of it, it is remarkable. The Corrs have established themselves as a brand that has become famous almost the world over. They have provided image-makers with a product that sells instantly, a sound, perhaps, that is clearly recognisable. In many respects they are a phenomenon.

From a financial point of view The Corrs' have been incredibly successful. They have achieved almost universal success. They have not produced an album that has not sold well and have reached the stage in their careers where they could release virtually anything and it would sell. Although they have yet to reach the 30–35 million sales bracket that establishes an act as being at the top of its profession commercially, like Shania Twain or Celine Dion, The Corrs have sold enough records to be safely regarded as being a brand and not just as a group of musicians. As Sir Richard Branson, the founder of Virgin

Music, has written, the aim of any record label is to establish brand loyalty to their artist:

> One of the things every record company aims for is to transform its brands into household names. When a band has reached a certain stature it is more like a brand name and people start buying its new albums on faith. Although two bad albums will dent almost any star's career, once you have built up a following it is quite easy to predict how many copies the next record will sell. New artists have a high failure rate, but once they have crossed a threshold they have far greater potential for growth than books or films, or indeed almost anything else I can think of.

That is exactly what has happened with The Corrs. Their *Unplugged* album and their third original album, *In Blue*, both sold well, thanks to in part the brand loyalty that The Corrs had established worldwide with *Forgiven Not Forgotten* and *Talk on Corners*.

*   *   *   *

I can't say that The Corrs were the reason why I came to Ireland. That would be too simplistic and far too obliging. What I would say, however, is that when it came to selling the Emerald Isle, they did a pretty good job in pointing me in the right direction.

Towards the end of 1998 the opportunity to leave New Zealand's distant shores for a time became too appealing to ignore. I had always wanted to travel — being a New Zealander it is almost bred into you that you must at some stage take the plunge and have a look overseas. So there I was at the end of 1998, at the ripe old age of 27, with no commitments, enough money to at least get me to the other side of the world and a little bored with the economic depression gripping New Zealand.

But where should I go? I had always had a love affair with everything American, but I had been there before and it was difficult to get a work permit. Everyone was going to Britain and, although I felt a twinge of cultural association, it seemed big and daunting. I dreamed about spending a year in Italy before waking up to the reality that they all spoke Italian and I didn't. My younger brother had spent time in Belfast and had fallen in love with Dublin and Ireland on his travels there. When I was granted a work permit I made up my mind. It was Ireland where I would be heading.

*   *   *   *

As much as anything else, The Corrs are a product of their environment. The true Corrs sound is essentially an Irish sound, comprising both the proud traditional musical tradition and the changing landscape of Irish society.

The children of Gerry and Jean Corr grew up in an Ireland that had opened its shutters from the internal retrospection that had prevailed since the Republic of Ireland was founded in 1922. A child growing up in Ireland in the 1970s and 1980s was freer from the shackles of Church, State and colonial repression that had affected earlier generations. It is easy to forget that the Dublin and Ireland of the late twentieth and early twenty-first centuries was not necessarily the Dublin and Ireland of the majority of the twentieth century. As house prices continued to rise at an alarming rate, social commentators talked relentlessly about the Celtic Tiger and Ireland's place in the world. The days of hardship in Ireland appeared over as a new and vibrant economy heralded new prosperity. To many, Dublin symbolised this new and exciting environment. As American tourists rushed to buy cheap and over-priced Irish memorabilia and took trips on big, slow buses, the irony was obvious: Dublin had become as international as any other large city. In a sense these tourists were buying a relic of Ireland's past.

*   *   *   *

The Corrs came to New Zealand in February 1998, and yet I was not rushing out to buy a ticket to see them. In fact, they came and went and I didn't even bother going to the concert, as I didn't know who they were. For someone who had paid to see Joshua Kadison a year or two before, I now look back in horror. The Christchurch Press *certainly did its part in advertising that the band was in town: they splashed the good-looking foursome across the front page one Saturday morning, with a story on the inside, while after the concert they published a rather flattering review. The Corrs' journey to New Zealand was also notable for the concert in Auckland that was played in a city with large electricity shortages. The next day the band shot the video for 'What Can I Do' north of Auckland. The New Zealand scenery appeared to agree with them.*

*   *   *   *

There were numerous signs throughout Irish society, some more obvious than others, that Ireland had embraced the world marketplace with more passion than could have been expected. What in days gone by could have passed for cultural cringe was a case of the Irish tuning into what the world was tuning into.

In the middle of 1999 the MTV Awards arrived in Dublin in an almighty blaze of publicity and hype. Puff Daddy, Britney Spears and

The Corrs were on the playlist. Children spent hours outside hotels trying to get glimpses of their heroes, while a few select stores closed so that American stars could shop in privacy. There was a desire by the Irish to make a good impression on their overseas visitors. When the assembled European media, which had been corralled into a room behind the main stage, were given the opportunity to ask questions of each award winner, the most frequent questions of the night were along the lines of 'Are you enjoying Ireland?' followed swiftly by 'Why are you so wonderful?'

Brian Boyd in *The Irish Times* wrote that 'the awards were organised right down to the last ad-lib. They are a corporate, sales-boosting, clap-ourselves-on-the-back event. And judging by last night's performance, new levels of banality were scaled ... Britney Spears told us how 'happy and surprised' she was to win an award, sentiments echoed by every other act/solo performer who won a gong. And still they kept on asking them "Are you enjoying Ireland?", maybe in the forlorn hope that one of the acts would say "No, it's an awful dump".'

This was the perfect example of modern Ireland — embracing the world and yet still wondering what the world thought of it. Big enough to stand up but still concerned about being knocked down again. A nation that had produced one of the biggest rock bands of the last thirty years (U2), one of the finest solo artists (Van Morrison), and a host of traditional Irish musicians, was showing a fair degree of cultural cringe towards a seventeen-year-old American named Britney. The Irish weren't so much paying homage to the latest stars of the day, as paying their respects to the modern music industry that has mass marketing as its primary feature. The Irish were acting the same way as their English counterparts would have, had Ms Spears and company graced their shores.

In the year 2001 Ireland is at a crossroads. It has not totally let go of its colonial or insular past, while on the other hand it has embraced Europe and the wider world with passion. The result is a nation that has undergone dramatic economic change in the last 40 years, but which socially has taken its time to catch up. Historians suggest that the modernisation of Ireland took place around the time Sean Lemass became Taoiseach (Prime Minister) in 1959. Lemass realised the only way to halt the large number of Irish emigrating was to provide jobs and opportunities. The Irish economy continued to develop throughout the 1960s and 1970s, maintaining a steady growth rate of 4 per cent and the population of Ireland began to increase again, from about 2.8 million in 1961 to 3.4 million in 1981. Perhaps most importantly, half this population was under 25, suggesting the return of a vibrant and energetic workforce.

*   *   *   *

Then one Sunday night it happened. I was working at my desk, the TV to my right screening another Pavarotti special somewhere in the depths of Italy. Oh how I longed to explore Italy! I looked on with mild interest. I saw in the preview that The Corrs would be playing, although that alone did not make me watch the show.

   But they were playing 'Dreams', the Fleetwood Mac classic that was one of my anthems and would always be on my all-time personal greatest hits CD. I have to be honest: I was struck by the looks of the girls. Okay, I panicked and for some reason flicked the video on. I caught three minutes and 39 seconds of the performance and was at first amazed that I had not paid these three gorgeous girls more attention. In the heat of an Italian summer in June, they were stunning.

*   *   *   *

The social culture of Ireland also began changing in the 1960s. Television and modern advertising began to have an effect, while the range of goods in stores widened. Foreign holidays and dining-out became commonplace amongst Irish society and not just for those in well-paying jobs. Tennis and golf became popular sports and a large number of golf courses appeared on the outskirts of Dublin.

   Ireland's outlook on the world further developed with its entry into the European Community in 1973. Before that the Irish had tendered to ignore the Continent. Through the European connection the Irish have developed new links. Where in the past emigration had been more or less reserved to Britain, the USA and Australia, now the Irish were emigrating to other countries too.

*   *   *   *

Being anything but a technological boffin, I did not hold much hope of getting 'Dreams' on video. I wound the tape back and it was gone! Not giving up hope, I wound it back and on my screen was an incredibly striking girl wearing a black top and a blue skirt. That night I played the tape back about fifteen times. There was no one reason why: certainly the three girls were pleasant to look at, but there was more to it. There was a charisma about the band; a passion I learned was just waiting to be inhaled by the British music public. Andrea Corr radiated optimism. I guess from my own perspective The Corrs represented the thrills of travel and chasing your dreams. Whatever, I wanted to find out more.

*   *   *   *

The modern, cosmopolitan Dublin of the year 2001 is due in part to Ireland's passionate embrace of the concept of a European community. In a referendum in 1972, 83 per cent of those voting wanted their nation to become part of Europe.

A modernised, vibrant economy has emerged on the back of Europe. Ireland is getting all of the benefits with few of the drawbacks of union. While European money continues to flow into the Irish economy, Ireland has been left to its own devices in cultural areas. It is questionable whether the Irish would have been so quick to embrace Europe had their way of life, their cultural privacy, been disturbed. Although the benefits of being in Europe have become obvious to the Irish, in many respects socially the Irish have remained Eurosceptic. While the mobile upper-middle class may jet off to France or Spain for their holidays, Europeans who venture to Ireland visit a place where few Irish speak their languages.

*   *   *   *

The more I read, the more The Corrs began to symbolise my forthcoming overseas experience. The more I discovered about their lives, their music and their hopes, the more I realised that they were normal people with musical talent. It was a talent that I wanted to ask questions and write about. The more I read, the more I realised that the background and rise to fame of The Corrs was closely connected with the broader trends of Irish music. Although they weren't Clannad, they were brought up on similar foundations and within a burgeoning Irish cultural renaissance. After spending much time devouring every media report I could find, communicating through the Internet with Corrs' fans from throughout the world, and watching two videos, I set about contemplating how I would write a book on The Corrs.

*   *   *   *

Ireland is now a consumer society, as opposed to a traditional society. Ireland is no longer — especially in the cities — a God-fearing place where social and cultural repression is prominent. It has changed to the point where Irish society is in some ways hard to distinguish from English society. A music journalist at *The Irish Times*, Kevin Courtney, has lived in Dublin for the majority of his life. He says the changes in Ireland in the last few years are in many respects the maturing of Irish society:

> Maybe it's the shedding of our inferiority complex? I
> remember our parents always encouraged us to take the
> safe things, discouraging us from taking too many risks. I

didn't feel confident making it in the wider world the same way young people in Ireland feel nowadays.

The Ireland in which The Corrs grew up in was significantly different from the Ireland that their parents had matured in. Modern Ireland, as it has been neatly termed, was about opportunity, diversification, and marketing and looking out into the world as opposed to the retrospection that had gone on before.

* * * *

I initially thought it might be possible to write an authorised biography on The Corrs. I easily found a number for the band's management and late one night in January 1999 rang them. 'You have reached The Corrs' office,' the answerphone told me. I left a message briefly outlining my proposal, before offering to fax the details across. I made a follow-up phone call the next day, and was asked to post my proposal to John Hughes, The Corrs' manager. That was the last time I had contact with The Corrs' office before I left New Zealand. Despite sending them a lot of information from New Zealand and phoning and faxing them from Dublin, they didn't bother to acknowledge my calls, let alone respond. With hindsight it was probably not surprising. I must admit that it did have some effect: I did reassess my writing plans more times than I care to remember, but then figured that there was still a story to be told and that I would write it without their help.

* * * *

As Irish society changed, so did Irish music, moving from being something that was inherently unfashionable to something more upbeat, and decidedly trendy. 'In my experience Irish music was always old fogy music and I just wanted to get away from anything to do with trad [traditional music] or Irish music,' says Kevin Courtney. 'I just wanted to adopt anything that was American or English. I was a fan of English punk or American rock. I found that it was probably a sense of shame in a way because in the end chasing after American rock was not very cool at all and in the early 1980s developing our own identity as Irish was in effect the stamp of a new Ireland.'

Several Irish bands of the time, such as Horslips, combined traditional Irish music with folk and rock, making them accessible. What these bands did essentially made them the precursors of The Corrs. 'Horslips grew up with traditional music and combined their love of rock with it, which is effectively what The Corrs are doing at the moment,' suggests Courtney. 'They love pop music but they grew up with trad influences and they mixed it together in a more mainstream fashion.'

Around this time, a number of musicians combined their desire for quality musicianship with their pride in Irish music. Christy Moore and Donal Lunny's Moving Hearts, for example, was set up to present contemporary music that at the same time was compatible with the rock aspirations of traditional Irish music. Within the concept of modern Ireland there has been a rise in confidence that has seen Irish culture move outside its national boundaries. Where Irish culture once was inward looking and self-fulfilling, now it is progressive, confident and ready to embrace the larger markets of the world. What's more, the Irish did not necessarily have to leave home permanently to make their mark internationally.

Ireland has long been a major exporter of creative, talented people. Numerous folk musicians left Ireland for the USA, while writers of the calibre of George Bernard Shaw and Oscar Wilde settled in England. This exit was perfectly understandable: most of the publishing houses and venues for music of any type were situated in either Britain or the USA. Probably because of this exit, traditional Irish music appeared to be dying a natural death as recently as the late 1950s. The problem was that even the Irish regarded traditional music as being part of Ireland's past and not likely to be a factor in a new, vibrant Ireland. There were now other recreational pursuits, such as ballroom dancing and pop music. Television was also starting to beam in overseas acts.

In the 1950s and 1960s the Irish duly went out and rescued traditional Irish music. In 1951 an Association called *Comhaltas Ceoltóiri Éireann* (CCE) — the Irish music movement — was formed. The association had as its main goal to restore and develop Irish music, as well as developing the Irish language. CCE established music classes and its influence eventually led to a music explosion in the 1960s. Due to this renaissance, numerous Irish music groups were formed, most prominently the Chieftains in 1962 and the Dubliners, both of whom were to leave lasting impressions on the Irish music landscape and on the world music scene.

Part of the reason why music in Ireland developed so extensively was the tax breaks given to artists and performers. In 1969 the Minister of Finance, the later disgraced Charles Haughey, instituted a scheme whereby earnings on creative works were free from income tax for anyone living in Ireland, whether Irish or foreign. Naturally enough, this led to several artists, writers and entertainers living in Éire.

*   *   *   *

It was never my intention to write a tell-all book and, to be frank, I never thought The Corrs had much to hide. What I did want to do was find answers to a number of questions and write a serious book that studied their work, influences and objectives. Where had they come from? Were the looks of the girls an advantage or a barrier to the band being taken seriously as musicians? Should it matter? Why had there been such a dramatic shift in emphasis from the first to second albums? Where on earth was Dundalk? Why had they influenced me so much when their music was clearly pop? What force was telling me to head to Ireland and write this book?

*   *   *   *

Given its impact on Irish nationalism, just what is traditional Irish music? The principal instrument is the fiddle, while others include the flute, the tin whistle and the *bodhrán*, a small goatskin drum that is beaten with the knuckles or a stick. Other prominent instruments used in traditional Irish music include the Irish version of the bagpipes — the *uilleann* (pipes) — and the harp, which is the traditional emblem of Ireland and is featured on Irish bank notes.

Today the soothing sounds of traditional music can be heard throughout modern Ireland. Even in Temple Bar, in the very heartland of Dublin's inner city, session musicians come together most afternoons to play. Their fee will often only be token, suggesting that their satisfaction comes in the actual playing and the companionship. Ironically enough the attitude of playing for virtually nothing has forced many professional Irish bands to go overseas in search of paying audiences.

This cultural renaissance of Irish music has also been manifest in the annual *fleadh* in London, where a combination of folk balladeers combine with the new breed of Irish rock stars, such as Sinead O'Connor and The Corrs, in celebrating the historical traditions of their rich culture. Putting Irish music on a larger stage was the best thing that could have been done to promote Irish music aboard. Not only were there thousands of Irish in England keen to celebrate their heritage, but it undoubtedly gave the Irish confidence in their own culture.

Some suggest that classical music never really took off in Ireland because it was brought over by the English and that traditional Irish music was a way for the Celts to maintain their own culture. Like Catholicism, Irish music has become a cherished expression of national identity. But at its heart, Irish music is about passion. Nothing more, and certainly nothing less. It is also about capturing the beauty, innocence and glory of the land. As Maíre Ní Bhraonain of Clannad has said:

> You know that when we've made an album ... the judgement day for me is when I'm going home to Donegal and ... I put the cassette on then, and I feel it's worthy of

the area, then I'm happy with it ... so that's how I judge
my music ... I love going home to Donegal; it is definitely
the sole inspiration of Clannad in the long run.

The proud history of traditional Irish music has undoubtedly played an
important part in the success of Irish musical acts over the last 30
years. As mentioned, Horslips, a middle-class, educated group,
performed a mixture of traditional, folk and rock that proved very
popular and saw the band pioneer what was neatly termed 'Celtic
Rock'. Likewise, the Pogues and the Saw Doctors crossed the barrier
from being just Irish acts to mainstream artists, although the influence
of traditional Irish music was still clear and obvious. The Saw Doctors'
music was heavily influenced by their origins in Galway and the
traditional Irish music that emerged from the West of Ireland.

The influence of traditional Irish music on the more mainstream
Irish acts is perhaps less obvious. Van Morrison, from the North, was
certainly influenced by his Celtic origins. Morrison has said that in his
early days he resented traditional Irish music, but now feels that Irish
and Scottish music is soul music: 'I think it can be dangerous to not
validate the music of where you're from, for anybody ... For me it's
traditional. I'm a traditionalist. I believe in tracing back to the source
and finding out what the real thing was, and how it changed.' Van
Morrison celebrates his Celtic roots on some of his later albums, with
No Guru, No Method, No Teacher and *Irish Heartbeat* being the most
prominent. After the release of *No Guru*, Morrison commented that
out of necessity the album contained a number of influences: 'Now
you get all these crossovers. People have to make connections because
in this modern age we live in, which is the video age, you're allowed
five minutes. You have to make more connections than that,
otherwise you're gonna starve.'

That is the crux of Morrison's music and of Irish music in the last
25 years: as *Irish* music it certainly has appeal, but it also has a more
general universal appeal that most people can relate to.

*   *   *   *

*I left Christchurch, New Zealand on 5 March 1999 and felt like I was going
to war. In fact my grandfather had left New Zealand at roughly the same
age 58 years previously and had spent four years fighting for his country in
North Africa and Italy. I wasn't going into battle, but I was going to find
myself and discover some sort of independence and, hopefully, in the process
work out who the hell I was. I remember saying goodbye to my Nana,
wondering whether I would ever see her again, and my parents at the airport
and knowing that the next time I saw them the dynamics of our relationship*

would be different. I can imagine how The Corrs felt when they left for the USA to record Forgiven Not Forgotten *in 1995.*

*   *   *   *

Like Van Morrison, the careers of Sinead O'Connor and U2 have less clearly relied on traditional Irish music. But the way to look at the Irish influence on their music and careers is to suggest that, like Morrison, their music has crossed the borders of nationalism. What the traditions of Irish music did was provide motivation and a cultural springboard, which encouraged a love of music and a passion that established both U2 and O'Connor as world class acts.

U2 were the prototype for the expansion of the Irish music industry onto the world market. Four lads from Dublin with a clever manager took on the world and became one of the biggest rock acts of the last 30 years. Socially committed, U2 sung songs about imperialism, war, human rights and drugs. Their strength was not just in their vast musical abilities, but in their passion for what they were doing. They broke into the lucrative USA market because, quite simply, they were world class and they had raw ability that was appreciated by the Americans.

U2 have given mixed signals about the extent of the influence traditional Irish music has had on their sound. Lead singer Bono has said: 'I rebelled against being Irish, I rebelled against speaking the Irish language, Irish culture.' Yet in a documentary on Irish music, *Bringing It All Back Home*, Bono has suggested that traditional Irish music has had a positive influence: 'I think there's an Irishness to what U2 do; I'm not quite sure what it is. I think it's something to do with the romantic spirit of the words I write, but also of the melodies that Edge makes on the guitar.' There is, however, not a great degree of Irishness about U2's music. But U2's influence on the Irish music culture has been huge in two main ways. Firstly, through their success U2 have provided inspiration and created the pathway for other Irish acts. There have been numerous interviews in which Irish singers and pop musicians have said that not only were U2 a major influence and inspiration, but that the band proved what could be achieved on a world scale. Any successful musical act in Ireland today appears to have some connection with U2. The Corrs are friends of the band and in the summer of 1999 were reported to have spent much time with U2 in a trendy nightspot in Dublin. Clannad have sung a magnificent duet with Bono, while Boyzone have also been known to hang out with U2 and at various times have been given advice. But despite their influence, it is perhaps sad and systematic of the modern music industry that no other Irish band has been as successful as U2. Clannad were musicians of the highest quality and in their own way every bit as talented as U2. But traditional Irish or Celtic music was never going to sell as many albums as U2's pure rock.

Secondly, U2's influence on the next generation of modern Irish musicians was to provide a shop window from which the talents of others could blossom. Part of the appeal of The Corrs has been their ability to sing songs about universal themes. Love, destiny and being in love don't hold the same level of importance as some of the songs sung by U2, but their appeal is nonetheless universal. What U2 did was open the door for other Irish acts to make a name for themselves in England and in the USA.

U2 also proved that you did not necessarily have to go and live in England or the USA if you were Irish and wanted to make it big. *Irish Times* music journalist Kevin Courtney has said:

> I think there was this kind of perceived wisdom that there was no point in trying anything because you would only fail. U2 totally overturned that completely. They became ridiculously successful, beyond anyone's wildest dreams. Nobody could have believed that U2 could be successful. Their friends in the pub sitting there in Dublin were sitting there saying: 'You're in a band? What do you call it? U2? ****ing hell! You're going to try and be big and sell a lot of records?' There was a change to this self-belief where you didn't listen to begrudgers; you gravitated towards other people who were fed up with begrudgery. These people stuck together and the effect was that they changed the attitudes a bit.

In early 2000, the members of U2 were granted the freedom of Dublin. This civic reception was just reward for a band that had altered the boundaries within Ireland as to what could be achieved. Although to many in Dublin, U2 were overexposed and appeared bored pop stars, they opened the international doors that acts like The Corrs were only too quick to jump through. Their influence on the Irish musical and cultural tradition cannot be underestimated.

*   *   *   *

I arrived in Dublin one cold, grey Sunday morning in late March 1999. I had come over on the ferry from Holyhead in Wales after spending three tiring weeks in Europe. I had travelled the last part of the way from London to Dublin with two American girls, who were sisters. They were good craic (an Irish term for fun and enjoyment) for most of the trip. They were even laughing at my jokes and flirting in a non-offensive sort of way. One of then was attending Cambridge University. We arrived in Dublin port having had three hours' sleep on the ferry over. Comfortable it was not. Despite the time, the conditions and the fact that there was anything but a welcoming committee to greet me, Dublin felt like home. I really didn't know why. We bussed into the centre of the city and it too was dead. I desperately needed to sleep. Then the fun started.

Some say the Americans aren't the best travellers. Well anyway, the girls (who were in Dublin for just two days) hadn't had any sleep and it was starting to show. We went to a hostel to book in and they found they couldn't sleep in the same room. Despite living on different continents for most of the year, they didn't want this and so we tried to find another hostel. The bitching now really started. To them everything about Dublin was wrong; from the weather to the fact that there was nowhere to eat. They eventually found another hostel to stay at. I had had more than enough, said I was staying at the first hostel and looked forward to finding a job and a place to live. Welcome to Dublin.

*   *   *   *

In the early 1990s Irish music also became hip through the success of the movie *Titanic* and the now legendary *Riverdance*. *Titanic* helped make Celtic music fashionable and romantic. However it was *Riverdance* that proved the greatest influence and was the most obvious example of the Irish cultural renaissance.

The phenomenon of *Riverdance* was something of a surprise. In the early 1990s Ireland played host to the Eurovision song contest. As part of the entertainment, a twelve-minute entertainment package of Irish dance was organised by Moya Doherty. With Michael Flatley and Jean Butler in the lead roles, *Riverdance* was a celebration, full of energy and passion, and an instant success.

Bill Whelan, a great friend of the manager of The Corrs, John Hughes, suggested that *Riverdance* become a fully-fledged show. It was written as a high tempo, celebration of traditional Irish dance. Although Flatley left *Riverdance* in 1995 after creative differences (he would subsequently write and star in *Lord of the Dance* and *Feet of Flames*), it was *Riverdance* that stole the imagination of Ireland, Europe, Australia and New Zealand and the east coast of the United States. *Riverdance* would go on to be the highest grossing musical in history, partly due to its subject matter, its high-octane performances and helped no end by its rave reviews. In many respects *Riverdance* kept on fuelling its own fire. As it moved around the world to sell-out audiences, it was continuing to reinforce this Irish cultural renaissance, which in turn continued to produce a demand for *Riverdance*. It was its own individual success story.

Although it cannot be said that the phenomenon of boy bands in the 1990s changed the face of popular culture as much as U2 did, the trend again saw Irish bands to the fore. British band Take That effectively started the boy band era. Five clean-cut young males sung harmless songs that had a wide audience and, in an age looking for purity and non-offensive role models, it was the right ticket at the right time. When Take That disintegrated, enter Boyzone, a creation of music promoter, and some would say manipulator, Dubliner Louis Walsh.

Ronan Keating aside, Boyzone was as musically talentless as the thousands of other bands that had tried to make it in the industry and failed before. Three of the band had virtually no talent and did not even sing; backing singers had to be hired by Walsh to provide some sort of reasonable sound. What Boyzone did have was the personal charisma and charm of Keating, the shrewd marketing of Walsh and the knack of being mass produced for a market that was just ready to lap them up. The success of Boyzone was hardly due to the fact that their music had a strong Irish sound. Their appeal was universal, their sound inoffensive. They were the cornflakes of the industry: easily consumed but not terribly remarkable. Yet their clean-cut Irish accents were used positively to promote the band. It made them slightly different, a tool to set them apart from the rest. The important thing was that being Irish was anything but a disadvantage.

Westlife was an extension and an improvement of the formula established by Walsh. More than two members of Westlife could sing, they were better looking than Boyzone, their sound more crafted, more universal. Like Boyzone, the fact that three of Westlife came from Sligo in Ireland and two from Dublin was irrelevant. The sound was again universal and palpable to the picky world market.

Girl band B*Witched was also formed and marketed along similar lines as the boy bands. Their members looked good, had some talent and they were catering for a specific demand in the marketplace, achieving four number ones on the British charts. Again, being Irish was in many respects irrelevant, as B*Witched performed 'magic, fun pop' and it was this that established their large following. But, when asked about their musical influences and the importance of the traditional Irish music tradition, they were quick to suggest that their act was traditionally Irish. 'People's perception of the Irish scene are always beardy types,' Sinead O'Carroll of B*Witched has said.

'Traditional Irish music hadn't been done by a young group before, so it was a challenge to us.' This sort of statement shows the lengths some musicians go to in order to catch every conceivable market. Although B*Witched were undoubtedly genuine in their desire to pay homage to their Irish music traditions, they were successful because of their image which was of anything but an Irish band. If The Corrs were the vanilla of the music industry, B*Witched were the bubble gum.

Kevin Courtney notes that, while being Irish gives these young bands a twist to make them more interesting, their heritage is largely irrelevant to their success: 'Boyzone's Irishness has helped them from a PR point of view because they come across as charming young Irishmen; they have a good easy rapport with the media that has worked in their favour. A lot of the interest in Boyzone, especially Ronan Keating, has been their soft Irish accent, and their easy-going attitude. There is nothing wrong with that. If people were to buy an Irish boy band, or an English boy band, or an American boy band, it really makes no difference. B*Witched might have a few Irish fiddles, but getting all precious about throwing in the odd fiddle solo is not going to really worry the traditional Irish musicians.'

But haven't the traditional practitioners of Irish music been sold down the river? Courtney argues that traditional Irish music has always 'sold out', in the sense of using its Irishness to help its commercial success. 'Traditionally trad music has sold out, from the Clancy brothers playing Carnegie Hall in their Ireland sweaters to the Wolftones doing their neo-military style of ballads.'

Although the modern Ireland was a key reason why these new Irish bands were making such an impact, as was the worldwide achievements of U2, their success could also be attributed to the changing technological environment in which they were operating. MTV, the Internet, faster computers, the mass marketing industry and countless other innovations were making the supply and delivery of information significantly faster. An obvious example of this new technological environment was the British music charts. Where in the past a popular tune would stay at the top of the charts for several weeks, in some cases months, now the average lifespan for a song at the top of the charts is one week.

About the time 'Breathless', the first single off The Corrs' *In Blue* album, was released, Ronan Keating's 'Life is a Rollercoaster' was also released. It was followed a few weeks later by his self-titled first solo album. Keating knocked The Corrs off number one on both charts but he himself only lasted a week at the top of the singles charts. Forty different acts were UK number ones in the year 2000, suggesting the fickle nature of the British music business. Furthermore, songs that appear at number one often not only get knocked off top spot after a week, but are also dropped off the ever-important Radio One playlist a week or two after that.

*   *   *   *

The Irish were also internally gaining the confidence to celebrate the success they had had worldwide with their music. It was fitting that in March 1999 an Irish Music Hall of Fame was officially opened, close to the banks of Dublin's River Liffey. Designed to celebrate the rich tradition of Irish music, one of the first inductees was Van Morrison, who was given a heart-warming tribute by Bob Geldof. Included in the museum is a huge amount of memorabilia that in itself gives the visitor a detailed history of Irish music. What is striking is not so much the number of exhibits dedicated to well-known Irish acts, but the attention given to acts that would hardly be known outside Ireland.

Barry Walsh, Operations Manager of the *Hot Press* Hall of Fame, notes that the more well-known Irish artists have helped out substantially in the creation of the Hall:

> When the idea was further mooted the response was largely reliant on the response of the musicians. I think what made it possible was that the patron of the place was the *Hot Press* magazine, which has been running for around twenty-five years and has been the bible in terms of Irish music and culture. They had created a goodwill with the artists that in the end was vital in that the Hall was reliant on people donating items of memorabilia that were going to be rare and have huge appeal to not just Irish people but people the world over.

Walsh believes that the Hall of Fame is another symbol of Irish music and culture finding its own voice and identity in the world:

> The culture of the last thirty or forty years has been very different than it was before then. It's only been in the last 30 or 40 years that we stopped imitating the rest of the world. The traditional genre was always there and had a huge influence throughout the world on the likes of Woody Gurthrie or Bob Dylan, but in the last 30 or 40 years people like Thin Lizzy and Rory Gallagher have gone out and put their stamp on music. For young people that is a very vibrant and recent culture for them to aspire to.

*   *   *   *

I was fortunate enough when arriving in Dublin to get a job as a sub-editor with The Irish Times, *undoubtedly the best daily newspaper in Ireland. Although the first three months were difficult, learning Irish names and places, I eventually picked up the methods and came to enjoy my work. It was in many respects the perfect way to learn about Ireland and what was going on. I could have, however, done without paying 48 per cent of my wages in tax. But, like any job, it was the people I worked with who made the job what it was. The sub-editors in the sports department were interesting: almost exclusively male, they varied in their approaches, their temperaments, their life experiences and their ability to relate to other people. Subbing is a strange job: you work in your own little world, just you and the screen and yet there are people three or four metres away. In many respects it is lonely work. Being younger than most of the subs, and being a foreigner, it did take time for me to get accepted and fit in. When I did, however, I felt more at home that perhaps I ever had in New Zealand. Ireland is like that.*

*   *   *   *

Being Irish and growing up in the 1970s and 1980s had two specific effects on The Corrs. Firstly, the changing environment in Ireland influenced their early careers and made international success more likely than it would have been before while, secondly, external changes in the Irish music industry itself paved the way for The Corrs to be successful. With the advent of the concept of modern Europe, Ireland found itself with a more certain place in international affairs and the younger generation perhaps benefited from this more than any other. No goal or possibility could be ruled out. If you were growing up and Irish you were as good, if not better, than anyone else was. No longer was there a consciousness about who or what you were. You were as good as the next person.

Undoubtedly, a reduction in importance of the Catholic Church in society had some effect, as did the modernisation of Irish society. When all these factors are combined the barriers that had been placed in front of any Irish endeavour in the past were now largely eliminated. There was still a fair degree of begrudgery — so fundamental to the Irish character — but no longer could being Irish be regarded as an excuse for not reaching your goals. This phenomenon was perhaps stronger in culture than it was anywhere else. The Irish had always had a strong cultural tradition, especially in music. It had been their lifeblood for as long as Ireland had been a Celtic nation. But somehow Ireland hadn't had the confidence to showcase its resources on the rest of the world to any great degree.

It was the talents of Thin Lizzy, Van Morrison and a host of other talented Irish musicians that paved the way for an Irish band that would change the face of popular music and at the same time positively influence Irish artists. The Corrs were of the generation that was inspired by U2's international success and in that respect the world's biggest band in the 1980s has played a significant part in the rise to stardom of The Corrs. The success of U2 in virtually every market proved that being Irish was no predicament in achieving international success.

CHAPTER 3

Running Wild and Free

The Corrs are like any family: we eat, we drink, we have the Christmas turkey, the Baileys, the presents. It's just us and our parents.

Andrea Corr

We are all products of our upbringing and the environment in which we grew up. The Corrs are from Dundalk, almost halfway between Dublin and Belfast on the east coast of Ireland.

You get a whiff of brown ale when you arrive in Dundalk by train. It's perfectly understandable — the brewery is right next to the station. An Irish flag greets you at the station as you slowly ramble into downtown Dundalk. The 35,000-strong community has had its fair share of bad press in the last few years and you get the feeling that people look over their shoulders when you walk by. This does not make them any less friendly, but you know when you are an outsider.

Despite the image problems that have affected Dundalk, it is a very safe town, homely, friendly and secure. You detect a feeling of contentment on the faces of the people, the mothers and the fathers, the grandparents, the young people who whizz around on their bikes. Everyone knows everyone in this town. It is reassuring in this town that people care about you. In the depths of a city, like Dublin less than an hour south on the train, they not only don't know who you are, they don't seem to care.

But it is nice to just watch locals do their shopping and stop to talk to other locals, actually listen to what they have to say. Share a laugh and a smile. Although the weather is often grey, the craic is reassuring and homely. The town feels to the outsider as though it hasn't lost its 1950 beauty, echoing times much more innocent. But somehow the beauty of Dundalk is not in what there is to do, but in the fact that people actually take the time to talk to each other. When you start to explore it you realise that Dundalk is a pretty town nestled near the heartland of national uncertainty, but distinctly Irish in its culture. The steeples on the local churches appear more Anglican than Catholic and the lined streets have the same sort of small-town, bored feeling you would expect in some small British towns. It is not until you speak to one of the locals that you realise that this is Ireland and given the passion the townsfolk feel for their town and their country.

*   *   *   *

I first went past Dundalk on the train from Dublin to Belfast. It was a nice day and the cream train station looked pleasant enough. I first visited Dundalk outright with friend Tom Cosgrave two weeks later. We arrived at Clarke Station, Dundalk (Dun Dealgan) just before 10.45 one Saturday morning.

Dundalk immediately felt like a comfortable sort of place to live. The architecture, with its red brick look, appeared British. The people, though, looked, spoke and had the spirit of the Irish. This is a border town, although from the start of our visits there Dundalk appeared more Irish than Dublin.

We stopped at the leabharlann (library). We went inside, grabbed a map and bought tickets to visit the museum. The Irish president had just opened a new exhibition. One of the exhibits was a copy of a concert ticket from a Corrs' concert in Dublin the January before.

*   *   *   *

Many locals regard Dundalk as being 'terminally unfashionable'. Its location may not help it, nor the adverse publicity generated late in 1998 following the Omagh bombing, although at around the same time Xerox was formulating plans to open a plant just outside town, creating 1,500 jobs. Dundalk is a down-to-earth town. This down-to-earthness is undoubtedly also due to the history of the town. Dundalk is steeped in tradition and was home to the mythical hero Cúchulainn. It was a market town throughout the Middle Ages, as much for the Old Irish of Ulster as it was for the Old English town of north Leinster. It emerged into the modern era in the 1740s and 1750s by means of a town redevelopment plan initiated by the town landlord James Hamilton, the Earl of Clanbrassil. This plan saw new roads built to the east of the town and the creation of Market Square, still a feature today. Contemporary Dundalk, however, has always been known as an industrial town, which was inevitable given its location between Belfast in the north and Dublin in the south. Industrial towns aren't normally regarded as being the pick of places to live and maybe this is why Dundalk has always been regarded as being unfashionable.

There is a unique feel about Dundalk. It is neither that big nor that small. As journalist Tony Clayton-Lea has written:

> There is no affectation about the townspeople. Urban
> enough to have a thriving arts scheme that is happy and

clear-minded to embrace the full range of creative pursuits (from indie bands to poetry readings), it is also rural enough to have its own inherent bullshit detector.

It is in the pubs in Dundalk where the true passion and spirit of the local community can be felt. There are many lies told and the pubs themselves are more a hub of the local community than they are merely drinking holes. A place to share experiences and reflect on the day — or night — that has just been. A place also in which to grow up. In the pubs, the young people will mix with those of more experienced years. The trend continues even when jobs and other opportunities move some of Dundalk's young people to the cities. When they return to Dundalk they spend their weekend drinking and socialising. They will start off at the pubs, then move to a nightclub, then on to a party, often getting home when the sun rises. Socialising and drinking are part and parcel of the fabric of life in Dundalk. As is traditional Irish music, played regularly in the pubs and the clubs of Dundalk.

It is within these musical traditions in Dundalk that Gerry and Jean Corr decided to raise a family. Jean Corr (née Bell) was one of ten children and was a beautiful child with dark, angelic features and a ready smile for everyone. Her father was from Dublin and her mother from Donegal, in the north west of Ireland, but still in the Republic. Her father worked for the Customs and Excise department, in those days a highly respected profession within Ireland, and was stationed in Donegal where he met his future wife. He was later moved to Dundalk where his children were raised.

In Jean's family there was a strong musical tradition. Her aunts and uncle on her paternal side all enjoyed and played music, while her mother loved music but did not sing. Jean and her siblings grew up following the music of the day and whatever their friends were playing. The big thing at the time was rebelling against the traditional piano and singing lessons that had to be endured. The in-thing was to play the guitar. This was due largely to the popularity of The Beatles, who had played in Dundalk, and the Rolling Stones.

Jean Corr was described as being a very determined person, although very soft at the same time. Many Dundalk locals suggest that the Corr siblings get their determination from their mother and their artistic flair from their father. Friends of the family say it was the drive to perfect whatever she did that made Jean stand out. Whatever task she applied herself to would be completed and she very rarely said that something could not be done. Jean was also the rock of the Corr family. Whenever there was a crisis it was her strength that provided the family's backbone.

Both the Bells and the Corrs have traditionally been family-orientated people. Accordingly, Jean and Gerry's families were much the same. If there were a bit of fun to be had they would have it and enjoy life at the same time. But the Corr children would also realise when it was time to be responsible. What was a feature of both extended families was a strong work ethic and a fierce determination of mind.

*   *   *   *

Tom had mentioned that the musical career of The Corrs developed at a pub called McManus', owned by Jean Corr's sister and her husband. We expected plenty as we walked silently through the streets of Dundalk trying to find this establishment. Eventually a blue building with a small doorway greeted us. It could have been the corner bar in any British or Irish town. Two blokes sat at the bar, a Hot Press cover of The Corrs sat in pride of place at the top of the bar, like a trophy. As I ordered a Guinness I noticed pictures of Gerry and Jean Corr to my right. We were very much in Corrs territory now. As we sipped our drinks and took in the atmosphere, we were both surprised by the quaintness of the place. With the amount of second-hand goods behind the bar it could have easily been a pawn shop, although the spirit of the Corrs appeared alive and well in the four walls that were waiting for Saturday night. Even the parrot that strutted itself behind the bar did not look out of place.

*   *   *   *

Gerry Corr, creative in the extreme, has always been a joker and does his best to catch out friends and relatives with practical jokes, often taken to elaborate lengths. Gerry's willingness to indulge in pranks seems to have been inherited by Jim Corr. Jim and his sisters think nothing of ringing their Aunt Lillian from a tour bus in England and putting on a voice to confuse her. They would have perhaps spoken to Gerry and they will know what issue to raise to get her attention. It always seems to work.

The Corr household was never short of excitement, amusement and general entertainment — musical or otherwise. Family friend Barry Henry reflected on the family, before Jean's untimely death:

> Their parents are lovely, lovely people. There was always hype going on about the house. Andrea was always on form. She was always hyped is the way I would describe it. And there was always this great slagging match going on in their house. It was all good fun. You would go up there and there would be these great slagging matches

going on. I would start slagging them back, just about anything. They were always great like that. In many respects it would be very similar to our house.

Although these days the Corr siblings seem united in their quest for world musical domination, as they grew up the differences in ages between the four ensured that they were never close in the sense that they spent time together. Because of the year between them, Caroline and Andrea were raised like twins and had some of the same friends, while Jim and Sharon were older and had their own social circle. Only when they formed The Corrs did the siblings have more in common and as a result stronger bonds developed.

Friends of the Corr family consider that Jim has taken after his father, both in his approach to life and in much of his personality. Jim was a spontaneous, happy child who always enjoyed having a good time when the time was right. He could also be serious and as he matured he became more and more entrepreneurial. On one particular occasion he proved to be, in the short-term, one step ahead of the rest of his family. As a child, Jim would often not attend school. His maternal grandmother lived about ten minutes from school and often Jim would pay her a visit — without her knowing. Jim would enter the house through a small bathroom window and spend his time up in the top bedroom without his grandmother hearing. He would know just the right times to come down to the kitchen and raid the fridge and generally make himself at home. Eventually, however, his uncle Paddy caught on to Jim's cunning plan and he was forced, begrudgingly, to attend school on a more regular basis.

Suggestions have been made in earlier books on The Corrs that Jim Corr had a reputation as being something of an arsonist in his youth. It has been written that he set off a bonfire dangerously close to a chemical plant and that the Gardaí (the Irish police) came calling. The truth is that Jim was indeed questioned by the Gardaí but, although present at the scene, he hadn't lit the fire and had merely poked it, which had led to it flaring.

Jim attended Coláiste Rís, or the old Christian Brothers School, in Dundalk, for his high school years. The school was strong in music and the arts and performed several Gilbert and Sullivan shows during Jim's time there. Eamon Ó Huallacháin, now deputy principal, says that Jim was a good student who 'did not cause any trouble'. He is remembered as being 'decidedly keen' on music and it was clear to the Christian Brothers that that was where his future lay. The school does not recall Jim's academic prowess, suggesting that he was not viewed as a scholar.

Jim only spent three years at high school. Although unusual these days, in the early 1980s it was quite normal for a student to stay for such a limited time. Jim sat his Public Examination at the school, but did not take his education any further.

The second Corr child was born on 12 August 1966. He was named Gerard Patrick Corr, a reversal of Gerry Corr's official names — Patrick Gerard. But tragedy struck on 2 April 1970 when the three-year-old Gerard was hit by a vehicle when he went out on to the street to collect a ball. He child suffered substantial head injuries as the result of the accident and died the following morning in the county hospital in Dundalk. Friends of the family say the tragedy naturally had a dramatic impact on Gerry and Jean and that the months after the accident were 'bad days' for them, although close friends of Jim say he was too young to have suffered. Sharon Corr had just been born and the impact on her would also have been minimal. Even to this day Gerry Corr does not talk about the death of his second son.

$$* \quad * \quad * \quad *$$

I wanted to help her and I felt guilty for my good fortune in life. She told me she had lived in Dundalk since year dot, that she was 29 (around the same age as me), had two children and was seeing 'A British fella'. She was a waitress in the Café du Paris in Dundalk, a restaurant that provided grills and snacks. Despite the posh sounding name and the cheap and filling food, it was nothing more or less than what you would find in millions of similar establishments throughout the world. I had eaten there before and asked to interview this waitress on her break about what it was like living in Dundalk and what she knew about The Corrs.

Although we made a time, when it came she ignored me and instead sat on her own eating lunch. Miffed, I went over and sat down. She didn't say much at first, but when we got to talking she opened up. She enjoyed talking about Dundalk and The Corrs. I still felt as though I was bugging her with my questions and after fifteen minutes I left.

I thought about her all week. It wasn't what she had told me about The Corrs or Dundalk that had made me think, it was her own situation. She told me she worked six days because she had to provide for her children. I felt lucky, able and free. I wanted to help her, open her eyes to the world and open her mind. I felt I had a cause. There had been only a few occasions like this when I wanted to be the knight in shining armour. It was as if she was switched off from the rest of the world in order to get through it all. I said I would drop a copy of the book in when it was finished. She said she hoped it had plenty of pictures. She said her cousin went to school with Andrea Corr, and I asked her to pass on my number. Being new to Dublin, I was unsure of what my number was. The following week I dropped it in. 'I have no time to talk,' she snapped as I walked through the door. I felt like a tabloid journalist and hurt because she had been on my mind. I quickly gave her my telephone number to give to her cousin and left, a potential hero shot down in flames.

*   *   *   *

From the time she was a baby, Sharon Corr has always been seen as slightly more cautious than her three siblings. She says she is weary of being referred to as the 'ice maiden' and, although certainly not cold as a person, friends say she is watchful with those she does not know. Always remembered as playing the fiddle, she was a splendid looking child with angelic features. Sharon was also well known for having a beautiful voice. A friend recalls her coming round to their house and, after listening to a CD, singing the song perfectly.

Sharon has often said in interviews that she struggled at school and at one stage was abused by a nun who told her that she would never amount to anything: 'I didn't take it seriously at the time,' Sharon told *Q Magazine*. 'And I'm not the kind of person to go "Hey you said I was a failure and look at me now." I could be internationally famous but totally devoid of personality and just an absolute ass to everyone. I don't think there is any such thing as failure — if you're trying you're not a failure. But I think I annoyed the nun, so I wouldn't like to be vindictive about her because I don't think she meant it badly.'

It is true that Sharon, like her brother Jim, was never an academic. But friends say that she was streetwise and from an early age had an understanding of how the world worked. She was certainly not stupid.

Given her angelic looks and her willingness to enjoy life, it is not surprising that she had her fair share of boyfriends as she was growing up. One former boyfriend, who did not wish to be named, says that Sharon took the responsibility of being the oldest Corr daughter seriously and was forever worrying about her two sisters. He also says that the bond that she had with Jim was very obvious, particularly when they played together as a duo in pubs and clubs in Dundalk. 'I liked Sharon for a number of reasons,' said the former boyfriend. 'Obviously she was very beautiful and that didn't hurt, but there was much more to her than that. She was intelligent and had an understanding of the world around her that I liked. But perhaps the most striking thing about her was that she knew how to have fun. Not all the time, but when the occasion was right. She was someone whom I would call social, but not overly social if you know what I mean. She had a reserved side that I liked and I wouldn't necessarily call her an extrovert. She was a lovely girl though and I enjoyed the time I spent with her.'

Sharon is the most down-to-earth Corr and the sibling who in both looks and attitude is the most Irish. Although arguably the most beautiful of the Corr girls, she is also the most opinionated. In 2000 she was quoted in the media on a range of non-music issues that reflect the fact that she is someone who thinks about the world around her and does not live in a bubble like so many other stars of the music world.

Caroline Corr is more reserved. As a baby she was a gentle and quiet child. She was always very sensitive. Barry Henry has been a friend of Caroline's for over ten years. Henry says Caroline is good company, totally relaxed and fun to be with, but is also a unique individual:

> She would be sitting there and be so engrossed in a conversation with you that another person could be talking to her and she wouldn't hear a thing. Caroline is great craic and a very genuine person. If Caroline is pissed off she'll let you know that she is pissed off. In saying that, she is the best of company and I always love her company. She is not blunt or anything like that, but when she is happy with things she's just delightful. She has this infectious laugh and she will just roar with laughter. At times she will be sitting there and things will be happening around her and because she is so engrossed with what's happening, she will be laughing away and miss everything that's going on. It can be quite comical at times.

Although she may not appear to be particularly intellectual, Henry says that in the last few years he has begun to appreciate how deep Caroline can be:

> You may sometimes think that 'Jesus, this girl is dizzy, she is not taking in a thing I'm saying here,' and then she will turn around as if she's not listening and come out with the most outstanding facts and point of view and opinion and I'll be going, 'Jesus Christ where did that come from?'

Like all the Corr siblings, Caroline is very comfortable with company. Following The Corrs' Lansdowne Road concert in July 1999, Caroline caught up with a couple of her closest friends from Dundalk at a party back at her boyfriend Frank's house. Caroline and the girls started talking as if nothing had changed in the last ten years, exchanging the same banter as they did when they were teenagers. It was far removed from the concert she and her siblings had headlined in front of 44,000 people earlier that evening.

Although certainly not stupid, Caroline, like many students, performed below her potential at school and her results were distinctly average. Like many of her classmates, Caroline only did the minimum amount of work required to get through and was more than happy having a good time. In this sense Caroline and Andrea Corr differ remarkably. While Caroline was happy to cruise, Andrea was a diligent student who did very well in her leaving exams and could have picked any of the third level (university) courses on offer.

Being similar in age, Caroline and Andrea spent time together more than with Jim and Sharon. Although the four siblings are described as being close, friends of the family say there is an obvious bond between Caroline and Andrea and that the pair were raised almost like twins.

Andrea nearly died a few months after her birth. She contracted a kidney infection and from there picked up gastro-enteritis. 'They thought I was going to die,' she says. 'I was shifted around all the different hospitals. So for that reason I got an awful lot of love because I was brought back from the dead — literally.'

After a shaky start, Andrea soon developed a natural talent for entertainment. She was always the natural entertainer of the family and from an early age was terrific at mimicry, apparently doing a terrific Frank Spencer. Described as giddy as a child, Andrea was a 'breath of fresh air from knee high', according to her Aunt Lillian.

Friends describe Andrea as always being 'hyperactive'. Normally good fun, she had the ability to take a slagging, while at the same time give her fair share. With people she knows well she is always relaxed and good company, but she is reserved and shy around people she doesn't know. She has said herself that around the time of *The Commitments* she was more outgoing than she has been in subsequent years. Friends say the success of the band and the fact that she is the front-person has placed extra responsibility on her. The price of fame, however, is that although naturally comfortable with those she knows, come interview time and the barriers will often go up. 'If anything [Andrea] is quieter than she ever was,' says Henry. 'I get the impression that in interviews she is quite tense. That as the front person for the band she feels the pressure. However when she is with people she knows, or has known for a long time, she is so relaxed. She'll give you loads of shit and she'll take the shit. If she gives you loads of shit, you throw it straight back at her and she will take it and laugh and have great fun. It's just in interviews she appears quite tense. Maybe she lets the pressure get to her.'

At school Andrea was well known for her academic prowess and her theatrical ability. She was also known as a drama queen. Friends who went to school with Andrea say that she was never necessarily happy to fit in with the rest, unlike Sharon and Caroline, and always believed that she was something special. This was not necessarily a bad thing, it was just that she was different from the rest. The differences were more obvious once she landed a part in *The Commitments*: 'We were not allowed to wear cardigans to school, which was fair enough,' recalls one school friend, 'but when Andrea won the part in the movie she was allowed to. There seemed one set of rules for her and one for the rest of us. That's just the way she was. She was certainly very pretty though and when it came to drama and that sort of thing, she was obviously, even back then, a talent.'

*   *   *   *

Looking at Jean Corr's sister Lillian McElarney was like looking at Andrea Corr in fifteen or twenty years' time. She too was striking. I had arranged to meet her one Saturday morning on one of my regular jaunts to Dundalk. She was defensive at first, as most people are when you interview them, as we sat in a corner of McManus' bar. She eased up as we talked, but I don't think she ever felt totally easy with me, as if I was going to ask a difficult question. She showed me early photos of Andrea and Sharon. I loved her Irishness, the fact that family, drinking and socialising seemed the important components of local life. I would have loved to have been a part of that. She appeared busy and my questions couldn't linger. She seemed a nice person, although there was a determination and toughness about her that I both admired and feared.

*   *   *   *

All three Corr girls attended Dún Lughaidh Convent in Dundalk, a school well known for its strong musical tradition. Music is compulsory for students there up until their Junior Certificate year, while the school combines with boys' schools in Belfast and Newry to form a strong school symphony orchestra. Sharon and Caroline took music in their Leaving Certificate year, while Andrea, who was acknowledged by the school as being good at a number of things, chose not to. One of their music teachers at the school, Irene Barr, recalls that all three of the girls were talented at music: 'They had a natural affinity for music and were highly skilled at anything they put their minds to. They were all very good students and were never any problem.' Mrs Barr says the girls would take part in anything musical that was happening at the school, whether it was the choir, the orchestra or musicals. Although she has a great deal of time for all of the girls, it is Andrea that she reserves special praise for. 'Andrea was a special talent, there is no doubt about that,' she says. 'As well as being very good musically, she was also superb on the stage. She had a leading role in one of our productions, *Love From Judy*, and was quite outstanding. We have had a lot of good dramatists and musicians through the school but she would be one of the very best.'

Despite Andrea and, to a lesser degree, Caroline, winning parts in *The Commitments* and the girls composing music with Jim and Sharon in their spare time, they had no problem finding time for other activities. 'You find that with musicians,' says Mrs Barr. 'They tend to fit everything in to their schedule and it [the music] enriches them as people.'

To say that the Corr household was musical is an understatement. With Jean singing and Gerry playing keyboards in their own band, it was natural for their children to be inspired by the environment in which they grew up. Gerry and Jean's band, The Sound Affair, played a range of contemporary covers around the Dundalk and County Louth area. Those that heard them say the band was nothing out of the ordinary. But their strength, as opposed to some bands today, was that they played their own musical instruments. The Sound Affair created 'good wholesome entertainment', playing lounge music, a number of traditional and folk songs and cover versions of popular tunes 1970s tunes. With Gerry working as a wages manager at the local power board, the money that was earned performing was also undoubtedly a handy second income. Although they provided plenty of entertainment for the people of Dundalk and the surrounding area, perhaps their biggest achievement was creating a musical environment in which their children could thrive.

Today when looking at Jim Corr on keyboards and Andrea Corr singing lead vocals, it is not difficult to imagine their parents in those same respective roles twenty years previously. According to Andrea, the Corr household was always filled with music, although she didn't consider it any different from any other family home. 'As a child you think your household is like everyone else's,' she told one reporter, 'so we grew up thinking that everyone sang and played instruments as part of family life. Singing was just always there because our parents had their own covers band, The Sound Affair, and they'd rehearse during the week and play pubs and bars at the weekends. They were very good and did a lot of melodic stuff like the Carpenters, and the

Eagles and Abba. Abba were huge for them, my mother did a mean "Super Trooper" ... '. The musical influence appears to have affected all the Corr siblings early. A defining moment for the Corr family came when Gerry Corr was given a piano by his father. He has said: 'I was the only person who ever played it, so my father gave it to us. After we had our first child, Jim, we put it in his bedroom. He took to it like a natural. He had perfect pitch right from the beginning. It seemed easy.'

'We were always singing along instead of going out and playing with the other kids in the street,' Caroline says. 'My father taught us all how to play the piano from the age of six, and Sharon was taught violin from a very early age.'

Gerry Corr used to display his talents at his local church, the Church of the Redeemer, nestled in the heart of Dundalk. Father Brendan McNally recalls that Gerry was the best organist he ever had. 'He used to play the organ at late Mass on Sunday morning and he would do a mixture of things, it wouldn't be strictly hymns, but it would be appropriate music, maybe just as a background and people would come in happy and it would settle people down and put them in the right frame of mind.'

Close friends of the family say that Gerry and Jean took the success of The Corrs in their stride. Part of the reason was undoubtedly the environment in which they have continued to live. It would appear the local community has, to some degree, made an informal pact with Gerry and Jean: we'll leave you alone, but you don't change and act as if anything is different.

Music aside, the Corrs children had no different an upbringing from anyone else in Dundalk. They appear to have been raised with sound morals and good ethics and, perhaps most importantly, an appreciation that people come first. This settled upbringing would pay dividends later in their lives when time after time they would be regarded as being amongst the nicest people in an often cut-throat industry. But still throughout their backgrounds there was always the music: a passion that appears to run almost deep as their love for their parents.

CHAPTER 4

A Musical Education of Sorts

We grew up listening to our parents rehearse to 1970s pop-rock songs. Later on we got into different types of music, of course, but I think that's where it started at a young age.

Caroline Corr

Close friends of Caroline and Andrea Corr say the family 'was always very quiet' about its music. Those that spent time with them, however, realised that the family possessed musical talent but it was all taken for granted. One friend recalls:

> When I used to ring Caroline, I would hear the piano in the background and I would think it was Sharon playing, when in fact it was probably Andrea. There was always music in [their] house — there was always a guitar sitting there, or someone playing the piano. They didn't talk about their music often, which is still the case these days. Caroline will forget to tell you they've done whatever. I would ask how things were going and she would say things like 'oh, we've sold half a million albums', and I would say 'that's ****ing incredible', and she would say 'I forget to mention it'. She's so used to people interviewing her the whole time that we'd heard it all before, the same as I would forget to mention it to other people.

If Dundalk has a reputation for being dour, it also has a reputation for being a centre for quality music, especially traditional Irish music. Father Brendan McNally, who served in Dundalk for a number of years, was one of the leading music teachers in the town and taught a large number of talented classical musicians who have gone on to play with leading symphonies in Ireland and in England. He also taught Sharon Corr and she has often mentioned McNally in interviews.

A modest man with an analytical mind, McNally taught Sharon once a week for the best part of ten years. Undoubtedly McNally saw the oldest Corr sister develop over that period, both as a musician and as a person, but if he did he does not recall much. Part of the reason could be that over the time he taught Sharon he taught hundreds of budding musicians. It also could be that because he saw her each week it was difficult to notice change. Regardless, when asked about her he is non-committal. He does not speak of her fondly; but he has no negative things to say about her either. He says that Sharon's musical background was helpful, although to a great extent a talented violin player is born and not made. The manual dexterity, the feel for the music and the patience required to spend hours each day practising are more important than whether one is born in a musical household or not.

Sharon appears to be the only Corr sibling who learned the violin to any great extent and McNally believes that she was possibly the only one of the four who had the natural ability to take it up. Caroline appears to have flirted with the instrument for a brief time, before getting bored.

McNally's passion for classical music developed at high school and continued when he joined the priesthood. He took up the violin at the age of 25, thinking it would be an easy instrument to play. He says the Irish have a great tradition with finger instruments, although that does not make the violin any easier to perfect. He is a fan of rote learning, in which the student's best assets are time and patience. Being methodical, he developed a programme for bringing the students up from the very beginning to a reasonably advanced level. He refined his programme over the years as he studied more. McNally believes it takes ten years of hard work to learn the violin and that playing it is as strenuous as athletics, gymnastics or any other sport and also requires a great deal of concentration and hard work. 'You need to have a very good ear, you need to be well co-ordinated and able to handle the instrument physically, together with the musical prowess of course and the individuality that everyone looks for.'

To become a top violinist and to make a career out of violin playing a student would have to practice for at least three hours a day from an early age. McNally feels that, while Sharon was born with ability and had the hand/eye co-ordination required, she did not put in enough time to become a professional violinist:

> I knew that Sharon wasn't going to play the violin for a living. When I left Dundalk she hadn't started singing, so I had no idea what she was going to do from there. She wasn't going to be advanced enough for the age that she was at. The standard for getting into a top music college is very high, I don't know to what grade Sharon did, perhaps to grade six or seven. She would have done a certain

amount of practice. I probably would have liked it if she had done a bit more. She was satisfactory, she was relaxed. A lot of the kids that I would have would do a certain amount of work and that's all they would get out of it; you would be looking for them to do an hour every day and they would do, say, half an hour every day, and then there would be the few who would be very dedicated.

He admits that Sharon was a talented student who had all the basics, including good timing and good posture, but McNally questions how interested she was in taking her violin playing to an advanced level. McNally is not critical of the music that The Corrs play, but feels that Sharon's playing is, in violin terms, reasonably basic. 'What she is doing with the violin is technically very simple. I'm not saying that to take anything away from her, because her sound is beautiful and she does play beautifully, but there would be a big difference between playing that and playing a top classical piece.'

McNally says with The Corrs it is the singing that makes them special and the violin is an addition. This is undoubtedly true when the mass market appeal of The Corrs is considered, although at the heart of The Corrs in numbers such as 'Toss the Feathers', 'The Joy of Life' and 'Erin Shore', the violin is the lead instrument and should not be underestimated in creating the fundamental sound of the band.

Sharon was a member of the Dundalk Youth Orchestra that visited the USA in 1988, led by McNally. Because all the young Irish musicians were billeted, McNally says he can't remember much about Sharon on the trip, apart from the fact that she was friendly with the other musicians and appeared to have a good time. He does recall that Gerry and Jean Corr were supportive of the trip and helped with the fund-raising.

McNally has not kept in touch with Sharon. He is delighted with the success the band has had, but admits that pop music is not his thing. He is surprised to learn that Sharon refers to him occasionally in interviews, although he doesn't have a TV and gets most of his information from the radio. Although there was an obvious pupil/teacher relationship between the pair, Sharon was certainly not the prodigy that she has sometimes been portrayed as in interviews.

McNally, though, knows the family reasonably well and as the local priest used to call in on the family from time to time. It is obvious that he still has a soft spot for the Corr family and that that would be the case even if they hadn't ended up famous.

*   *   *   *

I knew that she had met someone, but it didn't make it any easier. A friend of mine had seen a letter to the editor of my local newspaper back home. It had a past lover of mine's name on it. I read it on the paper's website, and it hurt me, stung even, and brought home the reality that love never ends, it is merely hidden and replaced — hopefully — by new love. I was angry, wild ideas of ringing my long lost love back in New Zealand and telling her that I still thought about her, loved her even, going through my head. That somehow this would make it easier and not tougher.

I was fired up and walked the streets of Dublin at an alarming pace trying to work off some tension, some hurt. I needed to sit down and compose myself. I went into a darkened bar, ordered a BLT and a double rum and coke, sat down and tried to drown my sorrows. I was very much alone and wanting it that way, and what should be the in-house music? You guessed it, The Corrs and almost the entire Forgiven Not Forgotten *album. It sounded superb. I would love to say that it made me feel better. It didn't.*

*   *   *   *

While the girls were growing up, Jim Corr was doing his own thing. Music was always his main focus and old friends of his realised that his determination to succeed in the music business was almost second to none. Nicola Matthews, a very close friend of Jim's since the age of fifteen, says Jim always knew he was going to be famous:

> We used to work together at Tesco's and even back then when he was small, skinny and very quiet, he knew what he wanted to do with his life. It wasn't a matter of if; it was a question of when. He had this driving ambition and never thought about what he was going to do. It was always in this one direction and I admire that about him.

Matthews had a very strong friendship with Corr, which included discussing dealings with the opposite sex. 'When we were younger we were close confidants, talking about everything including relationships,' she says. 'It was good to get someone of the opposite sex's perspective. We were more or less like sister and brother.' Matthews could also turn to Jim to solve her problems and to be there as a sounding board. 'I would tell him things that I wouldn't tell other people and he would tell me things ... nothing ever happened between us, but we were and are close friends.'

However, music underlay the upbringing of all four Corr siblings. As Jim started to do his own thing and make his own way in the world, the girls were having their own musical education of sorts. The Corr sisters worked in McManus', nestled just off the main drag in Dundalk, which was and is a nice enough corner bar. The locals say McManus' is one of the best bars in Dundalk to get some Irish craic. Traditional Irish music sessions are held each Monday and Friday night. The patrons are a combination of locals and students from the nearby Institute of Technology. It is one of the better-known pubs in Dundalk, undoubtedly because of the great traditions of music that have been built up there throughout the years. It is a very busy establishment and is only one of two or three pubs in Dundalk where music is played during the week.

Lillian McElarney, the sister of the late Jean Corr, and her husband Brendan have been the proprietors of McManus' since 1981. Lillian herself sang, mostly in the folk scene in the late 1960s, although modestly says it was only around Dundalk and a couple of times in Dublin and Belfast. After leaving school Lillian worked in Dublin before coming back to Dundalk to get married. She and her husband looked around for a pub to buy. Their requirements were specific: they were just beginners in the industry and thus nothing too big was suitable. McManus' fitted the bill perfectly. Not only was it the right size, but Lillian had a history with the bar: it was the first bar she had had a drink in and had adopted it as her local long before she even thought of purchasing it.

McManus' was being run by Peter McManus when the McElarney's expressed an interest in it. Although he wasn't initially interested in selling, McManus changed his mind and Lillian and Brendan have been running McManus' ever since. It has changed under the proprietorship of the McElarneys from being an all-male pub (without even a women's toilet) to one where everyone feels at home.

There are various zones to McManus'. At the front is the musical area, where traditional music is played, while the middle section is for the older crowds who enjoy chatting. The newly renovated back section is for the younger brigade, including the large number of students who drink there. Locals say that you can tell what sort of person someone is by what they drink and where he or she drinks it in McManus'.

It was at McManus' where Sharon, Caroline and Andrea (to a lesser degree) worked behind the bar. When Lillian returned to Dundalk from Dublin in 1979, one of her few remaining friends in the town was her sister, Jean. Naturally they remained close and Lillian was able to call on any of Jean's children to work in the bar whenever things got tough. 'Andrea was only a baby when we took over the bar,' says Lillian, 'and as they [Jean's children] were growing up I was getting busy and having my children. My first girl came along in 1981 and my sister's children were looking after my children and it was like that ... these things just happen. They helped me out with babysitting and when they were older they helped me out in the bar. They were really great. At a drop of a hat they would come in and help me out as there were times when with the children, and with my mother living with me, I just couldn't cope. All I would have to do is ring and they would be down.' Lillian would also spend a lot of time with her oldest nephew Jim, although he only worked the odd shift at McManus'.

None of the girls worked at McManus' full-time (Sharon also worked in a record store called The Record Sleeve in Dundalk, while Caroline and Andrea were at school for most of their careers at McManus'). There was no denying their strengths, for the attraction of beautiful young girls behind the bar obviously brought more patrons through the door, including a number from the Institute of Technology. Students would sit and drink and sit and watch the Corr girls serve. Like other young males, some made no bones about their attraction to the girls and why they were there. 'We got a reputation in Dundalk because there were three of us behind the bar,' Sharon has said. 'The students would be there ogling.'

In fact, when the girls got parts in the movie *The Commitments* the regulars got hold of a video from the local army lads back from peace-keeping in Lebanon. They all came down to McManus' to watch it, even though it was dubbed into Arabic.

*   *   *   *

Barry Henry walked past me, which was not surprising, as we had never met before. We eventually shook hands and I couldn't get over how big he was. An electrical contractor by trade, he'd been mates with Caroline and Andrea Corr since they were all teenagers. He hadn't, as I had originally thought, been a past boyfriend of Caroline's. We lunched at Café Metz in Dundalk, a swanky place that despite its grandeur (on a Dundalk scale) still only charged £3 each for both of us to have a pretty decent meal. We sat talking and I immediately liked the fellow — he was down to earth, funny, entertaining and could talk the hump off a rhino. Which was just perfect as my tape recorder was humming away as he spoke. His affection for Caroline and Andrea was obvious and they appeared good friends. It gave me insight into the normality of the Corr family. Given that Barry was friendly with two of the Corr girls and that Sharon Corr went out with his brother, I began to appreciate what a small town Dundalk was.

*   *   *   *

Pat Dunn was bar manager at McManus' between 1985 and 1997, before leaving to open another bar, Courtney's, in central Dundalk. Like many managers he was very much hands-on, making sure everything was done right. He started in the job when the shoe factory where he worked closed down. His best friend, Brendan McElareny, came to the rescue with a job offer. Dunn talks with undeniable pride and fondness about the days when he worked at McManus'. It's a fondness not derived from the fame the Corrs have subsequently achieved, but rather from the memories of the good times at McManus'. 'It was a lovely atmosphere, a lovely family. We all got on well,' he recalls. 'It was lovely working there. It was a very busy bar; it still is. I hated leaving it, but opportunities came along and I took them and luckily things have worked out well for me.'

Being the eldest, Sharon was the first of the sisters to start working behind the bar, from the age of fourteen. As Caroline and Andrea grew older, they also began working at McManus'. Because it was a family establishment and the girls would do a range of jobs and not just pour drinks, age restrictions for serving — which are sixteen in Ireland — were not rigidly imposed. These rules, like closing time in Ireland, were flexible. 'It was great craic,' Dunn says, 'brilliant atmosphere. There were differences all the time, but that was part of the craic. It was great. Everyone got on well. My two sons worked in the bar ... we also had a guy called Jimmy working behind the bar and he would [often] come to work in fancy dress.

'The girls themselves would serve as well as doing some of the more unpleasant jobs that went with working behind a bar, including cleaning the toilets. The girls would have learnt an awful lot from their time at McManus'. But there was no denying that it was hard work. 'People say that working behind the bar is easy,' says Dunn. 'Well it certainly isn't. It's bloody hard work and McManus' is the type of bar where everyone rolls up their sleeves and gets stuck in. It involves everything. As well as being friendly to customers, your presentation behind the bar is important, as is the way you greet people, the way you serve people, talk to people and then the various topics that you can handle. Plus when everyone goes home at night all that cleaning that has to be done ... that would include things like toilets and jobs that weren't very nice, but they [the Corr girls] did it ... they would come out from the toilets some nights and go "yuk" ... but they did it.'

The Corr girls were very good behind the bar and worked extremely hard. Dunn says that their ability to handle the job was the main reason why they worked at McManus' and not because they were the nieces of the proprietor. Lillian McElareny, for her part, is in no doubt that the looks of the girls were good for patronage. She used to look at men looking at the Corr girls and know what the guys were thinking. They just couldn't take their eyes off them:

> They could handle all the attention ... that's how relaxed they are, no matter how many guys were drooling over them. They would handle it in the most beautiful way, in the fashion that any girl should do ... in a nice way and to appreciate the attention without making it difficult for themselves ... they were in control of it because if you are pretty from when you are born you have all of your life learning to deal with it, people paying you attention and all ... when they came to McManus' it was just a continuation of that.

'They had no trouble getting the punters in,' adds Dunn. 'They are lovely looking girls, but when you are working with them and you know them the very last thing in the world you think about is the fact that they are stunners or anything like that. You just take them as they are. They are very good with people and they were very friendly. They still are in fact. I am amazed with how well they are handling their fame.'

* * * *

Nicola Matthews met me in a side street not far from McManus' in Dundalk. I had had a tiring day interviewing people and somehow had to get myself up for this last interview of the day. It began to rain and I backed into the doorway of the pub waiting for my interviewee. It was not a busy stretch and I took the time to think how the lack of activity was both reassuring and at the same time utterly boring. The best and the worst of small-town living perhaps. I knew that it was Nicola (a friend of Jim Corr's) even before she stepped out of her car. She was striking and I immediately thought this wasn't going to be such a bad interview after all.

I bought us both a drink and we sat down and chewed the fat. She pointed out that there had been a recent murder in Dundalk and the victim had been drinking in this bar the night he died. I gulped, looked around me and then back at my tape recorder and pad. No I wasn't the local Garda conducting inquiries. Nicola was amazingly hesitant at first and I did my best to make her feel at ease. 'Tell me what you want to tell me,' I said, stating the obvious. Gradually Nicola started to open up and talk about her relationship with Jim Corr. She asked that I did not put my tape recorder on. Why? As it turned out she had been interviewed by the Garda that week as she had been in this very pub the night of the murder.

* * * *

Friend Barry Henry witnessed Caroline Corr behind the bar many times and was often amazed with her ability to think on the job. 'It was one Christmas Eve,' he recalls, 'and the place was jammed. There were a good twenty of us sitting in this one group and someone had just got his Christmas bonus. Well, everyone was shouted a drink and so I was asked to get them all. Caroline was on her own and I say, "I've got a massive big order here, can you take it?" She says, "Yeah, no problem", and then I list off this huge number of drinks and she goes and does it one by one and then reels each drink off one by one. And I'm thinking: how the hell?'

Such was their expertise behind the bar that even today, Pat Dunn says with a cheeky smile, that he would have no hesitation in hiring them to pull a pint at his new bar, Courtney's. But it wasn't just hard work at McManus'. At one McManus' Christmas Party at a Chinese restaurant in Dundalk, bartender Jimmy went to great efforts to make the occasion memorable for the then vegetarian Sharon Corr. 'Jimmy decided that Sharon would enjoy herself,' Pat Dunn says with a laugh. 'He arranged it with the chef that all her vegetables would be done in the most delicate matter ... brought out to Sharon were carrots in the shape of a rose and other works of art. Sharon got quite a shock: "What on earth is this?" she said.'

It was a long-standing joke that Jimmy played the saxophone in *The Commitments*, as he looks somewhat like a character in the film. The Corr sisters found the whole joke very funny. Even today Jimmy, who followed Pat Dunn to Courtney's, still gets comments about his outstanding performance in the movie.

It wasn't as though the bar work was detrimental to the outside careers of the girls. Andrea did extremely well in her leaving exams and a university career was certainly available to her, should she have chosen to go down that road.

'When they decided to form this band and they started practising,' says Pat Dunn, 'I often wondered. They were very clever girls ... I was amazed at the time ... you would ask them how their exams went and what they were going to do, whether they were going to go to college, and they would say "we are going to work on the music". You sort of wondered whether it would all work out. In saying that, I never doubted them as musicians ... they were top class musicians and their voices were superb ... listening to them at Lansdowne Road and hearing one of their CDs and all this equipment that they use ... they might as well be sitting at McManus' or behind the bar singing a song because they sound no different ... they just have it, they can play their instruments, they can sing, they can perform.'

Dunn says there was never any question that music was the girls' first love. Often after work they would gather around the piano and have a session. 'One of the lads might sing a song on certain occasions and the girls would join in. They would sound no different than they do today. They could lift an instrument ... they would batter the piano down the back of McManus' just the same as they do today on stage.'

It was at McManus' where Andrea first learnt how to play the tin whistle. 'I was working at McManus' and this guy was playing a traditional Irish wooden flute and it's a lovely sound,' Andrea told *Hot Press*. 'So I wanted to learn it and the whistle is the same fingering. But the whistle sounds better with the violin because it's shrill.'

Although Caroline and Andrea did not play at McManus' officially, Jim and Sharon did. They would play on certain Sundays and have the punters flocking in to hear their traditional music. The pair didn't have a name for their duo — word of mouth was enough to make the numbers grow whenever the pair played. 'We had the piano here,' says Lillian McElarney. 'Jim is great on the piano. This place just used to bounce. The piano used to belong to my mother and when we brought it in here we had it sprayed pink and so it became the pink piano. Jim and Sharon were really a super combination. A bit of trad [music] would come in there, along with Dire Straits, who were big at the time. There was a great combinations of sounds, it was fabulous.'

Lillian recalls often retiring upstairs to bed in order to get up early the next morning and hearing 'wonderful sounds' being played down below as the staff would have an almost all-night music session that would contain a bit of everything. Pat Dunn says although The Corrs never played any of the *Forgiven Not Forgotten* album at McManus', from time to time the girls hummed melodies they were practising at home. 'A lot of the songs from the first album were played here in some form ... when the album was first released I knew some of them ... when they were sitting around the bar they would be humming to themselves some of the tunes that would later end up as songs ... it was very normal for them to be singing away.'

Dunn says even today the Corr family has not changed. Speaking before Jean Corr's death he commented:

> Even when you see them today they are nothing but friendly. They would come into me here and it will be as if nothing has changed. That's a tribute to their parents and the way they were brought up. Jean and Gerry are great people and I am not just saying that. They are genuinely nice people. The girls have been reared very well ... they have got respect for people, they obviously have great

respect for their parents, you know they have, and I don't think they will ever change ... they have always been like that ... the family is great support. I just know from my observations that they are a very close family. They will never pass you. They will want to know how you are getting on, whether you are keeping well, how the family is doing, all the bits and pieces ... we would never be talking about show business or anything, it would just be more about catching up with all the gossip.

He gives an example of how the Corr family has kept their feet on the ground:

I was working here [at Courtney's] on a Saturday night. I was walking home after one shift to have my tea and then return for another. I heard this beep, beep, beep, I looked and I didn't know who it was ... it was a 1993 red Peugeot ... I still didn't know who it was and so I walked on ... and then I realised it was Andrea ... she came over and gave me a great big hug ... it's lovely isn't it ... they love meeting people and their friends from the old days.

It is telling that among the very first customers when Courtney's opened in late July 1997 were Sharon, Caroline and Andrea.

*   *   *   *

I had wanted to interview Ollie Campbell almost more than I had wanted life itself. He has been a boyhood hero of mine, his rugby exploits famous the length and breath of New Zealand. When I was eleven he was, in my eyes, bigger than the President of the United States. Campbell had come to my town with the Lions and one wet, cold Friday afternoon I had watched him practice like a disciple.

Years later I found out that Ollie had a connection with The Corrs. The fact that Ireland is such a small country was brought home to me by the news that Ollie Campbell was good mates with Corrs' manager John Hughes, himself a strapping winger in his time. I now wanted to speak to Ollie on two counts.

I rang the great number ten and got an answer machine. Nervous as hell, I left a message and asked him to contact me, which he did later that evening. We talked for over an hour, my hero and me, and covered as much rugby as we could fit in. Talking to my hero, I felt eleven again. Eventually I brought up the second topic: 'Ah Ollie, I'm doing this book on The Corrs ...'

*   *   *   *

Dundalk journalist Margaret Roddy says that although many in Dundalk were proven wrong with the success of The Corrs, she was not surprised that a musical entity from Dundalk has made the big time. 'There has been such a long tradition of music in the town, going way back to the 1940s and 1950s,' she says. 'There were always bands, always people playing music so at some stage there was always going to be a band from Dundalk who were going to make it big. But I don't know whether we would have said it was going to be The Corrs. In saying that they have worked very hard over the years preparing for what they are doing.'

Although Dundalk has a strong musical tradition, there have been plenty of restrictions on the local music industry. Perhaps the biggest problem has been a lack of places for bands to practice. In the 1960s and 1970s there were a couple of major venues that hosted Thin Lizzy and Eric Clapton, but there has been not a lot else. As people became more upwardly mobile and the costs of bringing big names to Dundalk became unrealistic, the venues became uneconomic to run and, as a result, local bands suffered. This was one of a number of issues dealt with in a report commissioned by the Arts Council of the Louth County Council and released in June 1999. One of the people who made a submission on the report was Jim Corr.

Even today The Corrs feel very much part of Dundalk and locals regard the Corr family as being normal townsfolk. Recently a local asked Jim Corr to sign a birthday card for a young friend in Kilkenny. Jim asked him the address, when the birthday was and said he would take it down to Dublin for the girls to sign. Amazingly enough on the day itself a birthday card and signed photograph arrived from The Corrs. It undoubtedly made the friend's day and reflects as much as anything the good upbringing the Corr children have had and how they haven't forgotten their roots.

Coming from Dundalk was particularly relevant in the musical education of The Corrs. One of the more musical towns in a musical country, Dundalk provided the platform for the Corr children to develop and test their talents. These days they may underplay the role of the town of Dundalk in their careers, but there can be no denying its importance. It is impossible to truly understand The Corrs without understanding Dundalk.

CHAPTER 5

Committed to *The Commitments*

Jimmy Rabbitte is a man with a vision — to bring soul music to Dublin. His friends Derek and Outspan ask him to manage their band. Jimmy agrees, but on his own terms. He places an ad in the local paper: 'Have you got Soul? If so the World's Hardest Working Band is looking for you … ' Jimmy weeds out all with impure musical tastes and the pieces begin to fall into place.

Promotional material from *The Commitments*

Throughout their childhood and early adult years, music was always a passion for the Corr siblings — always in the blood and always a likely career in some shape or form. Thanks to the influence and piano lessons of Gerry and Jean Corr and the musical environment in which they were brought up, the Corrs were always going to be involved in music somehow.

The Corr girls themselves seemed happy living in Dundalk. They were, on the whole, level headed and rarely went off the rails. They liked to have their fair share of good times, including a number of boyfriends, but always seemed to know when to stop. Although not prudish, friends say they could certainly be defined as sensible. They didn't have much time to get into trouble, as the Corrs siblings became 'The Corrs' when Caroline was seventeen and Andrea only sixteen.

*   *   *   *

Ollie Campbell was everything I imagined. In his tone and manner he was distinctly Irish, he was polite, analytical and, like me, deeply in love with rugby. He was everything I had wanted him to be. I didn't have the guts to ask him whether he remembered me, because I am sure that he didn't and that would have broken my heart. I told him that he was probably respected more in New Zealand than in Ireland and that in some shape or form he had changed my life. He appreciated my comments and was as gracious as any hero should be.

I asked him for an interview both about rugby and his involvement with The Corrs (he had been acknowledged on their first album). He said he would think about both requests and get back to me. He did so one Monday evening. He said that he wouldn't be able to talk to me about rugby because he was contracted with another company, but that he would be prepared to talk to me about The Corrs. That was fine with me. Being an unbelievably busy man, we had trouble connecting for the next two weeks.

When we spoke again we talked about getting an interview with The Corrs' manager John Hughes. He said he would ask him, that I probably would be able to get a meeting with Hughes and that it would be then up to me to sell myself and convince him to agree to an interview. And all this through rugby connections. I wouldn't have thought this possible when I watched my hero methodically kick rugby balls back at Lincoln College in 1983.

*   *   *   *

The foundations of The Corrs were laid when Jim Corr decided that he had had enough of school and that he wanted to be a musician. You have to wonder what the conservative Gerry and Jean Corr thought of their son's decision to forgo what their generation had regarded as safe career options and aim for a career in music. Perhaps the only reason why they allowed it to happen was that their own passion for music was so strong. But, then again, they may not have had a choice in the matter.

Jim had begun performing with Gerry and Jean in Dundalk's bars and clubs when he was fifteen, but it wasn't until a few years later that he started to gig seriously. A spell in Germany with a local band provided a sound musical foundation, but the work and the hours were harsh. It was not an experience Jim remembers fondly and it provided him with an early lesson in the pitfalls of an often fickle industry. Friends of Jim say these were important developing years for him. When the later success of The Corrs is put into context, it's clear that the degree to which Jim has savoured his success is in part due to the time that he spent on the road, working for little and learning that many musicians make a meagre living.

Life soon got better for Jim. He worked with a variety of traditional Irish bands and was lucky enough to tour at one stage with the legendary traditional Irish musician Dolores Keane. Gigging to various parts of the world was a forerunner to Jim's ultimate destiny, but it was clear that something special would need to happen for Jim to ever reach the lofty goals that he had set himself.

*   *   *   *

Ollie rang me one Tuesday morning. I had been asleep but this was the phone call that I had been waiting for.

'Yes', he said, 'John [Hughes] is prepared to meet with you.' I was pretty rapt although not as excited as I would have been nine months previously.

I rang Hughes that afternoon and told him how much I admired him, which was perfectly true. He asked me whether I was playing rugby in Ireland. It was pretty obvious he was a big picture sort of man and not a details sort of bloke. The mobile phone connection wasn't great and I had trouble hearing him. He told me to ring him back the following week. I did that, but he was busy that week and said to ring him the following week. I did that too, but couldn't get hold of him and so I left a message. I thought I'd get to him eventually. At no stage, however, did I want to meet The Corrs. Either the book was authorised and I got full access, or I did it on my own and had no access. Still, it would have been kind of fun having a beer with them.

*   *   *   *

Jim had his first taste of success when he joined an electronic pop and rock band called The Fountainhead. The band was a five-piece fronted by Steve Belton and Pat O'Donnell. China Records signed The Fountainhead and they had one Irish hit, *Rhythm Method*. The band were notable for being the first techno band in Ireland and, while never scaling the heights that many had predicted, they developed a strong following.

Wayne G. Sheehy was the drummer with The Fountainhead and another band that Jim Corr would soon become involved with, Hinterland. He was and remains a close friend of Jim's. 'Jim was the second keyboard player in The Fountainhead,' Sheehy recalls, 'and he was an extraordinary musician, the consummate professional and perhaps most importantly, a good laugh as well. He also had a great passion for music, was superb on stage and was a master at the keyboards. As a keyboards player he was my type of musician in the sense that he played atmospheric pieces,' says Sheehy. 'He would kill me for saying it, but he was also something of a showman. I have a video or two of him in action that I am sure he would die of embarrassment if he ever saw. But he did know how to entertain an audience.' The rest of the Corr family was also noticed from time to time. 'We would often drop off Jim in Dundalk and catch a glimpse of his sisters, who would have been fourteen or fifteen at the time. We would go away drooling about what they would be like in a few years' time!' Sheehy continues: 'He would also talk very fondly about his family and the days when he would play with his parents around Dundalk. I think he learned a lot by doing that.'

The two founders of The Fountainhead, Steve Belton, and Pat O'Donnell, were guitarists. Belton remembers that they were looking for a quality keyboard player. 'In those days both Pat and myself played everything on the albums, so when we went out and played live we needed to hire musicians. Jim Corr was perfect for what we were looking for. He was a terrific musician, he looked good on stage and he was one of the most enthusiastic musicians I have come across. It was one of the reasons why we had Jim on retainer.' Both Belton and Sheehy recall Jim being the right type of person to tour with. 'He's a great guy to be around and he's fun to be with,' says Sheehy. 'We spent around two years with the band going backwards and forwards to Switzerland to concerts and that sort of thing and we always had a great time. I think we still hold the record for the number of people in attendance at the Cave of the Manor venue in Switzerland. I think there were 50 per cent more people than what the fire regulations allowed. We all thought we were going to pass out that night.'

The Fountainhead dissolved after parting with China Records and struggling to get a new record deal. Although very popular in Switzerland, the band never reached its goals and, when this became obvious, the motivation of band members waned. 'I think we were all very disappointed with what happened,' says Steve Belton, 'but we did our best and we did have some success.'

After playing with The Fountainhead, Jim received an invitation to play a couple of gigs with Hinterland, a duo established in 1986 and that had one critically acclaimed album, *Kissing the Roof of Heaven* released by Island Records. He got the gig not only because was he a highly regarded session musician, but because Hinterland had the same manager as The Fountainhead. Donal Coghlan was half of Hinterland and to this day speaks fondly of Jim Corr the musician and Jim Corr the person. 'Jim played with us at a couple of gigs during that time, including one at the Town and Country venue in London in front of 1,500 people,' he says. 'Obviously, coming in cold Jim had to pick up everything and I was amazed how quickly that he managed to learn the music. At one of the performances there was all sorts of music being played, some of it programmed and some of it live. He played his part effectively note perfect and afterwards we slagged him about whether he was playing live or not. He says he was, even to this day! He was quite simply an excellent keyboard player and an amazingly talented musician. Of all the people we worked with during those years, he was certainly one of the best. As a person he was one of the nicest people you could meet. He was always very serious about his music and I'm delighted that he has achieved so much success subsequently, because the music business is one of the hardest areas in which to make your mark.'

With Hinterland coming to the end of its days, Wayne G. Sheehy and Jim Corr sat together one night discussing what they would do next with their careers. 'And Jim says to me that he is going to move back to Dundalk,' says Sheehy, 'because he was sick of being a gunslinger [session musician] for other people. He said he was going to put a band together with his sisters and go for it. He said, basically, that he was going to bust his balls to make it happen. So that's what he did. He went away and bought some equipment and started to produce. I didn't see him for three years after that. To be honest, when he told me it didn't surprise me at all. Jim was good like that: when he said he was going to do something, he would go away and do it. In saying that, I'm not sure whether Jim always had it in mind to create a family band. In that respect he kept things close to his chest.'

Sheehy thinks the reason why Jim treats Keith Duffy and Anto Drennan, The Corrs' backing musicians, so well is because of his earlier experiences. 'He has been on both sides of the fence. He also has been a gunslinger and worked for other people and knows how hard it is. I think that is why The Corrs have held their musicians for so long.'

Jim decided to work independently and rented a cream-coloured, two-storey house close to his parents on Mount Avenue in Dundalk. In a dark back bedroom he created a studio and he split his time working as a session musician and playing in a variety of local bands. It was with one of these bands that he went touring around army bases in Germany. During this development period in Jim's life he crossed paths with a man who was to play a huge part in his future. A chance meeting between Jim and John Hughes led to the start of the story of The Corrs.

Jim met and then played with Hughes in a band called The Hughes Version, a short-lived outfit put together when Hughes' previous band, Minor Detail, ended. At the time, Hughes was also involved in casting for The Commitments and Jim had an idea. 'John was a friend,' he has said. 'I told him I had some sisters ... '.

It appears that the idea to form a family band had been with Jim for some time. In many respects this was not the most natural way of thinking for him. Like most session musicians, Jim's musical tastes could never be regarded as middle of the road and it is doubtful whether at the time he saw into the future and the style of music that The Corrs would go on to create. What he does deserve credit for is seeing the potential in his three sisters. Having done the local circuit with Sharon, he undoubtedly knew of her musical ability. Andrea's talent, even at the age of sixteen, was obvious. The little sister, the drama queen, she was the ideal lead singer; just like her mum and aunt. Caroline was a little more difficult to stereotype, although also clearly musical. How she fitted into the jigsaw would be defined later, although Caroline was only too happy to go along for the ride.

The Corrs' rise to success began when the foursome went to an audition for the Alan Parker movie *The Commitments* — a screen adaptation of Roddy Doyle's novel of the same name. The story tells of how a group of down-and-out, working-class north Dubliners try to make it big by playing soul music. While eventually there were comparisons made between The Corrs' story and *The Commitments* script, the band in the movie didn't go on to have huge worldwide success.

Up until this stage the Corr family had not performed together in public. The audition for *The Commitments* was an opportunity for the Corr siblings to come together as a musical unit and, just like their parents, do what came naturally to them. Sharon Corr explained to Australian magazine *Drum* how it all came about. 'We were in *The Commitments* but they were blink and you'll miss us roles. Just wee cameo roles, except Andrea had a few speaking lines, a few rude lines and was the lead character's little sister in it. Jim was in some avant-garde band and I was in a country and western band playing the violin and Caroline was in a crowd scene — major roles, you know. It was really good, meeting somebody like Alan Parker, but it was just tiny roles. Apart from playing for our family Christmas, the first time we performed together as The Corrs was at the auditions for *The Commitments*,' Sharon says. 'We heard Alan Parker was coming to Ireland to hold auditions for the film and, like most Irish teenagers, we decided to go along. Looking back we must have looked and sounded horrific.'

The Commitments was not just the big break for The Corrs, but also for casting agent Ros Hubbard. She recalls John Hughes telling her that he knew Jim and that he had some sisters. 'And so at the casting for the movie I met this protective brother and his three stunningly beautiful sisters,' she says. 'At that stage Jim Corr was a reasonably well-known musician and was even a member of the musicians' union. But it was obvious from early on that they were all remarkable talents.'

Auditions for the movie took place at The Waterfront in Dublin. In an effort to relax the hopefuls, Hubbard and director Alan Parker would get them to sing first before letting them show their prowess at acting. Hubbard recalls that each of the Corr siblings gave superb auditions and although Jim, Sharon and Caroline did not win major parts, it was not an indication of their ability. Part of the reason why

The Corrs weren't hired as a band was because there was no place for a family band as such. She also suggests that they may not have had the right look. 'Perhaps The Corrs, as they would become, were a little too refined. I think what the producers were looking for were earthier people. So what they ended up doing was putting a band together.'

Until *The Commitments* Jim had been struggling to make his mark in the music industry. Although reasonably successful as a session musician, his individual music career was effectively a dead-end street. The audition for *The Commitments* was the opportunity to do something that would provide a career lifeline. But forming a family band was still a punt. There were now four careers on the line. If the Corr family had not been so obsessed with music, if one of the girls had had a driving ambition to do something else, if Andrea or Caroline had established careers and not been schoolgirls at the time the band was formed, The Corrs may not have happened.

Following the audition, something more important developed. In an interview in *Hot Press* in 1999, Hughes recalls that 'When they were finished, Ros Hubbard barged into the room and said "I'm going to say something in front of John Hughes that he's not going to like — but I'm going to say it anyway". And she said: "You've got to manage them". And then she turned to them and said, "He'll do it right. He's honest; he's straight, and he'll look after you, you've got to let him." Which was highly embarrassing. Because I hadn't even made my mind up to be a manager yet.'

Hubbard downplays her role in connecting Hughes with The Corrs:

> There are so many crooks out there and The Corrs were so young that I felt that John would have been ideal. I felt that John being the man that he is, a family man with very high values, that he was the right person to manage them. He's a nice guy, someone with good morals and he had of course been a musician himself and he knew the industry. Generally though he is a good egg, someone whom I would trust with my daughter. I think also at that early stage he believed in The Corrs and perhaps saw that they had some potential.

Hughes took a weekend to think over the offer to manage The Corrs. For all their innocence, even from day one the family had its fair share of talent. But to take a risk and put everything on a chance that they were going to be successful? That takes some guts. It was obvious that the arrangement would be for the long haul.

As for *The Commitments* itself, it says more about the Ireland of the time than it does about The Corrs. Its acceptance across the world and the chord that it struck with so many was part of the developing Irish cultural phenomena that would develop so significantly in the following decade. There was an innocence about the movie, a sense of passion and community that proved so popular. It was a sweet movie, founded on strong foundations. Still, Andrea's performance as Jimmy Rabbitte's sister was noteworthy. It was clear from the limited number of scenes that she was in that she had a charisma for performance, an ability to feel comfortable and strong in front of a camera. Not only that, as a teenager she was visibly striking. 'My role was more substantial [than the others'] in that I spoke a few rude lines,' Andrea told *Hot Press*. 'I'm not embarrassed about it, it's just funny. They're lines that live with you forever. When I got the part in *The Commitments* I thought I was very pretty, which was hilarious, checking my hair and doing everything that a fifteen-year-old would. Luckily, my parents were there to protect me from the people I was drawing towards me without even knowing. I suddenly became aware of my body and men.'

Hughes is a visionary and deserves credit, as few businesspeople at the time would have looked at the Corr siblings and seen possibility. When it comes to listening and producing music he is also something of a master. He has an ear that can pick up things that others can't. He also has an understanding of the traditions of music.

*   *   *   *

For some reason (which will be explained later) I never did get to see John Hughes. For a journalist like myself trying to see this bloke was all a little bit confusing: he was harder to get to see than some of the most powerful people in Ireland. But, then again, according to The Irish Independent *he was the 23rd most powerful person in Irish entertainment. As a journalist I was used to being able to get to anyone I wanted to interview. I continued to try: more out of frustration of not being able to see him than an actual need. Good management in the entertainment industry is as much about protection as it is about anything else. I would have thought Hughes would have been interested in what I was writing. However, as this book demonstrates time after time, Hughes is not interested in the small details.*

*   *   *   *

Hughes met the Corr family after they had discussed the idea of a band and asked them if they wanted him to take up the reins? They said they did. Hughes replied: 'Okay, I'll have a go. I've got a ten-year vision.' 'After we'd agreed,' he told *Hot Press*, 'I had to go to Dundalk to say hello to the parents and to figure out what we were going to do. So I went up and Jim said "We'll go and get Andrea and Caroline". We went to a school and two girls with schoolbags, green uniforms, shirts, ties, blazers — the whole bit — appeared and suddenly I realised that they were children. It wasn't what I expected, having seen the girls on stage. Andrea was in fifth year — she had two years to go. And Caroline had all of sixth year to do. But it was too late to think was this madness or what. I was involved. And so we just took it from there.'

Then the hard work started. The family had some idea about the type of music that they wanted to create. It was a blend of pop with traditional Irish music. The vocals would be a key feature. But they lacked a drummer and, although Sharon's violin would provide a distinctive traditional flavour, it was the creative talents of Jim and Andrea that were providing the drive.

It came as no surprise to most when the siblings decided to form The Corrs. 'Jim had always planned that. It was there from the beginning,' says aunt Lillian McElarney. 'I was not surprised. It was taken for granted given that they were into music. That was just progressing from Jim being on his own with his music, to Sharon and Jim together ... I knew that it was always going to happen, despite not having talked about it. It was always there ... it was just like [saying] that they were going to grow up, they were going to be a band. That was their life, I knew that.'

But connected with the work came the drive and determination of John Hughes. The reluctant manager was a musician before he was a manager, so knew what the band would go through. Hughes learned his musical trade with Dublin band Ned Spoon and he emerged into national prominence in Ireland during the 1980s with Minor Detail, an electronic duo comprising Hughes and his brother Willie, 'doing a majestic kind of pop that captured the imagination of A&R scouts at Polygram's New York headquarters'. Minor Detail's debut album went top 75 in the USA, although it wasn't commercial enough to make the breakthrough that Hughes and his brother craved. Hughes has said that the project got bogged down in the familiar mire of record company politics, although in reality the music was neither commercial enough nor good enough to achieve worldwide success. Despite a positive early showing, the project ran aground, and the Hughes brothers became just another Irish act that had tried their hand at the big time and failed.

Minor Detail's lack of success in many respects ironically paved the way for The Corrs. Music industry insiders say a major problem with Minor Detail was the management of the band. Close friends of John Hughes say the relative failure of Minor Detail was a major motivation for Hughes in managing The Corrs. And it was perhaps a further stroke of luck that The Corrs found a manager who *did* have the ruthless desire to make something of a young band. 'I think he knew what it was like to fail through a lack of quality management,' says one friend of Hughes, who did not wish to be named. 'I am sure that part of John's motivation was to ensure that that never happened to The Corrs.'

*   *   *   *

Travel for me was about experience, developing as a person and meeting some of the nicest people in the world. After I had met Tom Cosgrave, a fan of The Corrs, I soon met his family. Such was the nature of the Cosgraves, I was quickly made one of the family and in my early days in Dublin went and visited them every Sunday. On these occasions I was treated to a roast meal, friendship and fantastic hospitality. I know that I could have turned to them had I ever got into trouble. I spent two Christmases with them and in years to come I will look upon those times with real fondness. I learned from the Cosgraves that what makes Ireland special is its people. That the Irish understand perhaps more fully than any other nation what it means to be alive.

*   *   *   *

John Hughes is a hard man to classify. Few people in the music industry are so full of contradictions and have such diverse strengths and weaknesses. On the one hand Hughes has an amazing sense of energy. Connected with this, Hughes has an appreciation of both music and the music industry that comes from his experiences with Minor Detail and from a natural affinity with sound. As well as being entrepreneurial, Hughes is a man with huge vision and understanding of the world around him. A prolific reader, he is also a shrewd trader and one of the hardest working managers in the music industry. Friends say that he is also a quality communicator and able to relate to people of all ages and backgrounds.

However, on the other hand Hughes has a total lack of ability when it comes to details and doing the paperwork, often leaving those around him pulling their hair out. Record industry sources say that Hughes' lack of attention to detail proved embarrassing after the Lansdowne Road concert in Dublin in 1999. With a host of record company guests at the post-concert party ignored, one senior record company executive left in a huff. Meanwhile transport that was supposed to be provided didn't turn up, while some specially invited guests didn't even get in to the bash afterwards.

Hughes left the patch-up work to the band, says a well-placed Atlantic Records insider. 'Jim Corr called ... It seems that someone spoke to him and told him exactly how the label people were treated. Jim was apparently horrified and had no idea. So, he called to apologise and asked who exactly didn't get in to the party. Bottom line is, professionally, it was very nice of him to make the personal calls. It wasn't really for him to apologise and it's pretty sad when an artist has to clean up after his manager's mess, *again*.'

Hughes often takes a long time to make up his mind and that can be frustrating for those he works with. But despite his failings when it comes to details, his vision has made him a vital component in the success of The Corrs. 'I never plan,' Hughes told *Hot Press*. 'I hate plans. I hate the tyranny of the plan. Planning is, as I read somewhere recently, based on the false assumption that you can predict the future. You can't. But you can have vision. And that's what we tried to construct. I hoped at the outset that within a ten-year period we could have a number one album in the world. It seemed like an eternity and they wanted to cut it back to seven years. But I said allow ten.'

Hughes is also loyal to those who have helped both him and The Corrs get to where they are now. 'John is a gentleman,' says family friend Barry Henry. 'When they were playing in these small places, John would always come up to me and say, "Thanks a million for coming, we appreciate your support". Some of us got tickets to see The Corrs play as support for Celine Dion. After The Corrs had finished we had no real interest in seeing the main act and so we disappeared back to the bar and I started talking to this traditional musician whom I knew. In the middle of our conversation, John Hughes walks along and walks straight up to me, shakes hands with me and says, "Thanks very much Barry for coming to the show". And I said, "Thanks a million for the tickets" and he says, "Barry you know with you, no problem". The fact that he went past everyone to say, "thanks a million" to me meant a lot.'

Music journalist Kevin Courtney says John Hughes has always been accommodating with him. 'He seemed very professional,' Courtney says of his dealings with Hughes. 'He has become a bigger figure having guided The Corrs to such success in Britain. I mean having the number one and two albums in Britain at the same time? I think if you do that you are going to become a pretty big figure. Those who like me didn't know about him certainly did know about him after that!'

Casting agent and friend Ros Hubbard also pays tribute to the job Hughes has done with The Corrs. 'Above all else I think what he has done is made sure that the band has retained its independence,' says Hubbard. 'It would have been so easy for them to have become manufactured, much the same way as many other bands these days. John has great respect for his fellow artist and I think he's taken the view that if it isn't broke, why fix it? When The Corrs were doing their stuff, people were telling them that they would not make it and that the Spice Girls were all the rage. Well with great respect to them, where are the Spice Girls now? John has ensured through taking a long-term approach that The Corrs have been no flash in the pan. This is mostly due, I believe, to the fact that they have been honest about their music and themselves.'

'There are two types of manager,' says Andy Murray, Vice-President for Warner Music International. 'One type has a relationship based on long industry experience, reputation and organisation. The other has a relationship with the artist based on absolute belief and support from the earliest part of the artist's career. If it works you can forgive them all sorts of personal faults. With John and The Corrs it works. Therefore, while I would much prefer it to have one word with his personal assistant on a Monday morning and not have to chase him [Hughes] all the way round Ireland or the world, that's the way it is. And, while I would have preferred it to not have had to call him twice a day for three months for him to confirm that The Corrs would be doing *Unplugged*, that's the way it is.'

Legendary record producer David Foster also has a lot of admiration for Hughes and says that as with many other popular musical acts, a feature of The Corrs' success has been the person guiding them. 'John Hughes would take a bullet for The Corrs, it's that simple,' he says. 'He has huge strength and is one of the most determined men I have met. He now has so much prestige that he can literally ring anyone up and say that it's John Hughes speaking and not necessarily John Hughes, manager of The Corrs speaking. Another reason why I have so much respect for the man is that he hasn't pushed himself forward and demanded some of the limelight. He has remained in the background and let The Corrs get all the attention, just like a good manager should. John said to me a long time ago that The Corrs were going to be the next U2. I laughed at him at the time and told him to get real. But he may very well be right. If that is the case I can see The Corrs being around for the next fifteen to twenty years.'

These days John Hughes has remained true to the lifestyle that he had back in a time when he was a simple unknown. He does not drink, drugs are out of the question and he does not jet around the world on expensive whims. His one luxury is being driven. Whenever he is going somewhere special he will arrange to be picked up, dropped off and then delivered home. It is not extravagant by any means (especially if you have experienced Dublin traffic) but it does reflect the fact that success, and not the trappings of it, has been Hughes's main aim; that seeing his own self as successful and as anything but a failure is more important than anything else.

Those who perhaps have been most affected by Hughes's relentless devotion to The Corrs has been his own family. Friends of the Hughes family say that it is a tribute to Hughes that his family has remained unaffected by the success of their father and husband. As Hughes' three children have grown older they have been able to participate more in the travel and success of The Corrs so have missed out on little. Also crucial in John Hughes's success is his wife Marie. Close friends of Hughes say Marie is the settled force in their marriage, keeping Hughes' feet on the ground. Hughes himself has publicly recognised the part she has played. 'My wife Marie was the real unsung hero,' he explained to *Hot Press*. 'When you say to your wife you are going to manage a band and there is no money, and any money you have is going to have to be spent on the band, and she says, "Okay, I don't know but I believe you and they seem like nice kids. Let's give it a shot," then she's a hero.'

Marie Hughes appears dear to The Corrs themselves. She receives a credit on each of their three original albums and the special thanks given to her on *In Blue* suggests that she played an important role in helping the Corr family grieve the death of their mother in October 1999.

The question remains: what motivates John Hughes? What motivates a man to manage two schoolgirls, a record shop manager and a session musician and see within them the potential to sell millions of albums? What motivates a man to put the rest of his life on hold to seek and achieve worldwide success? It would be taking the conclusion too far to suggest that Hughes was trying to make up for his lack of success with Minor Detail, although it is safe to assume that much of his motivation came from this chapter in his life.

Although Hughes was bright, willing and determined enough to have made it in any field that he chose to apply himself in, the talented (and attractive) siblings from Dundalk were perhaps his best and most obvious bet at making it big in an industry that he was so passionate about. Still, it would not be completely accurate to say that Hughes was an ardent admirer of The Corrs from the first day. Although he was certainly interested in the potential of The Corrs, it took him six months after deciding to manage the band to make his trip to Dundalk to meet the family. And it is unusual for Hughes to say that he found the fact that Caroline and Andrea were still at school surprising. After all, he knew their ages when they auditioned for *The Commitments.*

John Hughes, it would appear, is a man with a permanent sense of vision. He is not a dreamer, but rather a doer who sees the larger picture and, perhaps most importantly, knows what he has to do to make it happen. He does not seem overly concerned with being in the limelight himself. In fact, close friends of the man say that he purposely pushes himself away from the cameras.

Like The Corrs themselves, Hughes has been lucky, but even his harshest critic would admit that he has earned his good luck with hard work. He may be occasionally irritating for those who work with him, but as a manager the ultimate test is whether his charges have been successful. The Corrs have still gone on to sell millions of albums worldwide and there can be no denying that John Hughes has been crucial to the success of The Corrs.

*   *   *   *

It's funny, but the more travelling you do the more you realise that there are some cities that instantly appeal. Some years back when I travelled through the USA and Canada I separated cities into those I would like to live in and those that I would like to visit regularly. In the former category came Boston, San Franciso and Toronto. Into the later category came New York, New Orleans and Washington. Dublin appealed instantly to me. I am not sure whether it was the intrinsic literary feel on the streets, the bold architecture or the warmth of the people, but I fell in love with Dublin from almost day one. I would like to think that Dublin felt the same way about me. To me Dublin was the cultural magnificence of Temple Bar (although native Dubliners might disagree), the reserved good looks of the girls in their early twenties as they walked the streets in their lunch hours, the almost haunting images of Joyce, Wilde and Beckett in any of the cosy pubs that littered the streets. Yes, Dublin was my sort of city. I loved it almost as much as my own.

*   *   *   *

By this stage of their careers The Corrs were a band with unbridled potential, clear musical talent and a manager who had the drive, determination, experience and vision to take them places. There was also no question that they would all work hard to try to make their dreams a reality. All the ingredients for success? Perhaps, but there was still a lot of growing for The Corrs to do before they could realise this very considerable potential.

CHAPTER 6

Not Vogue, But Bloody Determined

We spent two years explaining to everybody what a bodhrán was, and a whistle. No one had ever seen them in the pop world. Nor did they want them. But we followed our instincts and it was a struggle and it wasn't welcome. It made it far harder to get a deal, not easier.

John Hughes

In the current pop industry it may seem surprising that a band has to work for years to achieve any sort of success. The Corrs have suggested time and time again in interviews that whatever success they have had has well and truly been earned. The Corrs probably say this in part because, where other bands have achieved chart success with relatively little hard slog, the Dundalk family took years to achieve their share of the fame pie.

To get a product that was marketable and could be sold to the record companies and the public alike, much work had to be put in to achieving what was essentially The Corrs' sound. Most of the distinctive feel of *Forgiven Not Forgotten* was created in Dundalk. The house that Jim Corr had hired became home to The Corrs and the hours and hours of practice that were required to craft their distinctive sound. Money was tight and any surplus was ploughed back into the music and purchasing recording equipment.

The house in Mount Avenue is known as Gate Lodge. It is owned by the Cox family, who are well known in the Dundalk area for their racehorses. The house where Jim spent around two years of his life is more frequently used for housing racing staff, although the Cox family were only too happy to rent the property to Jim. Bunny Cox says that he was a good tenant and did not cause any problems.

One of the first things that Jim did after leasing the house was to insulate it to ensure that it was soundproof. That way the sound made inside would not disturb the horses on the outside and nor would Jim be disturbed as he composed and produced his music.

Within walking distance of the Corr family home, Gate Lodge proved a perfect base for Jim and the three girls to compose. It gave

Jim enough room to be independent, while its proximity ensured that the girls could visit as often as they wished. It also provided an avenue for Jim to get some feedback on what he was producing. The Cox children — Jennifer, Richard, Suzanne and Michelle — would often leave sweets for Jim in his letterbox and then pop in to see what he was producing. 'Kids being kids, they would tell Jim what they thought of what he was doing: what they liked and what they didn't,' says Bunny Cox.

When The Corrs went to the USA for the first time the Cox family thought they would be seeing a lot less of the Corr family. 'But we got quite a surprise,' says Bunny, 'when Jim's dog kept coming back to us. He'd been sent to stay with Mr and Mrs Corr but, because we had quite a few stray dogs that used to hang around our place, he kept coming back! Gerry Corr would then come around and pick the dog up, as Jim was worried about it!'

Jim, now almost fully committed to the family band, undoubtedly saw its potential. Caroline and Andrea were still at school, combining schoolwork by day, working at McManus' at night and spending hours at Jim's house creating, crafting and developing sounds. Sharon was working in a record shop and at McManus', and she was as committed as her sisters. The hours the Corr family put into their music at this stage of their careers were clearly important. Not only did the whole concept of The Corrs develop at this time, but the bonds between Jim and younger his sisters, especially Caroline and Andrea, started to grow. It was music, however, that was the reason why they grew closer and this time was vital to the band's dynamic.

Friends of the Corr siblings say that as time passed the girls spent more and more time up at Jim's, although they still did not talk much about what they were doing. Other than the humming of some of the new songs off *Forgiven Not Forgotten* at McManus', that is. John Hughes, reflecting on this period, told *Hot Press* that the harmonies were a vital breakthrough. 'The voices melded in a way that only family voices do,' he said in 1999. 'They were out of fashion, no doubt about that, but the talent was blatantly obvious, or to me it was. So we were in a position of having to try to second-guess where the industry was going or just following our own instincts. Second-guessing is folly. Never second-guess. And so we had to do what we were good at, despite the fact that it was not in vogue.'

With enough songs to potentially get the band a record deal, Hughes pulled out all the stops in his efforts. But no one wanted to know them, not even local labels. 'I tried to get a record deal in Ireland and failed miserably,' Hughes told *Hot Press*. 'I tried to get a deal in England and failed just as miserably. My failures were tremendous and they were consistent — the rejection letters just kept on coming! And so I went to the USA to get a deal.'

The hardship that The Corrs and Hughes went through in those early days has been repeated many times in newspaper and magazine articles. 'I would have said John wouldn't have made me aware just how difficult things were as not to worry us, because we were a lot younger at the time,' Sharon Corr told Barry Egan of the *Irish Independent*. 'John also did things like give us money at Christmas. That was a real stress, especially when he himself didn't have much.'

For The Corrs, struggling to make ends meet and not having the experience in the industry that Hughes himself had, things must have been incredibly difficult. If ever there was a time when they would have packed it in and returned to the security of 'normal jobs' it would have been during these dark days. So the question is: what kept The Corrs going? Perhaps the answer lies in two directions. Firstly, the vision of Hughes, a man who possesses an exemplary ability to look at the possible. A dreamer perhaps, but a dreamer who works hard. Hughes tells a lovely story of drawing inspiration from Ireland's 1982 Triple Crown rugby win. Watching his friend Ollie Campbell score 21 points in the final game against Scotland, Hughes realised finally that the impossible could be achieved against the odds. 'The [Scotland] game was the deciding game and the Triple Crown had never been won at Lansdowne. On the day Ireland won 21–12. Ollie Campbell scored all 21 points. It was real Roy of the Rovers stuff,' Hughes recalled. 'When everyone said Ireland had no chance I valued the dream and thought this is do-able. When it was dark, when there was nothing, I would watch that video.' Hughes' friendship with Campbell would go further than providing inspiration. Although details remain private, Hughes has acknowledged that Campbell provided money for the production of *Forgiven Not Forgotten*. While not a huge amount, it was helpful, as neither the band nor Hughes had much at the time. Campbell is thanked in the credits of *Forgiven Not Forgotten*.

The second major reason why neither Hughes nor The Corrs quit is that, although they were all chasing a record deal, they were still musicians at heart. And so in the days where no one really wanted to know them, the days when it was only Hughes, family and friends supporting them, their music and their love for the craft was still intact. In many respects there was purity about those days. When the good times eventually came for The Corrs and Hughes, these often dark moments would not be forgotten. In this respect The Corrs

cannot be blamed for enjoying their success and all the trappings that
have gone with it.

*   *   *   *

*Contrary to what is said in many movies, I believe that life does not happen
in regimental blocks and is instead a gradual process. To say that I became
a fully-fledged adult in Dublin would not take into consideration all the
growing up that I did before I left New Zealand. But something happened
to me in Dublin that I am not sure I can truly explain. It was as if I started
to find myself in much the fashion that I had hoped for on that fateful day
when I left New Zealand. As if I now had enough confidence to go out into
the world secure in my ability, my belief structures and who I was. I guess
this is one of the great thrills and benefits of travel. As with The Corrs
themselves, development is often a beautiful thing. Slowly, but surely, I was
becoming the man that I wanted to be.*

*   *   *   *

During this period Hughes knew that he had to get the attention of
record company executives somehow. One of the best and most
obvious ways of doing this was by booking concerts in Dublin, asking
anyone who was anyone along and then hoping that something would
come from it.

The Corrs' first gig at The Waterfront in Dublin was a milestone
in their careers, if nothing else because it was the start of something
that would go on to blossom. John Hughes remembers the occasion
only too well. 'I remember their first gig,' he told *Hot Press*. 'I sweated
every single song with them. I was also the only crew they had at the
time. God, I was sick with nerves — I easily knocked five years off my
life that night.'

The Corrs performed twice at The Waterfront in Dublin before
the now famous concert at Whelan's which would indirectly
springboard them on to much greater things. At the time Caroline
Corr was still playing keyboards but it was clear that The Corrs
needed a drummer. With Jim playing keyboards and guitar, Andrea on
lead vocals and tin whistle and Sharon on vocals (and later violin), it
seemed obvious that the drumming would fall to Caroline, although
it came about by accident. 'I had a boyfriend from my hometown,
Dundalk,' Caroline recalls. 'He was a drummer, a crazy U2 fan —
Larry Mullen was his hero. We had the band going; we were just
writing together, but at the time Sharon wasn't playing violin in the
band, which is really strange. It sounds so hard to believe, but we were
really experimenting with our sound and instruments. Nobody knew
what they were doing, we just knew we were making music — we

didn't know how the live set-up was going to work. And he was playing one day and I said, "I'll have a wee go". So I learnt how to play just a straight eight beat or whatever, and I kind of liked it, so I started to learn a little bit more. And I think the rest — Jim, Sharon and Andrea — came in and said, "That sounds really good. That's what we'll do: we'll incorporate this into the band". And that was it, that's kind of how it happened — suddenly I was playing the drums. And the first time I remember playing live was on a TV show, and I was so bad — ha! It was a good few years ago and I was incredibly nervous — I remember it very well.'

Dublin musicians and journalists remember that plenty of promotion was done for The Corrs' performance at Whelan's, suggesting that Hughes went to extra lengths to get attention for the band and increase the chances of that much desired record deal. 'I don't think there was much media manipulation going on,' says one Dublin music journalist, who did not wish to be named. 'I seem to remember the whole phenomenon started with The Corrs playing at Whelan's and the word getting around town. A lot of people came up to me telling about The Corrs and telling me that I should go and see them. All the marketing people had to do was just guide the market to The Corrs. That was all they had to do. Close the gap, in other words, between the market and The Corrs. As soon as people knew about them they were going to buy them.'

For all the musical talent of The Corrs, it was the connections of John Hughes that got them their crucial break. It was at Whelan's in Dublin that the band became known to the USA ambassador for Ireland, Jean Kennedy Smith. Sister of the legendary JFK and Robert Kennedy, like many Irish Americans she identified closely with her Irish roots. Bill Whelan, an old friend of John Hughes and one of the key people behind the Irish cultural renaissance, had invited Kennedy Smith to Whelan's. Kennedy Smith liked what she heard. To her The Corrs appeared ideal candidates to join what effectively became the 'Court of Kennedy Smith' at the ambassador's residence in Dublin: they were young, talented, musical and on the up. 'I think it would be going too far to say that I discovered them,' she has said. 'What I saw was a very talented family who were wonderfully impressive. There were these beautiful girls and a handsome young man and there was terrific synergy between them all. They were also great musicians and that night they gave a gutsy performance. I really liked what they did and so I invited them to come over to Boston and play at the Kennedy Library. They did and, although the Library is not an easy place to play in the sense that it has high ceilings, they performed really well.'

Kennedy Smith says she is not surprised that The Corrs have gone on to achieve great success. 'It was obvious to me from the reaction they got in Boston and New York then that they had a special talent and the amazing thing was that they were all part of the same family!'

Going to the USA was the break The Corrs needed. Hughes had been there several times before in search of a record contract, but this opportunity ensured that the band themselves could go and help sell their music. Much has been written about Hughes's inability to get a record contract for the band. One school of thought suggests the band were holding out for a sizeable deal that would project them into the USA, in much the same way as the Irish band The Cranberries. However, although The Corrs were looking for a deal that would promote them internationally, it is doubtful whether they would have rejected any reasonable contract. As Hughes has said, The Corrs and their brand of music were simply not in vogue. Jim Corr has also stated that there were serious negotiations with record companies, with the band at various stages believing that they were 'practically signed'. The USA presented The Corrs with opportunities, much the same way as it had for the millions of Irish emigrants in the last two centuries. The trip went well, with gigs in Boston a hit. Still, the main aim of the trip was to somehow get a record contract. It happened on the last day of the trip in New York.

Enter David Foster, one of the top producers in the world. The Foster story is littered with success. Foster began piano lessons at the age of five in his native Victoria, British Columbia, and it quickly became obvious that he had remarkable musical talent. Living up to that early promise, he was enrolled as a student at the University of Washington at the age of thirteen, and three years later, when offered an opportunity to join the backing band for Chuck Berry, Foster embarked on his professional performing career. In 1971, Foster relocated to Los Angeles and within two years his group Skylark scored the top ten hit 'Wildflower'. Throughout the early 1970s he built a solid reputation as one of the best session keyboard players in music, performing with such superstars as George Harrison, Barbra Streisand and Rod Stewart.

Dissatisfied with life as a session musician, much like Jim Corr, Foster turned to outside projects, writing and producing hits for Hall and Oates, Boz Scaggs and the Average White Band. By 1979, Foster had won his first Grammy Award for co-writing the number one song 'After the Love Has Gone', recorded by Earth Wind and Fire. Foster's signature style of infectious rhythms and catchy lyrics became synonymous with contemporary radio, leading to hit after hit from the likes of Michael Jackson, Paul McCartney, Chicago, Neil Diamond, Alice Cooper, Manhattan Transfer, Phil Collins, the Pointer Sisters and Aretha Franklin.

On a business level, Foster became Vice President of Atlantic Records in 1994. Less than a year later, Foster established his first recording label, 143 Records, which was distributed through Atlantic and The Corrs were signed under. In 1997, Foster was promoted to Senior Vice President of Warner Music Group and Chairman of 143 Records, which was expanded to become a joint venture between Foster and Warners. Given Foster's background and success, it was hardly surprising that The Corrs should target him as a possible producer to work with.

The problems that The Corrs were experiencing in finding a record company to take an interest in them were difficult and certainly not unique. 'We'd done all of LA. We'd done all of New York — and no response' Hughes told *Hot Press* in 1999. 'It was: "pretty Irish girls, we love you, you're wonderful, go home". The whole trip was beginning to wear a bit thin, so there was no knowing how the collective might have responded if they'd gone home empty-handed. Jason Flom, head of Artists and Repertoire at Atlantic Records, was the exception. He took an interest in the group and decided that he'd try to hook the band up with David Foster, who was recording with Michael Jackson in New York at the time. So I rang Jason three times a day and said, "When are we meeting David Foster?" And he said, "I can't get to him". What happens is that when he's with Michael Jackson he switches the phones off. So on the second last day I said, "Will you tell me where he is?" And he said, "I'll tell you — but don't tell anyone I told you".'

The Corrs were doing an acoustic showcase at BMG Records at lunchtime that day. 'Just the four of them standing there doing the songs,' Hughes recalls. 'No big deal. And I asked someone there where this particular studio was. And the guy there said just around the corner, why? And I said David Foster was there and I was bringing the band around, and he said I'd never get in. But we had nothing to lose — so I said to the band "we're going around the corner".' And so they trooped around the corner, instruments in hand and knocked on the door. 'The security was very heavy, as it always is around Michael Jackson, and I said, "I'm here to see David Foster. I have a kind of appointment. It's not confirmed but he'll know who we are." Basically I was bluffing. But we made a huge effort to look great and I have to admit that we got in because they looked the way they did. And so we sat in the lobby. We asked the receptionist which door he'd come out and we sat facing that door. He came out with his wife and kids and I just went straight up to him and said, "My name is John Hughes. I have this band The Corrs and we have a kind of appointment to meet you through Jason Flom". And he said, "I don't know anything about this but I'll listen to your music".'

And he did. 'When he'd listened to the tape, Jim Corr had the good sense to say, "Can we play?" Because we had the instruments with us, and there was a grand piano there. And he said, "Sure". So they sat around the piano and played and you could see he was thinking, "They're actually playing it and singing it, and they look like this!" So I said "What do you think?" and he said, "12 out of 10, A+, they're fantastic".'

Caroline Corr has a similar recollection of events: 'We arrived at the Hit Factory in New York, played one of our demos — it was actually 'Love to Love You' at the time, that we had done at home — and he loved it. We played around a piano acoustically, and from then on it all changed.'

'Love to Love You', one of the quality tracks on the album, was a good pick: it had that soulful creamy sound that The Corrs would almost patent in the years ahead. It was also the track that Jim had for some time thought would be the big hit off the album. David Foster himself recalls the occasion and describes it as a moment etched on his memory. 'It was a great day for me. Jason Flom had mentioned to me that he had this band that I should meet as they played my kind of music and he was more a rock and roller, but when they came through the door I didn't know who they were. I was working with Michael Jackson and there are always so many people around him that I was surprised that The Corrs had even managed to get in. But when I walked into the corridor to go the bathroom they were all sitting there. One of the girls came up to me and said they were waiting to see me. It was an amazing moment. I said that I had to finish up what I was doing but that I would be with them in twenty minutes.'

Foster then went and finished what he was doing before taking The Corrs up to the sixth floor of The Hit Factory. 'They played acoustically with the piano up there and I was flabbergasted. I felt exactly the same way as I did when I first heard Celine Dion and Bryan Adams for the first time. I just knew that they were remarkable talents. I was surprised that they had done the record company rounds and that no one had picked them up. Their sound was so unique, so real and I just knew that they were very special. There was no doubt in my mind that I just had to sign them before someone else did.'

Foster says that although he was amazed with their vocal talents and the way they harmonised, he was also impressed with their individual talents. 'Jim was obviously a superb musician in his own right and he struck me as being the organiser of the band. Caroline was the only chick I've ever met who could hold a beat, Sharon had lovely vocals, while Andrea could play a $6 instrument and make it sound beautiful. But even then it was obvious to me that they were special people. I am delighted the way their careers have developed and how they have continued to progress at various stages and it has not all happened at once. I think they are better off as people and musicians for it. Their careers have in many ways been textbook built.'

When Hughes phoned Jason Flom the next day the American began to apologise — he wasn't going to be able to set up the Foster appointment. 'It's okay,' Hughes said, 'we did it ourselves yesterday. He said you were to ring him wherever he was.' Hughes and the band went on packing their cases, getting ready to fly home and a little while later the phone rang. He explained to *Hot Press*: 'It was Jason again, and he said, "When you get home, darlin', go out and spend a fortune on a big meal on behalf of the record company because you've got yourselves a record deal. You're signed." And I put the phone down and turned to Jim and said, "We've just got a record deal". And he said, "Okay", and continued packing. He said, "Are you sure?" And I rang the girls and said, "We've got a record deal". But it didn't seem to sink in. And then I had six months of gruelling negotiations.'

It was at this point that Hughes' experience with Minor Detail became decidedly useful. Those in the music business say that Hughes knew the industry and knew what to look for in the contract. To this day no details of the first Corrs' contract have ever been revealed. Given the unproven nature of The Corrs at that stage, the fact that they were signing with a giant American company capable of pushing them into every home in the USA and further afield, the negotiations would undoubtedly have favoured Atlantic. Whatever the details were, The Corrs had a giant record company now backing them. 'It's one of the most gruesomely stressful aspects of the entertainment business — contract negotiations!' Hughes says. 'You've been through the mill and under the grill, you know what it's all about.'

Negotiating the first contract and sorting out the nuts and bolds of it all proved more difficult than Hughes had expected. Were there any moments when he was disillusioned? 'Moments? Every second moment,' he recalls. 'Because we were poles apart. Bones Howe is one of the great producers — he did the Fifth Dimension, he defined harmony — and he'd heard a tape from Bill Whelan, and had fallen in love with them, and we'd met and a friendship developed, so I rang him and I said, "Bones, they're beating me up something terrible here. Should I be with this record company or not?" And he said, "John, you've got two choices. You can stick around and it'll get worse or you can get the f*** out of there, fast and you'll get the deal". So I was out of there on the next flight. And he was right. It went on for months but he was right. They had me cornered, so I had to get out. And in the end I think the Chinese proverb applied: it was a win-win situation. And because of the nature of the business, it's the more you sell, you renegotiate your position. And we've been able to do that.'

*   *   *   *

There were numerous days and nights when I questioned whether it was possible to write a serious book about The Corrs and their impact on Irish society. I mean, you can write about U2 and suggest they had an impact on Irish society, but The Corrs? Perhaps pop music did not deserve or want serious attention?

I wondered why back in New Zealand I had paid The Corrs so much attention. It wasn't that I didn't like their music, nor that their music wasn't any good, it was just that the more I researched the more I realised that their music wasn't that important in comparison with that of Van Morrison or U2 or a host of other Irish acts.

Perhaps it was not their music, rather just the pop genre? The music of The Corrs gave satisfaction to millions of people around the world and in that sense it was important, but, applying a critical perspective, did their music stand up to close scrutiny? Was I being too cynical? Or had I just grown up?

*   *   *   *

David Foster believed that The Corrs were capable of creating hits. For their part The Corrs were naturally delighted that one of the most popular producers in the world believed in them. In the months ahead the Foster name would again open doors for The Corrs that would otherwise have stayed firmly shut.

The night before The Corrs left Ireland for Los Angeles to record *Forgiven Not Forgotten*, Jim Corr sat in a local restaurant with his old friend Nicola Matthews. She said to Jim that things were never going to be the same again, that he would in the near future receive the slice of fame that he so craved and as a result their friendship would change. She felt sad. He said that that was not going to be the case and that they would always be friends. She knew, though, that regardless of what he said, the days of them being the best of friends were coming to an end. Looking back, Matthews says that she was right: things have never been the same as they were before The Corrs signed a record deal and started to ride the musical merry-go-round. She remains hopeful, however, that maybe some day they will renew their friendship.

CHAPTER 7

Forgiven, But Now Not Forgotten

The real story of The Corrs development is not about dodgy haircuts and bad clothes. Looking back, it seems as though the band arrived fully formed. After the incubation period where hair was modified, clothes tailored and music polished, they landed the big record deal with the big producer.

Irish journalist Alan Corr (no relation) in 1998

In January 1995 The Corrs went to Malibu to record their first album over a period of five months at Foster's studio. Jim Corr was asked to produce the record with Foster, something he desperately wanted to do, as it was a concern of the band that the American production would water down the rich Irish sound that had been created at Mount Avenue.

'What Foster was afraid of was that he would take it far too much down his road and turn it into an American sound,' Jim told one newspaper. 'But he'd asked me to co-produce, which allayed our fears, because we knew then that we had a certain amount of control on the sound.'

David Foster liked the band, their songs and the harmonies. But the fiddles, the bodhrán and the whistle were another story. John Hughes recalls: 'I remember playing "Toss The Feathers" for him and he said, "That's great, but you're not putting that on the record, sure you're not?" He didn't want us to. And I said it's great fun, they like doing it — why would you stop bands playing something they like? But it was a struggle to get it accepted. This was before *Riverdance* or *Titanic*.'

Foster does not necessarily have the same recollections, but is adamant that the Irish angle is what makes the music of The Corrs special:

> I know The Corrs have moved away from the Irish sound in their last two albums, mainly with a view to making it in America. I would, however, encourage them to return to their roots as I think it is that that makes them distinct.

I haven't been involved in the productions of their music since the early days of the second album, but I would like to be involved in a fourth album. If that were the case, I would encourage them to return to some degree to the Irish music.

Recording in Malibu had its own set of pressures and expectations. There were occasional tensions, the result of four siblings cocooned in a compound in a foreign country with their manager for six months, but the work was generally productive after a settling-in period.

'So that's the way it was — five people together, 24 hours a day, seven days a week, for months,' Hughes told *Hot Press*. 'In the long run it was good for us because we did develop a bond which has sustained, but at the time it was very strange for everybody.'

Malibu was an important time for The Corrs. Not only did they continue to develop that essential sound that would, to many of their fans, be the true and original Corrs' sound, but the siblings learned to work with Hughes at close quarters.

From the Malibu partnership came an understanding, a trust and respect, between Hughes and The Corrs that would pay dividends later on. This was now not going to be a short-term project. The partnership that would eventually go on to sell in excess of twenty million albums now had firm foundations.

It is difficult to define precisely what the relationship between John Hughes and The Corrs is. Some suggest that it is a combination of many different relationships: father and daughter/son, best friends, mentor/students (especially in the early days).

Just as George Martin is often considered to be the fifth Beatle, John Hughes is essentially the fifth Corr. A father-like figure who guides, suggests, advises.

*   *   *   *

Every time I stepped off the train in Dundalk and smelled the hops of the brewery next door I would hear in my head those haunting sounds of 'Erin Shore'. As if it was an anthem to both The Corrs and Dundalk itself. I soon started to realise the reason why I was writing this book: in some ways it was as much about me as it was about The Corrs. This was also my journey, my passion, my experience. I loved the early days of The Corrs when they were trying to make a name for themselves in a brutal industry. When they were fresh, enthusiastic and raw. I always used to come back to Dublin from Dundalk on a high. There was something about Dundalk that I liked. It was the Ireland that I had read about in books, a town that was innocent, secure, devoid of bullshiters. I would have loved to have lived here, enjoyed my pint, my traditional Irish music, my English soccer results on a Saturday afternoon, my £4.50 haircut once a month. Life was lived at a pace I was comfortable at. The Corrs had led me to Dundalk, but my experiences there were not as much about them as I perhaps thought at the time.

*   *   *   *

David Foster downplays his role in creating the unique sound that so marked *Forgiven Not Forgotten*. He backs that up by saying that the demos The Corrs brought with them to Malibu were amongst the best he had ever heard:

> The demos were amazing and the quality made my job as a producer so much easier. It was a great start. They were very complete and certainly unique. I think the finished product in a couple of cases was not as good as the demo.
>
> What I tried to do was to make sure that this wonderful sound that The Corrs had created was not lost. What I did was minimal. I asked Jim to be involved in the production as he was, even at that time, accomplished on the keyboards and was the Corr most prepared to put in the time.
>
> I later learned that all of The Corrs could be capable producers in their own right, but at that stage Jim's skills were the most obvious.

Foster says The Corrs fitted into Malibu well and if there was tension during the recording, he did not see it:

> At that stage I didn't really think to myself how hard it must have been as a family being in the same place and doing the same thing all the time. I have six sisters and I love them dearly, but it would have driven me mad.
>
> But the talents of The Corrs were very obvious. I don't like comparing, but there are plenty of similarities between when The Corrs came to Malibu and when Celine Dion came here. There was this same feeling that I was dealing with people who were very special and who had a real talent for music.

Foster suggests that a major reason why The Corrs are so special is that they have been brought up so well:

> It was obvious to me early on that they had great love for their parents and that they got great love from their parents. I remember Jean and Gerry coming out to Malibu and all of us having a party at my house. I recall Jean

singing and having an absolutely lovely voice, Gerry laughing away after having one too many.

We had another party at the house after *Talk on Corners* had been so successful and I wanted to fly Jean and Gerry out from Ireland. Sadly someone from the record company vetoed the idea and of course it wasn't long after that Jean got sick. I could throttle the person who decided that.

The result of The Corrs' time in Malibu was *Forgiven Not Forgotten*, a seamless mix of pop, rock and traditional Irish music, the latter interspersed in snippets through the album.

'You write music that you love,' Sharon Corr has said in one interview, 'and naturally we've been very much influenced by the music that's in our environment. Every pub you go to on any street there's traditional music being played everywhere. Then also pop and rock music coming in from the US or from England — one of our favourite bands is Crowded House — so you get all different influences and our music is basically a mash of the three — pop, rock and Celtic.

'The reason we put in the traditional songs is we love those, and every time we played at a gig, no matter where it was, once we went into the traditional stuff, people went wild. So some of the company reps were at a few of the gigs and saw this happen and we really wanted them on the album and they really did as well. The way we put the snippets of traditional tunes in between songs was actually Bob Clearmountain's idea. So we went into a studio in Los Angeles, recorded those completely live and faded them in and out across the album.'

David Foster was vital in helping with the vocals as well as creatively giving the band ideas. His production expertise was also invaluable. He chiselled the roughness away from The Corrs and created a more secure, readily digestible sound. Although The Corrs had produced a vast majority of *Forgiven Not Forgotten* before they went to Malibu, it was there that they wrote 'Runaway', on their own, and 'Some Day', with Foster. Given the lasting appeal of 'Runaway', and the popularity of the first album, the time spent in Malibu was profitable.

For a Foster album it wasn't expensive; for a debut album it bordered on a binge. Reports suggested that the album would not have cost a lot more than a half a million US dollars to produce. Still, to recoup that the record company needed to sell a lot of units.

The result was an album full of originality, Irish passion and beauty. For a first album it was a stunning success, rich in quality. Analysing it several years later, its innocence and musical purity stands the test of time. In the music you can almost feel where The Corrs have come from, their influences and inspirations.

'Erin Shore' was a beautiful entry, as if it were recognition that The Corrs were Irish and had been strongly influenced by traditional Irish music. You can almost feel Dundalk in the sound, smell the hops when you get off the train and hear the craic in the 104 pubs.

One of the finest tracks on the album ('Forgiven Not Forgotten') came second. This was a haunting number that Andrea Corr acknowledges was anything but a feel-good song:

> The dark mode really dominates a track like 'Forgiven Not Forgotten' which is very morbid: it's death. I wrote it in the third person, but this woman has lost her love and she knows it's her own fault. So that person has gone and she lives with regret and disillusionment, constantly. 'Her days are grey/And the nights are black.' Then, in the last verse, when the music breaks down, it can be perceived that she takes her life, partly because, as I say in the second verse, he took his life, which is captured in 'a bleeding heart torn apart/Left on an icy grave'. Not exactly Baywatch, is it?

Third up, 'Heaven Knows' is a pleasant track, highlighting Andrea's sweet lyrics. There is a relaxed, spirited fun about this song, Sharon's violin leading the way. This is The Corrs playing with passion and soul and producing something that reflects their settled upbringing. The striking thing about this song is that The Corrs seem to be enjoying the music. It works well.

'Along With The Girls' is a brief but emotional Irish instrumental, Sharon again coming to the fore. In contrast, 'Someday' rocks the listener, this time Jim Corr taking centre stage with his musical organisation. There is a pleasant harmony amongst the girls' vocals with the song never losing any momentum.

'Runaway', originated by Caroline Corr, is perhaps The Corrs' most popular song with their fans. There is a romantic feel about this song: driving down country roads in the summer and being in love. Andrea's vocals on this track are superb, combining beautifully with Sharon's violin and lovely backing vocals. Some may suggest this song is too soppy, although it probably remains the best original song The Corrs have ever produced. If ever there was a Corrs' anthem, than this was it.

There is more gentle fun about 'The Right Time', the next track. There is a relaxed feel to the song, almost a Caribbean swing. Again

Sharon's violin is prominent, reinforcing the traditional Irish aspects of the fast emerging Corrs' sound.

'The Minstrel Boy', an old Irish instrumental, is vintage early Corrs. Once more Sharon takes centre stage, creating a sound rich in purity and deep in emotion. With Jim on piano also notable, this could only be performed by a family such is the texture of the vocals and the understanding between musicians. The song does not have a Clannad feel, although there is a richness that is familiar.

'The Minstrel Boy' leads nicely into 'Toss the Feathers', possibly The Corrs' best track live. Again the harmonies between the four siblings are superb, the music proudly Irish, the rhythm never easing. This song has all the heart and soul that has characterised Irish music down the years. It is amongst their best work and the joy on their faces when they play it live is quite obvious. David Foster had doubts about its accessibility, but 'Toss the Feathers' has become a Corrs' classic.

'Love to Love You' is a pleasant song, though it lacks the passion of 'Toss the Feathers' or 'Forgiven Not Forgotten'. Again there is a Sunday romanticism about it that takes the listener to another world. It is soft, polite and easy listening. It became one of the obvious anthems of *Forgiven Not Forgotten* and another crowd favourite.

The album then goes off on something of a tangent, suggesting that it would have been a much tighter production had it been twelve tracks and not fifteen.

'Secret Life' is a little bit of a hotchpot musically. The guitar chord is strong, as is the drumming. It is listenable, but without the mystical beauty of the earlier tracks. It is a touch immature and is only saved by Sharon's frantic violin playing.

'Carraroe Jig' is a nice interlude and once again appeals as an example of the true Corrs' sound. You can feel almost feel Dundalk in the magic of the violin sound.

Andrea's full vocal talents come into play on the thirteenth track, 'Closer'. Another strong song, this track conjures up connotations of Sunday afternoons in the sun. Still, by this stage the album has begun to lose its momentum. Despite that, the talents of Andrea are obvious: the passion of her voice, the ability to gently cajole the listener into another world, perhaps *her* world. She holds the song together, although musically it lacks punch and true spirit. It is the 'weak cup of tea' track of the album.

The next song, 'Leave Me Alone', wakes the listener. This is better: Jim stepping it up on the guitar, the backing vocals proving a perfect foil for Andrea to unveil her singing talents once again. In the middle of the song the music even starts to fly, Andrea really starting to find herself. Where 'Closer' lacked pace, this track has it. Still, The Corrs were perhaps a touch too cautious: a bigger sound would have seen this song reach its full potential.

'Erin Shore' rounds off an impressive first album. Again, this is vintage Corrs. Such simplicity combined with the utmost respect for the Irish culture. Sharon, so impressive throughout the album, sets the pace and the beauty of the music comes seeping through.

Although there were a number of very strong pop tunes on this album ('Runaway', 'Forgiven Not Forgotten' and 'Love to Love You'), it is the traditional numbers that were the most memorable. 'Erin Shore', 'Along With The Girls', 'The Minstrel Boy 'and the 'Carraroe Jig' gave this album its heart. Not only does the music pay great respect to the traditions that The Corrs grew up with, but it also pays homage to the Irish music culture that they were so clearly influenced by.

In the years to come when journalists and writers would write of a Corrs' sound they would write about these four traditional tracks in particular. Fans would also use these songs as the benchmark for future Corrs' efforts. The Corrs were Irish, proud of it and, it appeared, more than happy to use their rich traditions in their work.

Perhaps the most beautiful thing about this album is its integrity. There is a passion, a strength about this body of work that undoubtedly makes it an outstanding first album. Although too long and a little disjointed towards the end, it is an album created by four obviously talented musicians.

In late 1995, Q *Magazine* in the UK wrote about what it considered to be the intrinsic appeal of *Forgiven Not Forgotten*:

> Blimey. An American A&R man's wet dream. Three mouth-watering Corrs sisters (Sharon, Caroline, Andrea) and their brother (Jim) who can harmonise, play instruments and write radio-friendly songs with just enough blarney to sucker the ex-patriot transatlantic Irish, just enough new country to turn heads in Nashville, just enough AOR to guarantee saturation radio play, and sultry looks that MTV would kill for.
>
> Naturally, it's impeccably played, performed and recorded but too often the finished product comes uncomfortably close to a cross between The Bangles and The Nolans. That may be enough to shift multi-platinum quantities in the US from now until doomsday but it's unlikely to stand up to repeated plays if you like a bit of meat on your bone.

This report was wrong on both counts — The Corrs did not sell platinum quantities in the US initially, while *Forgiven Not Forgotten* remains the one album that passes the test of time.

The Spectator in the US also believed that the first album was decidedly good:

> The member most responsible for the Corrs' Celtic sounds is Sharon Corr on the violin. She draws out the age old melodies of their hometown in County Louth, Ireland, and with her skilful solos, creates a whole new appreciation of the violin as an instrument of modern music. If Sharon Corr is representative of the traditional, then Jim Corr elicits the contemporary sounds. The rough edges to the songs are given a voice by the electric guitar. There are some instances when the siblings indulge in a friendly rivalry between their styles.
>
> Caroline Corr's demure persona makes it easy to overlook her capacity as a drummer. Letting her hands do the talking, she lays all doubts to rest with her deft handiwork on 'Heaven Knows'. Lead vocalist Andrea Corr, who plays the tin whistle as well, has such a soothing effect that she gives an element of healing to the songs. She sings them like lullabies and calms all nerves, making *Forgiven Not Forgotten* incredibly relaxing.

What this reviewer misses is the fact that the drumming on *Forgiven Not Forgotten* is the subject of some controversy. Caroline Corr was not yet sufficiently advanced to truly master the art, so did not actually play drums on this album at all. All but one track was recorded using a drum machine. This fact is obscured on later releases of the album, which credit Caroline with 'Drums, Bodhrán, Vocals'.

Simon Phillips was in fact brought in to play drums for 'Toss The Feathers'. 'That song needed a special rhythm section, that's why we invited Neil Steubenhaus on base and Simon Philips on drums,' Caroline said some years later. 'He brought in this gigantic drum-kit and I thought Wow! What in God's name are all those drums for? It takes enormous discipline. He's brilliant. But I had a problem. I had to learn that part for live shows. That took quite some effort, but I can manage now. Yes, I also play that complicated break, although I do it my way.'

It would not be the last time questions were raised about who drummed on a Corrs' album.

*   *   *   *

*Although my passion for Dublin was unbridled and in some ways I loved it
more than any other city in the world, I was surprised by how snobby it was.
When you think 'snobby' you think English aristocracy. But when you think
snobby you should also think Dublin. If you lived on the south side of Dublin
you were okay. You obviously had money and you came from the right
stock, went to the right school. If you lived on the north side, you apparently
envied or resented those that had the above.*

*On the nights that I worked I would taxi home through the barren streets
of Dublin's inner city heartlands and see those that had nothing at all. You
could almost feel the drug culture, the quiet desperation simmering in the
housing estates. I would get home and thank my lucky stars that I had a job
and opportunity. I read up on Dublin's history and started to understand the
divisions. Still, one of the first things John Hughes asked me in one of our
two conversations was whether I lived on the north side or the south side.*

*   *   *   *

Producing a quality album is fantastic, but the second, just as
important, stage is to promote the product. The Europeans did not get
the opportunity to market *Forgiven Not Forgotten* until the Americans
had finished with their promotion. After the release of the album, The
Corrs did a huge amount of promotion in the US, including a number
of showcases and numerous radio and press interviews. At the time,
Atlantic Records was promoting 'Runaway' as the band's first single.
They got plenty of airplay throughout the US and did manage to sell
a large number of records.

The American system of record companies selling albums to
outlets is slightly different from the European system, in the sense that
they have a 'sale or return' policy, where in Europe it is straight
purchase. The result is that in the US it is possible to stock a large
number of records because stores know that if they can't sell them they
can return them to the distributor.

Half a million dollar budget or not, *Forgiven Not Forgotten* was less
than the kind of rip-roaring success in the US that Atlantic were
hoping for. The Corrs spent a lot of time touring and promoting the
album in the US and hit a plateau there at around 300,000 sales. John
Hughes explained to *Hot Press*:

> In the US you've got 5,000, 10,000 or a couple of million
> sales. 300,000 leaves you in a strange place where
> everybody goes 'that's a helluva lot of records' — and yet
> it hasn't succeeded or it hasn't failed. The record
> company's view was that we weren't getting radio to the

extent that we needed it — at least in part because of our fiddles and bodhráns. They loved us but we couldn't get into the mainstream. And so we decided: 'the best thing we can do is go to Europe'.

So The Corrs returned home to Ireland to try to rediscover some confidence; to try to make it at home before returning to crack the US. The momentum started, of all places, in Ennis in Ireland. No one knew who the band's audience were or how many had come to see them play, but The Corrs felt like the whole town was there. It was symptomatic of what was beginning to happen throughout the rest of Europe. Helped by an aggressive marketing policy by Atlantic, The Corrs were starting to make their mark.

'You could feel that there was something going on,' John Hughes recalls. 'In Paris, their debut concert attracted 2,000 people. The 'house full' notices went up in Stockholm. And then the word was out from Australia — there's something crazy going on, you've got to come down here.

'The record company had sold 40,000 albums there, and so our agent John Giddings said we'd do a short tour there, go back to Europe and then go back down to Australia. And so we did that — and by the time we went back to Australia, we'd sold 400,000 records, which was unbelievable.'

Although The Corrs had not played the major stadiums in their own country, suddenly they were making it big in Australia, Japan, Canada and Spain, encouraging local Warner Music outlets to promote and market The Corrs.

And their judgement was right. Very quickly, Europe was outselling the US by three to one. In Australia, *Forgiven Not Forgotten* ended up selling nearly 600,000 records, putting it in the top five international albums ever sold there.

Andy Murray, Vice-President of Marketing at Warner Music International, puts the success of *Forgiven Not Forgotten* into perspective:

> By 1997, The Corrs had sold two million copies. The album was Atlantic's biggest seller outside the US for 1996. A good selling record for Warner Europe across Europe is about 200,000 copies. The Corrs were big, even in the UK where the first album went gold. But there was this perception that they weren't big in Britain because they weren't on the radio. But gold is gold and they did do very well in the UK.

Despite being signed in the US and having initial aspirations to succeed there first, it was in Europe and in Australia where The Corrs would first receive wide acclaim. The Corrs' sound, their look and where they were as musicians and as people were part of the reason for this, but the smaller size of the European and Australian markets also helped.

In these territories, local labels were able to market them more efficiently, the media were easier to infiltrate than in the more brutal American market and the essentially soft sound of The Corrs had more of a natural affinity with European and Australian audiences. It does not follow, however, that the traditional Irish influence of the album was the reason why *Forgiven Not Forgotten* did not sell as well as expected in the US initially, as there are estimated to be 40 million Irish-Americans.

The success of The Corrs in Europe and Australia was more than just about having a quality first album. It was more than just working hard and playing wherever and whenever the record companies wanted. It was about having an image that was instantly accessible and as wholesome as, the Americans would say, mom, the flag and apple pie.

To help them become accessible in so many parts of the globe, it was helpful that The Corrs stuck to what Hughes has called the 'politics, religion and sex rule'. At this stage of their careers, The Corrs shied away from talking about any of these traditionally controversial subjects, especially avoiding the topic of Northern Ireland.

This stance also complemented the personalities of the band members and their sheltered upbringing. 'I don't think any of them would have felt comfortable talking about sex or anything like that,' according to a friend of the family. 'I know Andrea had trouble enough singing a mildly revealing line in "Only When I Sleep".'

The settled background of the Corr family and the almost sleepy nature of Dundalk ensured that what may have appeared good marketing to some was merely a reflection of who The Corrs were as individuals. They were entertainers, no doubt. But they were also children from a family where religion was important. Their father played the organ on Sundays and to get a bad reputation would make you an outcast in a town where almost everybody knew your name.

Leaving political references out of their lyrics had the effect, some critics suggested, of making The Corrs' music devoid of any greater meaning that set it apart from its contemporaries. Indeed, given their strong opinions on various issues, it would have been possible for The

Corrs to have written, sung and performed songs about issues of local and world importance.

Their efforts in 1998 to help raise money for those affected by the Omagh bomb in Northern Ireland was testimony to the fact that as a band and as individuals The Corrs do have a social conscience.

Despite this perceived failing, The Corrs' music was still going down well with a public ready to be embraced by their Irish sound, their melodies and their clean-cut good looks. It was also about Warners in Europe getting behind the band.

Andy Murray says right from the beginning The Corrs had great talent:

> I first saw some pictures of The Corrs in June 1995. I thought this looks interesting, don't know anything about them. Three girls and Jim, they were walking down a hillside. The girls were wearing long dresses. Andrea was playing something that looked like a wooden recorder and they looked oriental. They certainly didn't look Irish. But to me they looked interesting and so I put the picture up on my wall and thought no more about it.
>
> After about a month I called Atlantic and asked them whether they were going to send me the record. They said 'haven't you heard it?' and I said no I hadn't. They then said that while I was on holiday my boss had had a meeting with John Hughes and Brian Avnet from 143.
>
> I went and got the tape from my boss and thought it was very good. I have a Scottish background and I was into folk rock and I bored the pants off everyone by playing it [*Forgiven Not Forgotten*] constantly in the office.

After the US promotion, John Hughes and Brian Avnet had gone to the key territories in Europe with a view to getting as much exposure as possible for The Corrs.

In August 1995 representatives from all nineteen Warner territories in Europe met in Portugal and discussed what albums they had to promote. Coming up to the autumn and the blockbuster season, anything new and untried had to be very special for it to capture attention.

Steve Pritchitt of Atlantic International premiered the video for 'Runaway'. But there was a problem with the copy. Andy Murray takes up the story:

Although the pictures are okay, the sound is distorted. So what they do is they play the [audio] cassette of 'Runaway' and the pictures from Beta! Even though it is out of synch, you can see the band play and the upshot of it is that everyone in the room says they are fantastic.

So, first of all, there is an endorsement of the band from the community and secondly every single person in the room says 'we like "Runaway", but the big hit on the album is "Forgiven Not Forgotten"'. I personally didn't necessarily agree, but that was not the point. As the European marketing director that gave me a mandate to go out and market it. It would have been a lot more difficult if everyone in the room had said that they couldn't sell it.

Although neither of those two songs ('Runaway' and 'Forgiven Not Forgotten') were hits in their original form, that didn't matter. What was important was that people said those songs were going to be hits. At that kind of meeting you most probably would have found that there were two or three songs out of 50 a day that people said were going to be hits. The fact that my colleagues thought that there were going to be *two* top twenty hits on the album was relatively rare.

The countries that had a Celtic influence in their heritage, such as France and Spain, were naturally keener on the traditional music element of the album than the non-Celtic countries. Coming off the back of *Riverdance*, the Irish angle was particularly in vogue in Europe at that time. Atlantic has also had the critically acclaimed Celtic Heartbeat on the label and thus there was a knowledge and understanding of all things Irish within Europe.

'So there was some small amount of understanding,' says Andy Murray, 'and a large amount of enthusiasm on the part of some of those territories, especially those with a Celtic connection. *Riverdance* had also been big in Britain. So when The Corrs came along they were not coming completely out of nowhere. We had spent a certain amount of time discovering that there was a market in Europe. That there was a whole chain of Irish pubs. At least there was an angle that you would play up.'

The success of The Corrs with *Forgiven Not Forgotten* in Europe and Australia was due to two main factors. Not only did their music not profess to want to change the world, they didn't look as though they were taking themselves too seriously. There was a relaxed, almost

Not just good looks, but musical ability as well: Sharon, Andrea and Caroline Corr, performing at Virgin Megastore, Belfast, 1997. (Photo: Mervyn Smyth)

One of the two brains behind The Corrs: Jim Corr performing at Virgin Megastore, Belfast, 1997. (Photo: Mervyn Smyth)

A close relationship based on respect and almost mother-like fussing: Sharon and Andrea Corr also performing at Virgin Megastore, Belfast, 1997. (Photo: Mervyn Smyth)

The 'only chick' that David Foster ever met who could hold a beat: Caroline Corr performing at Virgin Megastore, Belfast, 1997. (Photo: Mervyn Smyth)

Consummate professionals: Sharon and Andrea Corr do their best to entertain at yet another in-store promotion in Ireland. (Photo: Mervyn Smyth)

Above: A town with a 'lack of bullshitters' and generally a pretty good place to grow up in for the children of Gerry and Jean Corr ... Dundalk, Co Louth. (Photo: Niall Carson)

Left: What could have been had Jim, Sharon, Caroline and Andrea Corr not been blessed with a talent for writing and performing music ... the Café de Paris in Dundalk. (Photo: Niall Carson)

Gerry and Jean Corr instilled moral values in their children that would stand them mostly in good stead in their professional careers … the Corr family home in Dundalk. (Photo: Niall Carson)

Dún Lughaidh Convent in Dundalk: where Sharon, Caroline and Andrea Corr were educated and where Andrea especially showed that she was more than just your run-of-the-mill music and drama student. (Photo: Niall Carson)

The Dundalk Youth Orchestra's visit to America in 1983 was the first chance Sharon Corr had to show off her musical talents internationally, although she was no child prodigy as has been suggested in the media. (Courtesy: Father Brendan McNally)

McManus' pub, Dundalk, where Sharon, Caroline and Andrea Corr often worked behind the bar and where Jim and Sharon gave some of their first public performances. (Photo: Niall Carson)

Pat Dunn, bar manager of McManus' from 1985–1997: 'They were beautiful girls who were great behind the bar and who were more than prepared to roll up their sleeves and do the hard work.' (Photo: Niall Carson)

McManus': a place where many stories are exchanged and where Jim Corr used to hammer a pink piano for all its worth. (Photo: Niall Carson)

McManus' … the Corr girls would hum the songs they were working on up at Jim's as they worked, while local students would come to stare at the pretty girls behind the bar. (Photo: Niall Carson)

Gate Lodge, Dundalk: rented to Jim Corr in the early 1990s, it was where the unique and passionate sound on Forgiven Not Forgotten *was first produced. (Photo: Niall Carson)*

The Cox family, from l to r, Richard, Sally, Bunny and Jennifer: owners of Gate Lodge and unofficial testers of the first tracks off Forgiven Not Forgotten. *(Photo: Niall Carson)*

Ollie Campbell in his playing days: part-financier of The Corrs in their early years, inspiration and best friend to John Hughes, and the author's hero. (Photo: The Irish News)

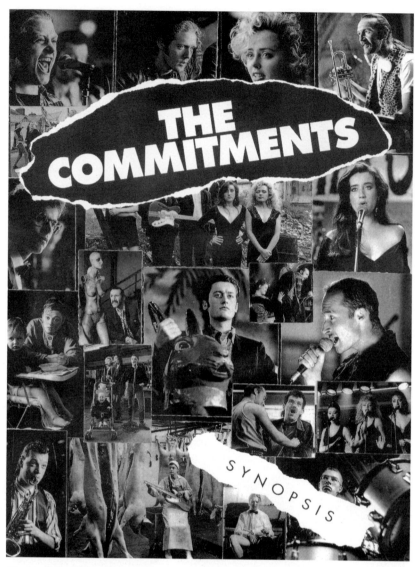

The Commitments: a slice of Irish life in the early 1990s, but also a significant period in the evolution of The Corrs, including the hatching of their relationship with John Hughes. (Photo: TRN Collection)

SHARON CORR   CAROLINE CORR   JIM CORR   ANDREA CORR

The Corrs in 1996: photogenic from the start, if you could have created the ideal family to market, then The Corrs would have been near enough perfect from day one. (Photo: TRN Collection)

The Corrs after one of their impressive 'home' performances at the Carrickdale Hotel in Dundalk in 1996. The locals turned out in droves to help celebrate their success. (Photo: Dundalk Democrat)

Whelan's pub, Dublin: where the then American Ambassador to Ireland Jean Kennedy Smith first saw The Corrs play. She liked what she heard. The Corrs were on their way. (Photo: TRN Collection)

American Ambassador to Ireland in the mid-1990s, Jean Kennedy Smith: an important individual in The Corrs' story and a more than useful business associate in opening the right doors, both in America and in Ireland. (Photo: The Irish News)

A first album and a first tour ensured that 'gunslingers' were needed: the under-utilised and supremely talented Anto Drennan was a shrewd choice by The Corrs. (Photo: TRN Collection)

Seductive, flirty but also the Corr sibling with the most charisma and star talent, Andrea Corr at the Europa hotel, Belfast, 1996. (Photo: Belfast Telegraph)

Proven performers even by this stage of their career: The Corrs in 1996. (Photo: Belfast Telegraph)

Left: The Corrs' career may not have got off the ground had it not been for the vision and outstanding talents of legendary Canadian producer David Foster, seen here chewing the fat with Andrea and Jim Corr in Scandinavia. (Photo: TRN Collection)

Below: 'Please tell me how we can get a hit record in America!' Andrea Corr with David Foster, one of the nicest men in the music business. (Photo: TRN Collection)

Sharon and Andrea Corr play at Langelands Festival, Denmark, 1996. It was a year and a world tour that for the band involved thousands of miles of travel and the selling of their first album almost from 'door to door'. (Photo: TRN Collection)

They called her 'Smiler' as a kid and with the smiles later came a classical elegance: Sharon Corr at Langelands Festival in Denmark, 1996. (Photo: TRN Collection)

All the hard work in 1996 did pay off: The Corrs, John Hughes and Warner Music representatives in Denmark at a Platinum disc presentation for Forgiven Not Forgotten, *1996. (Photo: TRN Collection)*

As a band, The Corrs have always known how to ignite an audience with their musical talent and charisma. (Photo: Ulf Magnusson)

Left: The days when they could walk the streets without being stared at: Andrea and a James Dean-looking Jim Corr, Belfast, 1996. (Photo: Belfast Telegraph)

Below: By 1997 Sharon was in a serious relationship with Belfast barrister Gavin Bonner and was able to combine a healthy personal life with the increasing pressures of her work commitments. (Photo: Belfast Telegraph)

A natural stage performer and the inspiration for millions of emotions, both male and female: Andrea Corr in 1997. (Photo: Belfast Telegraph)

Above: The Corrs arrive in Christchurch, New Zealand in February 1998: as in many towns and cities around the world, the Christchurch Press slapped the band all over their front-page the morning of the concert. (Photo: Christchurch Press)

Left: Andrea Corr performing in Christchurch, New Zealand, the author's hometown and one concert that he wished he had seen. (Photo: Christchurch Press)

'There is something special we are going to do now ...' If only she knew the impact that this song would have on The Corrs. Andrea Corr at the Royal Albert Hall in London in 1998. (Photo: All Action)

The beautiful strains of Sharon Corr's violin begin the concert that would change the destiny of The Corrs forever: Royal Albert Hall, 1998. (Photo: All Action)

Majestic, beautiful, charismatic, inspiring ... Andrea Corr, Royal Albert Hall, 1998. A night that to some degree would start the travels that would lead to this book being written. (Photo: All Action)

Voted the sexiest women in Ireland by one national Irish newspaper and a certified favourite of The Corrs' Internet fans around the world: Andrea Corr in 1999. (Photo: Belfast Telegraph)

Now world famous and one of the best front people in the business, Andrea Corr in 1999. (Photo: Belfast Telegraph)

The homecoming: Andrea Corr is all beauty, happiness and passion in front of 44,000 people at Lansdowne Road, Dublin in July 1999. There was no bigger concert for The Corrs to play than in front of their home fans. (Photos: Terry Thorp/ The Irish Times)

To cap an amazing year, The Corrs receive their BRIT Award for Best International Act in London in 1999. (Photo: Ian Coognan)

Death of the matriarch: The Corrs attend the funeral of their mother, Jean Corr, in Dundalk in late 1999. (Photo: Bill Smyth)

Devotion that knows no bounds: Dubliner Cormac Fox, the self-professed biggest fan of The Corrs. (Photo: TRN Collection)

Fans united before the Lansdowne Road homecoming concert in Dublin, July 1999. From left to right: Dubliner Alan Jacob, Swede Daniel Lindberg, Finn Mikko Hanninen and Dubliner Stephen Jacob. (Photo: TRN Collection)

Sensitive to what the media says about her and her family, especially her luncheon companions: the enigmatic Andrea Corr. (Photo: Mervyn Smyth)

The girl who could play a CD and sing it back almost as good: Sharon Corr. (Photo: Mervyn Smyth)

One of the main reasons why The Corrs have achieved what they have around the world: the charismatic and onstage talents of Dundalk's finest export, Andrea Corr. (Photo: Mervyn Smyth)

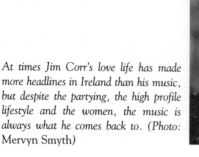

A girl who has never forgotten where she has come from and someone who close friends say hasn't changed since she has become famous: Caroline Corr does what she does best. (Photo: Mervyn Smyth)

At times Jim Corr's love life has made more headlines in Ireland than his music, but despite the partying, the high profile lifestyle and the women, the music is always what he comes back to. (Photo: Mervyn Smyth)

Sharon Corr and Gavin Bonner. The couple married in Ireland in July 2001. (Photo: Peter Morrison)

Above: Another day, another award: The Corrs are all smiles with their parents, Jean and Gerry, after being awarded another platinum disk for Forgiven Not Forgiven. (Photo: TRN Collection)

Left: Not only one of their biggest fans, but someone who keeps spreading The Corrs' gospel through the Internet, American Mark Szachara with Jim Corr in 2000. (Photo: Mark Szachara)

Tears, pride and a fair degree of emotion: the writing of this book ended in many ways for the author with a sterling performance by The Corrs at the Manchester Evening Arena in April 2001. (Photo: All Action)

'we're on this roller coaster and we're enjoying every second of it' sort of approach. Connected with that was a strong reliance and influence of Irish music, connected with universal melodies. As the Australian newspaper *The Irish Echo* suggested in early 1997:

> The Corrs' music merges west-coast American pop rhythms and harmonies with an Irish traditional gloss. It's like Wilson Phillips and The Go-Gos meet the Horslips. What is uniformly impressive about their live performance is that they look and sound great together (and I include Jim in that).

Nigel Williamson, a writer with *The London Times*, was one of the first English journalists to discover the talents of The Corrs. In May 1996, while holidaying in the West of Ireland, he was in the Wolf Tone pub and heard some pretty interesting noises:

> What I witnessed was astonishing,' he recalls. 'It seemed that the entire population, from great grandmothers to newborn babies, was packed into the tiny square. Farm lads from every village for miles around had hiked into town ... I had never heard of them but the square erupted. It was true that the band looked striking. Even more striking was the music: a rejuvenated Irish Fleetwood Mac — great harmonies, sublime songs and a Celtic folk-pop magic that soon had me doing *Riverdance* impersonations with strangers.
>
> They played 'Runaway', 'The Right Time' and 'Forgiven Not Forgotten': every song sounded like a hit song. Then they got out the tin whistle and bodhrán and played a selection of Irish jigs and reels. They were stupendous. At the end pandemonium broke out. The band's caravan was all but crushed by over-enthusiastic fans and they were rescued by the Gardaí.

Above all else, the success of *Forgiven Not Forgotten* was due to the fact that The Corrs were good at what they did. The almost unanimous opinion of those record company executives who had met in Portugal was that The Corrs were talented musicians who were producing catchy music that was of a high standard.

CHAPTER 8

Friends in the Right Places

Today our concern must be with the future. For the world
is changing. The old era is ending. The old ways will not
do.

John F. Kennedy (Los Angeles, July 15 1960).

As The Corrs furiously promoted *Forgiven Not Forgotten* in 1996, they
were riding on the back of an Irish cultural renaissance that was taking
place throughout the world. This celebration was obvious as far away
as Australia. There, it became popular to trace one's ancestry back a
century or two and discover whether one had relatives sent Down
Under for crimes of varying degrees. Although it was not solely the
Irish who were sent to Australia, this enlightenment was an important
part of the reason why Australians started to embrace everything Irish.
This Irish renaissance was also taking place within Ireland itself.

In early July 1996 the aircraft carrier USS *John F. Kennedy* arrived
in Dún Laoghaire harbour, to the south of Dublin. Local newspapers
heralded its arrival, while thousands went and took a look at one of
the biggest pieces of American war machinery.

It is difficult to understand why an American aircraft carrier should
cause so much fuss. Part of the reason could have been that Jean
Kennedy Smith was then American ambassador to Ireland. Being
American Independence Day, the timing was also appropriate.
Perhaps the main reason, however, was the cultural symbolism
attached to the visit. Maybe the American carrier symbolised the
historic relationship between the Americans and the Irish, a returning
home of sorts for one of Irish America's most famous names.

The crew of the *John F. Kennedy* celebrated Independence Day in
Ireland. A special celebratory party was held on the ship and was
attended by over 1,000 guests. Among the dignitaries was Jean
Kennedy Smith, who asked The Corrs along to perform. It was yet
another golden opportunity for the band to promote themselves.

Barry Gaster, the band's booking agent, believes that the
ambassador played a big role in the development of the band. As he

said to a Dundalk newspaper: 'It was a case of being in the right place at the right time, and it was all due to the ambassador.

Since then the ambassador has been more than helpful towards the band, and goes to see them play.'

The Corrs also played at an event called 'The Big Issue', designed to help the homeless in Ireland, and which was opened by the ambassador. The band also played three concerts around this time in aid of The Irish Fund, an American initiative intended to assist with the Northern Ireland peace process.

However, their performance on board the *John F. Kennedy* provoked the most media coverage. It also continued to put them in the picture with a number of prominent people: among the audience was the then Irish Taoiseach (Prime Minister), John Bruton, and Irish Minister of Justice, Liz O'Donnell.

Despite the value gained in publicity, The Corrs' performance did not go down well everywhere. An Irish human right organisation, Afri, publicly asked The Corrs to cancel their performance. In a letter to the band, co-ordinator Joe Murray said that because they were 'cultural icons and role models' their performance on board 'would glamorise the warship and will be seen by many young people as an acceptance of militarism and a glorification of war.'

*   *   *   *

I remember vividly when I realised that I would be leaving Dublin. I had expected that there would be no trouble renewing my work permit to stay in the Republic. I had a job, was earning good money and everybody seemed happy. But having done the honourable thing and tried to keep myself from becoming an illegal alien, I realised that the one thing that the Irish loved more than Guinness, smoking and telling wild stories is red tape. No I couldn't work in the Republic. It couldn't be proved that I had a full-time job, even though I was working and earning a good deal of money. It was a touch ironic that Ireland was stopping me from working in their country: How many Irish had gone out into the New World and done the same thing? After finding out the bad news from both my employer and some faceless official who chose not to show a hint of emotion, I spent hours walking around Dublin in a daze. It was a city that I had come to love and admire so much and feel very much part of. It had been the best sixteen months of my life. I had grown up, found myself and in part I had The Corrs to thank for it all. I was on the move to Belfast.

*   *   *   *

As well as playing on board the *John F. Kennedy*, The Corrs also performed a special concert at Jean Kennedy Smith's residence, another occasion for quality publicity and contact making.

A secretly-filmed video of the concert gives a useful insight into how The Corrs have not significantly altered their shows. It is clear from watching this performance that, although polish has been added to their act, six years on they are essentially doing what they did back in 1996. That is, providing good wholesome entertainment.

Dressed in black, Andrea stands with her back to the specially invited audience. It is a bit like a heavyweight title fight; there is an almost burning sensation of expectation amongst the crowd.

A slap of Andrea's thigh and 'Forgiven Not Forgotten' begins. The Corrs' performance is raw, honest and an ideal accompaniment to what is essentially an Irish celebration. On certain songs, such as 'Leave Me Alone', The Corrs loosen up and really start to rock. It is both refreshing and a classical example of what they could do if they were spontaneous more often.

On a traditional number The Corrs announce that they are 'kind of improvising'. The freshness of the occasion and the fact that they are playing from their musical souls is delightful to watch. It is, in fact, the highlight of the concert.

Out in the front, Andrea is her normal professional self. There is a touch of the philosopher about her. At this stage in her career she has sung these songs only a thousand times before, as opposed to the hundreds of thousands of times she will sing them in future. She is angelic and gives The Corrs' set presence and direction. At one point in the show someone shouts out 'I love you'. Andrea handles the statement easily and replies: 'The feeling's mutual'. As in future concerts, Sharon is notable for both her haunting violin playing and the fact that she likes the limelight much less than her youngest sister.

After having the week off before the concert, there is plenty of energy in the tanks and The Corrs really start to rock on the traditional numbers, especially 'Joy of Life' and 'Toss the Feathers'. At one stage Jim makes note of the fact that there are plenty of people from Dundalk in the audience. 'Suckers for punishment,' he says.

This 1996 concert shows clearly that all the fundamentals of The Corrs' sound, of their performance and presence, were there from early in their careers. All that they needed was refinement and polish. Furthermore, it showed that they were gifted musicians and performers and that they were certainly not manufactured. The individual and collective talents of The Corrs are natural. Although their wardrobes have become snazzier, their profiles better known, through it all their passion and ability to perform music is at the heart of their success and fame.

The concert also reflected the growing relationship between The Corrs and Jean Kennedy Smith that originated at Whelan's a couple of years earlier. The relationship between the band and the ambassador has been portrayed in the media as being a friendship. This may be misleading. A 'business relationship' would be a more accurate description. On the one hand, the band got exposure and invitations to increase their profile in the right company, while the ambassador got a ready-made Irish act that was only too willing to say yes to anything she asked. Both parties would help the other because they would get something in return. Accordingly, the ambassador receives 'special thanks' in the credits for *Forgiven Not Forgotten*.

*   *   *   *

It's the strangest thing standing in a music store and watching CDs almost walk off the shelves. In Blue had just been released in Belfast and literally everybody was talking about The Corrs. A little record store heralded the release of this so-called breakthrough album with a picture of The Corrs. You would walk down the main street in Belfast and see Jim looking like a pimp, Andrea pouting away softly, Sharon looking slightly dazed and Caroline ... well, wondering how on earth did The Corrs get here? Pretty standard Corrs stuff really.

For the purposes of research I bought the album. In I went, looking over my shoulder cautiously. I am not sure why I had so much trouble buying it, I mean there was nothing rude about it. But, well, as a bloke who should have been starting to develop a sense of style, it wasn't the most cultured thing to do. Just like the time when I was fifteen and bought a Madonna tape, saying it was for the sister that I never had. Before forking over my £10 and quickly placing In Blue in my pack, I had a look around. It was two minutes before someone came in and bought a copy, a girl of around twenty. A minute later the next album was sold, this time to another girl of around 25. They were selling like hotcakes. I stood in the record shop — pretending to look at Frank Sinatra's Greatest Hits — keeping an eye on what was selling. In fifteen minutes seven copies of In Blue were sold. I saw cash registers click and rested content in the knowledge that The Corrs would not be starving in their old age.

*   *   *   *

Given that The Corrs had spent much of 1996 touring out of Ireland, it was perhaps understandable that they did not fully realise the great interest and coverage they were getting in their home country. After returning from one tour that year, Caroline Corr got quite a shock while spending time with her friends, including Barry Henry. 'When they were away we had them non-stop over here and 'Runaway' was non-stop on the radio,' he recalls. 'A whole lot of us went away for the weekend and there was great slagging going on. Every time we heard the song we would all shout "Runaway, runaway". We were at some castle and Andrea goes running up to take the piss out of the video.

'A few days after that, after the Sunday papers had come out and we all knew at this stage that they were really going places, I get a call from Caroline and she rings me and she says, "Do you know something Barry, I think we are getting really big." and I'm thinking, "No shit Sherlock!" I said, "Why do you think this?" and Caroline says, "Well I picked up the paper yesterday and there was an article about us, there was also an article about something else that we were involved in and there was also an article with a mention of us that had nothing to do with us".

'And I said, "You haven't been here the last six months when we've been wrecking our heads every two minutes hearing you guys on the radio"'.

Caroline herself was surprised by the reaction. She told the *Argus*:

> We were home in Dundalk for Christmas and one night I was at a disco with all my friends, and the next minute 'Runaway' came on and I just wanted to run and hide. It really is weird. It's like the two worlds all of a sudden are united. You're at a club you've gone to for years, and all of a sudden this other part of your life comes in and just joins in.

This experience was not unique to Dundalk. Andrea recalled to *The Irish Times* an occasion when it happened in the US:

> One time, in an airport in the US, I heard 'Runaway' being played in a shop. I went up to the counter and asked out of interest what radio station was playing and the girl said that it was a tape of chart songs that was sent around all the airports. Then she said 'But I know who the band are, they're from Ireland and they're called The Corrs,' and I said 'Oh really?' She didn't recognise me and when it finally twigged I don't know whether she was more embarrassed than I was.

Still, despite their success, the Corr siblings remained largely unaffected. Caroline and Andrea continued to maintain their close friendships. In the early days of The Corrs, their friends travelled around Ireland following the band. It wasn't just for the music, it was to be with friends and share their success.

Barry Henry's favourite gig was at The Olympia in Dublin:

> Somehow I managed to be standing at the bar by myself,
> getting to see the band, drinking my pint, smoking a
> cigarette and getting a perfect view of everything. It was
> the best gig ever. They came off stage and Andrea walked
> in first and then the penny dropped as to the view I was
> getting. She says: 'enjoy the gig Barry?' and then Sharon
> walks in and says 'we might as well set-up a video link in
> Dundalk!'

In many respects, these days were golden for The Corrs. They had
already achieved some sort of success, but not the type of mainstream
chart success that would later change their lives and the way that they
viewed themselves. These were the days when they were accessible
and where touring, having fans and being in the spotlight was fresh
and invigorating. This was reflected in the way that The Corrs dealt
with the media.

'When I interviewed the band first it was in the early stages of their
success,' says journalist Kevin Courtney. 'They hadn't yet taken off. I
am sure Andrea was wary of the whole thing completely. How do you
deal with all these people? When I interviewed Sharon on the phone
a couple of years later they were a little more settled into it. At that
stage they had just taken off in Britain and they were kind of bemused
by that. It was great to see. They were enjoying the success that they
had achieved. It must have been very satisfying for them to get as big
as they had intended to get. They had certainly kept their promises.

'I think, unlike U2, who you can be sure are going to come out with
some deep and meaningful stuff, with The Corrs they like to talk
about their music, their record sales and they try and be as
accommodating to the reviewer as much as they can without giving
away their deepest secrets.'

It was during this period that The Corrs started to get a reputation
in the music industry for being hard workers. They would think
nothing of doing regular eighteen-hours days, promoting the album
everywhere and anywhere and, perhaps most strenuously, travelling
around the world at a drop of a hat. Although they had been brought
up with a sound work ethic, part of the reason why The Corrs adopted
this habit was the company they were keeping and the people they
were inspired by.

While playing support with Celine Dion in her European tour, The
Corrs were most impressed with the star, perhaps because she had the
same sort of energy. 'Celine would run around for two hours on stage

night after night,' Andrea told *Hot Press*. 'Then she would rush off and get changed and immediately afterwards be out meeting her fans to sign autographs and pose for photos.

'After that she would throw herself into endless meet-and-greets with representatives from her record company, as well as give interviews and do photo shoots for the press. And despite all of that, she was a lovely person 100 per cent of the time. She wasn't false about it either. As a person and as a performer, Celine is incredibly inspiring.'

Not only did Dion provide The Corrs with a role model into the benefits of working hard, playing with Dion provided a useful shop window for The Corrs in Europe. At that stage, Dion was almost at the height of her popularity and the audience that supported Dion was virtually the same audience that would appreciate The Corrs' middle-of-the-road music.

'I would consider playing with Dion, as well as the Royal Albert Hall and the remixes, as being one of the three most important things The Corrs did to achieve success in Europe,' says a music industry insider.

'I think John Hughes getting the gig to play in front of Dion was crucial in the career of The Corrs. People talk these days about opening for the Stones as being crucial in the career of The Corrs. While that was important, I think opening for Celine was even more important as they got more exposure than what even they though they would get.'

There was no denying that The Corrs practically sold *Forgiven Not Forgotten* door to door — even on their home turf. Another Irish tour was on the cards for The Corrs in August 1996, including a planned performance in Dundalk. Many in the old hometown had been miffed that they had missed out on the earlier Corrs' tour, although they were now delighted to pay homage to their most famous citizens. With demand being so great, an extra concert had to be scheduled.

The Carrickdale Hotel just outside of Dundalk played host to The Corrs. 'Hello everybody, it's great to be home. This is the Right Time', Andrea greeted the audience. The *Argus* in Dundalk wrote of the concert: 'Excellent musicianship and crisp, clear harmonies had the place going crazy from the outset ... everyone from kids not even in their teens, to their parents, were happy to be there, enjoying a night of pure entertainment ... '.

Along with their regular set that night, The Corrs played 'On Your Own', which was described as sounding like a traditional Irish tune crossed with a swirling Pink Floyd song.

According to Dundalk journalist Margaret Roddy, the show highlighted The Corrs' appeal: 'It was obvious by who attended that concert that they had wide appeal. Everyone from seven to 70 was there and that was, and is, the strength of The Corrs — their mass appeal.'

Although The Corrs were nervous about playing in front of their home crowds, the local community appreciated the Dundalk concerts. Such was the innocence of the gigs and the desire of The Corrs not to be aloof from their home crowd that the band joined some of the audience to chat a few minutes after the concert had finished.

It had been two nights to remember for a community with a great passion for music. Although there were many who attended the concerts who were not overwhelming fans of The Corrs, there was a large degree of pride that at last the locals were sharing in the success of The Corrs.

* * * *

It sounds mad, but I suffered withdrawal symptoms after leaving Dublin. It had been that good a sixteen months. The people in Belfast were nice, but if the people in Northern Ireland had even heard of the Celtic Tiger they were keeping the kitty hidden from everyone. I missed the passion of Dublin, the happiness on the streets that comes with economic prosperity, not having to look over your shoulder every second minute. I decided to go back to Dublin one Friday. I had a great day: I met up with friends, got inspired to keep on writing and thanked the Lord that I had been given the opportunity to live here for a time. This time I could feel U2 in the streets, smell the culture. If they had made a better city to live in than Dublin, well they hadn't told me.

* * * *

With The Corrs now constantly touring, two musicians were added to the band's line-up: Anto Drennan (lead guitar) and Keith Duffy (bass), two of the nicest people in the business.

Duffy was born on June 2 1966, in Drogheda, County Louth, in Ireland. The third of six children, Duffy's father played the trombone, while his brother Paul started on the saxophone when he was seven. Keith Duffy also started on the sax aged seven, playing for nine years before moving on to the bass. Up until the time he was sixteen, his family travelled Ireland with a circus Duffy's father and uncles owned.

In the mid-1980s, Duffy started a band with his brother Paul, who was also a singer, and his other brother, Jason, who played the drums. They toured in Spain and Ireland, wrote their own songs, but never got a record deal.

From 1990, Duffy played with Andrew Strong from *The Commitments*, for about four years. He then played with various bands and singers in Ireland, before touring with *The Commitments* for a year. In the middle of 1995, Duffy got a call from John Hughes, who knew him from his work with Strong. Hughes asked whether Duffy would be interested in playing bass for The Corrs. His first gig with the band was in October of the same year, when they played with Celine Dion. To the many fans of The Corrs, Duffy has gone on to become an integral member of the band, as much for his endearing personality as for his musical skills.

Anto Drennan has also become an important part of The Corrs' on-stage sound. Drennan is regarded as being amongst the finest guitarists in Ireland and this was part of the reason The Corrs were so disappointed to see him go on an assignment with Genesis for more than a year in 1997–98.

Drennan also comes from a musical family: his father was a musician, while he also has two brothers in the music field. One of them, Miles Drennan, is a talented jazz piano player.

Anto Drennan's reputation in Ireland grew while playing with a wide variety of Irish musicians, including the almost universally popular Clannad. Drennan had a reputation for not only being a top guitarist, but also a good person to tour with. Consequently, there was never any shortage of work for him.

Over the years Duffy and Drennan have become as close to the Corr family and the inner circle of five as it is possible to come. They have provided much to both the Corrs sound and on-stage performance, although there is a lingering suggestion that Drennan has been under-utilised. As it was, Drennan only played on two songs on *Talk on Corners*, while Duffy did not play at all.

With the tours of Ireland and the heavy promotion in the US, the year of 1996 was for The Corrs more about hard work than glamour. More about doing the donkey work than realising the benefits. Travelling the world sounds fascinating for those who don't have to spend hours on flights, constantly recovering from jetlag and often very little sleep. Promoting *Forgiven Not Forgotten* was anything but a picnic and close friends of the band say that, to this day, the siblings still talk about that year as physically the hardest of their musical careers.

The extent of the travelling that year was graphically illustrated in the band's own promotional video, *The Right Time*. A map showed the huge distance that the band had travelled during 1996. It took them to every continent, some on numerous occasions.

Still, despite all the hard work and the constant travelling, there was a delightful enthusiasm and innocence about The Corrs during 1996. 'We were touring with Celine Dion but, I swear to God — I mean I've had a little bit of experience but nothing like getting out in front of 10,000 people just like that,' Caroline told *Drum Media*, 'I was going "Oh my God, how did I do that?" It was great.'

The gruelling year that was 1996 for The Corrs ended with a concert at The Point in Dublin where, due to the cold and the constant flying, the majority of The Corrs were sick with the flu.

The Point had been for so long the biggest concert arena in Ireland. It was the venue that all the big bands from the US and Britain played at and at which the Corr family had dreamed of one day playing. It was yet another sign that The Corrs had made it in Ireland.

On this, perhaps their biggest gig to date, the fact that they were ill was cruel. Some of those who attended the concert say, however, that if The Corrs were sick that night then it wasn't noticeable in their performance. With the adrenaline pumping, they gave yet another non-stop effort and the Irish numbers were particularly well received.

The *Forgiven Not Forgotten* tour had been completed. It had been a success beyond The Corrs' wildest dreams, but had been a lot of hard work. Yet The Corrs had developed a firm following, especially in Ireland and Australia. Their efforts had paid off.

Andrea summed up the mood within the band at this time to *The Irish Times*:

> We want to make the best out of every moment, you know we are young and these are important years. And we really do see the benefit of all the work we do, and we can cope. It would be different if you did not see the fruits of your efforts, that would be soul destroying, but we do see it and we wouldn't want it any other way.

The fruits of their labours in 1996 were not to fully ripen until 1998. The foundations had, however, been very much laid for eventual and ongoing success in territories that had proved more elusive to crack.

Given their success it was natural that the band's individual talents would be noticed. Perhaps due to their experience in *The Commitments*, the acting world started to pay attention and given her charisma and personality, it was no surprise that Andrea especially started to get acting offers from production companies. In 1997, after taking in four continents in three weeks with the band, she took off for Budapest, courtesy of Alan Parker, director of *The Commitments*, where he was filming a large proportion of the film *Evita*.

Parker was inspired by the fact that Andrea's dark hair and exotic looks made her look almost Argentinean, while in *The Commitments* she had shown enough potential to suggest that she could act. Although Andrea appeared alongside Madonna in a scene, the relationship between the pair was almost non-existent.

'I was nervous about it,' Andrea told Irish chat show host Gay Byrne of the experience. 'But I just really did it and tried not to think of her [Madonna] as anything but focus on what I was doing myself. But I mean it was a fantastic experience, I mean wow!'

Andrea's performance was low-key and certainly not significant in the larger scheme of things for her. What it did prove again, however, was that Andrea did have acting ability and a certain star charisma that makes her unique amongst the siblings. What the event also showed was the willingness of band members to keep their options open and to look at the larger picture. This was partly due to the business they were in, but also testimony to the long-term planning and vision of John Hughes.

The completion of the *Forgiven Not Forgotten* tour was perhaps the end of The Corrs' professional innocence. It was time for The Corrs, John Hughes and their record company to start to assess what was important and what direction the band was heading in. The decisions that would be made would have long-lasting effects for all parties concerned.

CHAPTER 9

Making Sure-Fire Hits

We've been number one in Ireland, Spain, Singapore, Malaysia, Australia and New Zealand ... But it means so much more to be top in England. We've always been avid followers of the English scene and English acts. Watching Top of the Pops on a Thursday night was like a religious experience in our house.

Jim Corr

The difficulty in having a successful first album is then turning around and having to do as well, if not better, with the second album. *Forgiven Not Forgotten* had set a precedent, both musically and in terms of sales. It was clear that for The Corrs the aim of their second album was, first to foremost, to consolidate their position in the music industry in the territories where they had been successful and then, hopefully, try to expand their support base. It would not be easy since groups of the calibre of Oasis, The Verve and the Stereophonics were creating a following out of their harsher sounds. The British market especially would be difficult to crack.

The question of where, if at all, traditional Irish music would fit into The Corrs' second album posed a new set of problems. Although the traditional music on *Forgiven Not Forgotten* had gone down a treat in Ireland and Australia, it was prohibitive to the band's development in other markets. It was obvious to The Corrs, John Hughes and Atlantic Records that to achieve widespread appeal in the American and British markets the second album would need to move away from the distinct Irish flavour that so characterised *Forgiven Not Forgotten*. The sound would need to move towards a more universal, more mainstream feel that could easily be slotted into any radio playlist. Now that they had some brand image, they needed some accessibility.

'Definitely more progressive,' Jim told the *Dundalk Democrat* of the second album. 'Maybe with a slightly rockier feel. We know that we can't continue in the same style, but the next album will have The Corrs' stamp on it. But it will also be, in many respects, a progression from the first. Our influences are growing all the time.'

John Hughes also gave some indication as to what the aims with the second album were to be in his own commissioned video, *The Right Time*. Speaking at the end of the *Forgiven Not Forgotten* tour he stated that the aim was to write 'radio hits' so that the time spent promoting the first album 'door to door' would not have to be repeated.

Yet given the success of *Forgiven Not Forgotten* in Europe, Warner Music there were asking The Corrs not to change their sound *too* much. 'The European territories were so pleased with *Forgiven Not Forgotten*,' says Andy Murray, 'that we essentially said that what we wanted was more of the same. Except that we wanted it to be more rocky and more Celtic at the same time, if that was possible. As it turned out, *Talk on Corners* ended up being less rocky and less Celtic.'

Second-guessing what the public wants and is prepared to spend money on remains a risky business. The musical acts that have been the most successful have themselves set the boundaries. U2, for example, wrote and performed music that in many ways bucked the trend. But U2 were successful because their music was extremely good and because they believed in their talent and their message.

All the evidence suggests that The Corrs especially targeted the US and Britain with their second album. They aimed to make their mark in both countries by producing sure-fire hits that would earn substantial radio play and ensure that they would not have to work themselves to a standstill as they had in 1996.

In January 1997 The Corrs spent around a month demo-ing songs that they thought would go on the next record. These songs seemed very European in texture and lyrics. Some songs they recorded with real drums, others with drum machines. A problem, however, was trying to convince Atlantic in the US that there were any hit singles on the demo. According to press reports and comments made by John Hughes himself, the record company was anything but convinced that they had any sure-fire hits.

In order to understand why the Americans were less enthusiastic early on about *Talk on Corners* it is necessary to understand the American music charts. In the US, the music charts are basically columns of musical styles in which the most popular songs in each chart are rated. The most common charts are rhythm and blues, adult contemporary and country. There is a tendency in the American music industry to make records that fit into one of the specific categories, which is understandable as a record that falls outside the categories won't get radio play and most probably won't chart.

The Corrs took their demos to 143 Records in the US and 143 suggested that The Corrs should introduce some co-writers to try to produce these supposedly elusive sure-fire hits. Given some of the names suggested, The Corrs were initially enthusiastic about the concept. Oliver Leber, Carole Bayer Sager and Glen Ballard all had had credible success elsewhere and it seemed logical to collaborate with them.

Reflecting on the decision, David Foster says that the aim was essentially to create hits in America:

> We felt with *Talk on Corners* that the best chance The Corrs had of having hits was if we introduced some big name producers and co-writers. Although in many respects it was the forerunner for The Corrs to work with Mutt Lange on *In Blue*, I'm not sure looking back whether it was a great success.
>
> I know that The Corrs weren't real happy with it. I can recall there being occasions when they were tearing their hair out. I'm really not sure whether it was the best move on our part.

The Corrs found working with such seasoned professionals a mixed experience. On the one hand, they were producing music that appeared to have a good chance of getting played on the radio, but somewhere in the midst of production the album may have been too heavily influenced by their illustrious contributors. This fear had been with The Corrs before they recorded *Forgiven Not Forgotten* in the US and it now seemed as if it was coming back to haunt them. Jim especially was concerned that big-name songwriters were in danger of taking over the album.

The Corrs co-wrote and produced *Talk on Corners* in two sections. The first half was produced on the West Coast in the US; the end result being some songs they were happy with, others that needed further work.

They then returned to Dublin to work with Leo Pearson at Peak Studios. There, they produced: 'When He's Not Around', 'What Can I Do', 'Remember', 'Paddy McCarthy' and 'Radio'.

Around June that same year they went back to the US and completed the album. Although 143 on the West Coast of the US were happy with the album, the decision makers on the East Coast were less enthusiastic, fearing that *Talk on Corners* did not fit into any of the particular chart categories and would thus fail to get on the radio.

What developed as a result was a power struggle as to whether *Talk on Corners* would even be released. In a startling frank interview with

Hot Press editor Niall Stokes, a great friend of the band, John Hughes gave his account of what happened. 'It's true,' Hughes acknowledged. 'They were convinced we didn't have a hit single and so it came down to a very direct conflict. They were saying "It's not coming out, John. Get it straight." And I was insisting, "It is coming out. It's got to come out. If we miss this, our career's over. It has to come out." And they said, "We need a hit single off the record and we don't have one." I said, "Forget about the hit song. Nobody writes flops. You just don't like it. But that doesn't mean that other people won't."'

It went right to the final call. Hughes said that he knew the band had the support of the European territories, thanks to the success of *Forgiven Not Forgotten*. Warners International indicated that they wanted the album sooner rather than later too. In the end, Val Azzoli, Chairman of Atlantic Records in the US, and Ramon Lopez, the President of Warner Music International, eventually backed the album, no little thanks to the persistence of Hughes and his undying belief in the disc.

The album was released in Europe in October 1997, but not in the US. Hughes believed it was a high-risk strategy for Atlantic with so much at stake. A joint release would undoubtedly have reduced their risk in some respects; although not releasing in the US was a safety net and appeared to keep both sides of Atlantic happy for the time being.

'It's a brutal business,' Hughes reflected later. 'You don't expect any favours. You're going into war claiming we can't win: we'd better not fight. We're saying this is all we have. We're together, we're unified, we believe — we'll fight.'

Given the failure of Minor Detail to make any real headway in the music industry, Hughes's reputation was again on the line; his image of himself in an industry that he loved once again up for evaluation. 'Sometimes the industry wants it tailor-made, but they may not like the tailoring,' Hughes told *Hot Press*. 'And you have to insist and shove and push and plead. And so there were shouting matches. And the upshot was that we got the album released but we had to sell three million records or we were dead. Or I was, at least.'

*   *   *   *

Settling into Belfast was never going to be easy after the life-changing experiences I had in Dublin, especially in the month of July. And although you could point out as many positives as you want about Belfast, it just wasn't Dublin. I was fortunate enough in my first nights in Belfast to stay with Frances Lynch and Mark Harriot. Young, talented and hard-working, Mark and Frances made me feel right at home, their generosity, friendship and belief in me enabled me to feel confident enough to handle whatever challenges Belfast could throw at me. Still, there were some nights when I would lie in their spare room and hear the sounds of helicopters over head monitoring what was going on below. It felt and sounded a bit like Billy Joel's 'Goodnight Saigon'. This was a long way from home, a war zone of sorts. A long way from Dublin in any sense.

*   *   *   *

Even in hindsight, the fears of the record company were justified. Despite *Talk on Corners* ultimately selling millions of copies around the world, two facts remain. First of all, despite its eventual success, the original version of *Talk on Corners* still didn't have a hit single in Britain on it that would essentially achieve the sort of the promotion that everyone wanted for The Corrs. As it happened, the song that brought The Corrs that success was 'Dreams'. 'What Can I Do' was a massive radio hit around Germany and Continental Europe, and it propelled the album to number nine in Germany overnight, but there is no disguising the fact that until The Corrs started to remix their songs, they did not have a hit single in Britain until 'Dreams'.

Secondly, on the whole the quality of the album remained questionable. This was reflected in the fact that when it was first released *Talk on Corners* did not sell many more copies than *Forgiven Not Forgotten* had. It is in many respects ironic that, after the eventual success of *Talk on Corners*, John Hughes should feel as if his initial enthusiasm for the album was proved correct. *Talk on Corners* may not have reached the benchmark sales of three million had the album not been remixed and had a cover of a very successful 1970s Fleetwood Mac song not been recorded. While Hughes can take some credit for the latter, his initial faith was not especially well founded. Although *Talk on Corners* would go on sell well over eight million albums world-wide, it still had serious flaws; the most obvious being a lack of passion and originality.

A close examination of the original *Talk on Corners* gives a clear picture of just how much the album was directed at getting airplay and being as accessible as possible. It starts with one of its strongest tracks, 'Only When I Sleep'. This is a quality song: The lead guitar sets the tempo, while for once Andrea's lyrics are tested. She proves up to the task with an accomplished display of emotion. There is a strong story to this song and although it remains true blue pop, Andrea displays a passion and sensuality that would be particularly evident in live performances.

Second up, 'When He's Not Around' is the perfect example of a radio-friendly song that yet does not have the passion of similar tracks on *Forgiven Not Forgotten*. The lyrics are immature and could have easily been written by a thirteen-year-old girl:

> I find that I can't breathe and I can't sleep
> When he's not around
> Everyday is bluey grey
> When he's not in town

The lack of depth and insight is obvious. The argument that it is *only* pop does not stand up to scrutiny when one considers that 'Dreams' — a song with passionate lyrics and emotions — is also deemed pop.

'What Can I Do?' continues the fast-developing trend for weepy lyrics. This is better, but only slightly. Again the lyrics are mediocre, and although there is a pleasant innocence about this song, there is nothing behind it. The sentiment is almost see-through. It's as if Andrea is the listener's pleasant younger sister: we clap at the end but we wish she would go away. Despite that, the track is radio-friendly and if you stay awake long enough it is catchy. This is reflected in the fact that it was such a big hit around the world. Lloyds Bank in England thought so and went on to use it as a campaign jingle. It did not deserve a better fate.

'I Never Loved You Anyway' is another radio-friendly song. Produced by David Foster and written by Andrea and Carole Bayer Sager, this track moves at a brisk pace and has a clear story to it. It isn't groundbreaking, but the song flows along nicely and it is easy listening. Again, it is pure vanilla.

'So Young' was written by Sharon Corr and remains the catchiest track on *Talk on Corners*. Here, the lead guitar is to the fore. There is a joyful playfulness to this song and the lyrics combine beautifully with the melody. As well as the lead guitar, Andrea's vocals also stand out. This is a song that she obviously enjoys singing and the strength of her voice is obvious. As a pop song 'So Young' works well.

If the listener had begun to nod off by the time they reached 'So Young' then they might well be put to sleep by 'Don't Say You Love Me'. Although this is one of the better slow songs on the album, it is more of the same: weepy lyrics, a solid but unspectacular guitar wrap and pleasant backing vocals. Again it is Andrea and Carole Bayer Sager driving on a Sunday afternoon. Nice, but too much of the same.

By the time the listener gets to 'Love Gives Love Takes', another soppy tune is waiting:

> Love breaks and love divides
> Love laughs and love can make you cry
> I can't believe the ways
> That love can give
> And love can take away.

Talk on Corners is fast becoming predictable. Five slow dreamy songs in the first seven and if John Hughes had planned a dreamy, radio-friendly second album then he was well and truly getting it. No points for originality though.

The pace of the album increases just a fraction on 'Hopelessly Addicted'. Written by Andrea and Oliver Leiber, the theme of this song is the same as the others. It is hard to gauge how much anguish Andrea must have been going through with her love life at this time, but it all seems to be coming out in her writing.

By this stage the listener is almost crying out for something different. It's been a great trek so far if you're a teenager in love or like easy-listening music, but not for those who like variety. 'Paddy McCarthy' comes as something of a relief then.

A traditional Irish instrumental, 'Paddy McCarthy' is a return of sorts to what made *Forgiven Not Forgotten* special. This isn't classic Irish music, but there is an atmospheric feel to it, emphasised by the outstanding violin playing of Sharon.

'Intimacy', although not written by The Corrs, is another pleasant interlude and it would have even been more pleasant had this not already been an album of interludes. Still, this is one of the better slow songs on the album.

Suddenly *Talk on Corners* springs to life with 'Queen of Hollywood'. At last some passion from The Corrs! This song is about an aspiring actress who lowers herself to follow her dream. This is a much stronger song. There is a story to it; plenty of spirit and it is performed with real feeling. Sharon's violin complements Andrea's vocals and it is nicely produced.

The pace of the album is at last starting to pick up. It continues with 'No Good For Me' which is another quality track. The song begins with a catchy guitar rift, leading straight into Andrea's rich vocals. There is more depth to this song than to some of the earlier tracks. In short, it is a more mature song about more mature feelings. Even the lyrics are better:

> I see a home in a quiet place
> I see myself in a strong embrace
> And I feel protection from the human race
> It's not parental
> But it's a fantasy, not a reality
> And it's good for me you have no idea …

Written by Andrea, the key word again is passion. She sings the words as she means them, as if the words and the emotions belong to her.

The album finishes with perhaps its strongest track, the 1967 Jim Hendrix original 'Little Wing'. Combining with The Chieftains was beneficial: they provided the Celtic arrangements, while The Corrs provided guitars, bodhrán, tin whistle and vocals. It is a magic mix and once again The Corrs show how good they are at performing a song that has some depth. There is also a touch of Clannad about some of the backing vocals, while the music has a style about it that is worthy of the two groups performing it.

'Little Wing', which was a trade-off for The Corrs playing 'You Know My Love' on the Chieftains' *Tears of Stone* album, rounds *Talk on Corners* off nicely. With three strong songs at the end, the album has at least finished on a high. There are, however, too many weepy, melodramatic, immature songs to make it anywhere near as good as *Forgiven Not Forgotten*.

That said, however, the musicianship of The Corrs and their ability to bring to life what are some pretty average songs is impressive. On *Talk on Corners* the band once again showed that they could play.

Nevertheless, this 'softness' on *Talk on Corners* was noted by record executives, both in Britain and the US. Andy Murray stated that when the Europeans first heard rough mixes of 'When He's Not Around', 'Intimacy' and 'I Never Loved You Anyway' they were well received: 'So I was very sure and could say to my colleagues that there was a whole lot of stuff that we could market.'

'Only When I Sleep' as a single, followed by 'I Never Loved You Anyway' was the reason that the local Warner European companies thought that *Talk On Corners* could be released in autumn 1997 and do well, and 'When He's Not Around' was regarded as a good mix of modern pop with a Celtic edge. 'Our concern,' Murray says, 'was to get an album out as quickly as we could. By that stage it would have been two years since *Forgiven Not Forgotten*, but we were also concerned that releasing another album before Christmas would mean that we would be competing against numerous other artists, advertising dollars and space in the shops. We thought it would have been better to release the album early in 1998, when there was more room in the market-place.'

*   *   *   *

The summer of 2000 will always to me be the summer of U2. I savoured every word of Eamon Dunphy's excellent biography of the band; I listened to every U2 album I could find. I felt the band's passion, the chemistry. With Or Without You had always been a special theme of mine, but my passion for U2 was now more rounded. To me they provided a reason for our own existence. Okay, so I was about ten years late on the bandwagon, but the issue to me was not so much about what U2 was, but about what The Corrs had turned out not to be. Like the girl in the diner in Dundalk, you could demonstrate the importance of The Corrs by examining their contemporaries. It goes without saying that U2 achieved more success than even they ever dreamed. But the amazing thing was that they did this by staying true to their music, their image and, perhaps most importantly, themselves. They did not follow the trends, they set them. Did The Corrs do that? Were The Corrs mere products of a changing music environment that placed so much faith in Ronan Keating, Britney Spears and Posh Spice? Did real music count anymore? Would U2 have been successful if they had been starting out in 2001? These questions were whistling around in my head. The only answer I could find was that U2 had been true to themselves and that they had been hugely successful. They were the test, they were the role models and by any stretch The Corrs, although by no means the worst, were a poor comparison.

*   *   *   *

'What Can I Do?' and 'So Young' were not originally meant to be on the international version of *Talk on Corners*. '"So Young" at that stage wasn't finished,' says Andy Murray, 'they [The Corrs] had decided to record it, David Foster had approved it but they hadn't finished it. But at this stage I had heard all of the rest of the album and John Hughes and I believed strongly that the album needed an up tempo number. We weren't necessarily saying that it was going to be a hit, but we felt they needed to have it on the record. John spent a week working out of my office in London and we put together the suggested sequencing, in conjunction with the US. It was a joint effort. "So Young" was actually John's vision of a rabble-rousing, audience-pleasing showstopper, and he had stressed that the first time he played me the song. So when it came to discuss including it on the album, I reminded him of his original idea, and each time I see crowds respond to Jim Corr shouting "put your hands together" I remember John enthusiastically predicting it.'

John Hughes rang Foster telling him that 'So Young' needed to go on the international version of *Talk on Corners*. Although the album version of the song wasn't released as a single, the K-Class remix was a hit and fully justified the decision to include it. It was also a particular favourite of many fans at live shows.

Talk on Corners was released in Dublin in October 1997. The press release from the launch read:

> With their unique blend of contemporary and traditional Irish music, 143/Lava/Atlantic recording artists The Corrs have established themselves as true originals. On

their new album *Talk on Corners* Ireland's favourite sibling quartet — Jim (keyboards/guitars/vocals), Andrea (lead vocals, tin whistle), Caroline (drums/bodhrán/vocals) and Sharon (violin/vocals) have created a sound steeped in the folk music of their homeland, but invested with a vibrant and electric modern pop sensibility.

The album sees a remarkable growth and significant change from The Corrs' 1995 debut album *Forgiven Not Forgotten*, incorporating a more melancholy and adventurous tint to their musical palette.

The aim for Warners in Europe was to sell a million albums. Second albums normally either sell five times as many as the first album, or half the number of the first album, so *Talk on Corners* was very much going to be a test for The Corrs.

The reviews for *Talk on Corners* were mixed. *Sunday Tribune* journalist Michael Ross was perhaps the most critical of The Corrs and of *Talk on Corners*. He wrote:

Creatively timid to begin with, they have retreated further into the ideas and the musicianship of others to further burnish a music which, like that of Enya, is one of international superficiality from which all elements of the Irish tradition bar the merely vestigial have been expunged.

'Bland' was a word commonly used to describe The Corrs. Andrea said in an interview with *Hot Press* in 1997 that she understands why The Corrs get labelled with this tag, although she also took the time to berate the critics:

I get a sense of certain reviewers saying, 'Shit, I wish I didn't like this album, I wish I could totally resent it, but I can't', probably because rock critics do see us as so uncool. Rock critics are terrible snobs when it comes to pop music. They're all trying so hard to be alternative, to take a stand against whatever is popular with the majority of people. They're all very conservative themselves, in that sense. So I'm not really surprised when such critics attack us. But, yes, a lot of our critics are probably just rejecting us because we are presented in the media as so clean, so straight. Well, we are, so what?

Music critics tend to look for several things in both an album and a band. Obviously they are looking for musical talent. But also they are looking to see whether the boundaries of the art have been questioned, pushed, rocked or simply abused. Albums that tend to be popular with critics push the boundaries and question the very nature of our existence. They tend not to be interested in pretty faces, soft sounds, but whether an artist has truly explored within themselves and mankind and made a contribution that relates to us all.

In August 2000 the *Irish Star* surveyed four leading Irish music journalists and asked them what their ten top Irish albums of all time were. Several musicians were constantly included in the combined list: U2, Rory Gallagher, Thin Lizzy, The Undertones, Van Morrison. Out of the 40 albums listed, there was not one by The Corrs.

Despite music critics being less than overwhelmed with *Talk on Corners*, a constant word that was used in reviews was 'catchy'. As *Hot Press* reported late in 1998:

> The best of these acts was undoubtedly The Corrs. No matter how much the hyperati of the cities may have cat-called, spat and hissed at the Dundalk foursome, when it came to immaculately executed AOR pop radio fodder, there was no competition. 'Only When I Sleep', the first single from the *Talk on Corners* album remains the group's finest recorded moment.

CHAPTER 10

Talking On All Corners — Remixed

The Corrs won't leave you psychically disturbed, don't require concentration, but they're youthful and they like a bit of stadium thump, so they're on the money if you're not quite ready for Val Doonican.

Mojo magazine

One of the strengths of John Hughes and The Corrs themselves is never to settle for what other people might classify as success. Having sold over 100,000 copies of *Talk on Corners* in Britain alone, The Corrs would have been entitled to feel pleased that at least they had consolidated their reputation.

Still, *Talk on Corners* was not about consolidation; it was about development and progress. Then there was the small matter of the three million sales that were needed to get Hughes's neck off the hook with Atlantic Records in the US. Partially because of this, there was a feeling within The Corrs' camp that they had not achieved the success they were looking for with *Talk on Corners*.

Which is not to say that the original *Talk on Corners* had not sold well elsewhere. It had been a major success in Ireland, throughout Asia, in a number of countries in Europe and in Australia and New Zealand. Still, there was something about becoming a household name in Britain that pushed The Corrs on. It was as if they believed they would not have reached their potential had they not become a major success there.

The Corrs had grown up with the British charts and British music television programmes. They had watched their parents practice and perform some of the hits that they had seen on their TV screens. They themselves had imagined just what it would be like to be this famous. They had witnessed what it meant to be popular in Britain and it probably meant more to them than being big at home in Ireland.

While concentrating their energies on breaking the British market with *Talk on Corners*, The Corrs had to face up to a barrage of criticism from within Ireland. In a blatant attack on the band, the Irish *Sunday Tribune* made a series of accusations that shocked both The Corrs and their legion of Irish fans.

Entitled 'Bland on the Run', journalist Michael Ross wrote that their second album 'contains so relatively little of the four Dundalk siblings, and so relatively much of its three producers, its other outside songwriters and its many session musicians that it suggests a band with little inspiration or little effective control over their output or, quite likely, both.' He also claimed that the band only wrote five of the thirteen tracks, that 'Intimacy' was played entirely by outside contributors, and that Caroline Corr played drums on none of the tracks.

Ross was not completely accurate in his criticism. According to the first edition of *Talk on Corners*, five of the thirteen tracks were written by Andrea, one by Sharon, while three were written by Andrea and others. One was a Jimi Hendrix remake, another a traditional Irish instrumental. It was therefore only on two songs that The Corrs did not have a hand in writing the lyrics.

Andrea had her revenge against Ross in an article in Irish music magazine *Hot Press* in December 1997:

> I will be honest and say that was the first thing ever written about us that I felt was totally unjust. I believe in Karma, try to live that way. I get what I give. I'm not nasty to you so you won't be nasty to me, I believe. That's how my family lives, too.
>
> So we, The Corrs, are honest about what we are and everything we do. None of us have really done anything that was *that* wrong. So that article was so undeserved, unjust and incorrect that it hurt me because I hated things like that being said about my family, about my mother and my father.

The question of whether Caroline did or did not play drums on *Talk on Corners* has been a thorny issue for many critics of The Corrs, while fans of the band have also wondered what exactly happened. To answer that question, it is first necessary to describe how the music industry works.

In a highly informative article on the modern music industry, Tony Scherman wrote in *The New York Times* in January 2001 that the issue in modern music was less about who performed the music than who created it. His view is that 'records' of musical events were now recordings of something much more exotic:

> The music business has finally figured out how to do without musicians, those pesky varmints. Today, more and more pop is created not by conventional musicianship but

by using samplers, digital editing software and other computerised tools to stitch together pre-recorded sounds. From magnates like Sean (Puffy) Combs to innovators like the DJ and producer Roni Size, pop belongs increasingly to people who don't play instruments and have little or no grasp of even basic harmonic and rhythmic theory.

Even music that doesn't wear its computerised origins on its sleeve — the mainstream pop of Christina Aguilera, Britney Spears or, for that matter, of Madonna — relies far more on sampling and looping (programming a sampled phrase to repeat indefinitely) than on the rock 'n' roll staples of guitar playing and drumming.

The point is, music is an industry as well as an art, and once an industry finds a more efficient way to make its product, the clock doesn't turn back. It's as true of pop music as it is of the car business. And if something as fragile as taste is implicated, if the onrush of capital pushes performers, styles, genres into the margins — well, that's just too bad.

What Scherman was suggesting was that in the modern music age the emphasis has moved on from literally being four boys and some instruments playing on street corners, to something that has adapted with the technological age. Musicians still create music, but the means by which they do so has altered substantially. The musician is perhaps not someone who plays the instruments, but someone who arranges the programming. Music production would now appear to be more about composition than actual performance, although performance is still an integral part of musicianship.

As part of this musical revolution of sorts, many high profile producers and songwriters are accustomed to using their own musicians in the recording studio. The sound that they are trying to create, whether through artificial means or live performance, is their primary goal.

Given that The Corrs have proved beyond doubt that they can play music live, it should be irrelevant whether Caroline did or did not play drums on *Talk on Corners*. Still, the issue does require clarity.

As Michael Ross suggested, Caroline did not play the drums on *Talk on Corners*. Also, most of the drumming on *Forgiven Not Forgotten* was programmed, as at that stage Caroline had not been drumming for that long. Then again, Jim did not play guitar on all of the tracks on *Talk on Corners* and regulars Anto Drennan and Keith Duffy, both more than accomplished musicians, did not play guitars on a majority of the tracks on *Talk on Corners* either. However, The Corrs *did* sing on all of the tracks.

Record insiders say that not only did some of the producers employed prefer to work with their own people on *Talk on Corners*, but that it made 'musical sense' to utilise the talents of musicians who, in all honesty, were perhaps better than The Corrs themselves.

'It is a case of what is relevant to the track in question,' says one record insider. 'I think it would be foolish to suggest that The Corrs can't play just because they are not playing on every track on *Talk on Corners*. You could have said that it's a major change from the first album in that all the drums are programmed on the first album and they are played live on *Talk on Corners*. It depends on how you look at it.

'It's simply not an issue if you go to work with a big producer. You will find that even within session drummers there will be musicians who some producers prefer. Oliver Leiber prefers Matt Laug on drums and he was used on *Talk on Corners*. That's the way it works. You could argue that *Talk on Corners* would have sounded more contemporary had it been produced with drum machines,' the insider adds.

'In 1997 real drumming, as opposed to the drum machine, was viewed as not modern. Nowadays it is cool to have a combination of the two. In the end it will be up to who is producing the track to make the call whether to include a real drummer or not. If it's a drum machine, well then so be it.'

'There was one track, I think it was "Rainy Day",' says Andy Murray, 'and I said to Jim "that sounds great, who did the drums?" And he said it was a drum machine. I thought it was a drummer, so sometimes the difference can be quite small.'

Ultimately, The Corrs put their name on *Talk on Corners* and to say that the music wasn't totally theirs would be clutching at straws. Although it may not necessarily be artistically pure, it is the nature of the modern music industry. The Corrs were not the first, and they will certainly not be the last, musical act to utilise outside help.

Despite some criticism, The Corrs knew that with *Talk on Corners* they needed to continue to develop brand recognition. Although their major goal was to achieve success in Britain and the US, other territories were continuing to appreciate The Corrs.

The band toured Australia and New Zealand to wide acclaim in January and February 1998. As *The Christchurch Press* reported on Saturday February 21 1998: 'One by one the diminutive clan filed into Christchurch Airport's international arrivals area. Jim Corr stopped to sign a couple of autographs, and amateur photographers snapped some quick pics.'

And of the concert itself the next day, the same newspaper raved:

> Easy on the eye and the ear, the siblings Andrea, Sharon, Caroline and Jim delivered a performance equal, if not better, that their recordings. From the first strains of violin, enhanced by cleverly synchronised lighting, the eager audience was enveloped in a blanket of rich, positive sound.
>
> [Andrea's] sensual, cat-like movements and passionate vocals were captivating. She was admirably flanked by the elegant and classically influenced violinist Sharon, and brother Jim who laconically played sweet guitar riffs, interspersed with playing keyboards and giving occasional flirtatious glances. Caroline Corr spearheaded a fine rhythm section with fire and commitment.

It was during their tour of New Zealand that The Corrs achieved some success in Germany. The German branch of Warners had managed to get a booking on a well-known German television programme, which was made by a popular and powerful local producer. He wanted 'What Can I Do?' to be the track that the show featured. The Corrs had gone on the show and before they performed the presenter gave them a two-minute build-up, something unheard of on German television. The next week *Talk on Corners* went to number nine on the German charts. 'What Can I Do?' became the single and the video was shot in one day, north of Auckland in New Zealand.

By this stage The Corrs had also broken through in Spain. The record company there thought that, although the previous two Corrs' videos were fine, there was the risk that they might be viewed as too glamorous. Therefore, the record company asked the director of the video for 'What Can I Do?', Nigel Dick, to shoot them in T-shirts and jeans.

Dick duly told The Corrs that they had to wear this clothing for the video. Despite looking good in the video and it being one of the most popular Corr videos (including Caroline's cowboy hat) the irony was that The Corrs never really wear jeans in everyday life.

After the Australasian tour, it was time for another concentrated push in the British market. It was inevitable that The Corrs were going to make a major impact there sooner or later. It was just finding the right opportunity for them to showcase their talents and then let this huge market appreciate what they had to offer.

*   *   *   *

Belfast wasn't that far away from Dundalk, less than one hour on the train, although it could have been a million miles. I arrived in Belfast in July, just before the highly passionate marching season. I actually worked July 12, the day when Ulster's Orangemen take to the streets to celebrate their history. I had anticipated a historical, educational experience. I hadn't suspected that there would be so much hatred, so much negative passion. Belfast was not a pleasant place to be. The Orangemen met that day at a park just 50 metres from where I lived. I came home that night and was amazed by the rubbish that had been left. It was as if a football game had just taken place. I sat at my computer that night writing about The Corrs and started to wonder what they were writing about, singing about, preaching about. There was no doubt in my mind that what they were doing was making people feel good. But was it important in its own right? Were they doing what U2 were doing? Were they moving music into a higher art form?

*   *   *   *

Despite *Talk on Corners* eventually going gold in Britain, neither John Hughes nor the band believed that they had achieved their breakthrough. Part of the problem was that for all their good looks and catchy tunes, they had failed to gain enough exposure in the mainstream British media. They needed a hook or at least a platform from which they could express their talents.

Hughes believed The Corrs were not part of the sound of the day in Britain. The BBC wasn't playing The Corrs. Neither was Capitol Radio. And their only significant TV exposure had been on *Des O'Connor*. But all the hard work The Corrs had put in to establish themselves in the British market finally paid off. They got two lucky breaks: playing on the Fleetwood Mac tribute album, *Legacy*, and performing at the Royal Albert Hall in London on St Patrick's Day.

Legacy was the idea of Jason Flom, who had originally helped sign The Corrs. Flom wanted The Corrs to play on the album and he had discussions with John Hughes. The song 'Dreams' had become available and Hughes jumped at the opportunity.

The weekend after *Talk on Corners* was released, The Corrs recorded the vocals with Oliver Leiber. Following the recording, The Corrs started to tour. On the second night of the tour in Amsterdam they played 'Dreams'. Amongst the audience were chiefs from Warners in the US. Quite simply, the song failed to fire and the Americans asked whether The Corrs' version could be made more modern.

After some discussion it was decided that Leiber would produce a more modern-styled remix. Leiber produced the album version of

'Dreams', while Flom got Todd Terry to come in to mix the singles version, and Terry did five versions of the track.

By early March Rob Dickins, then Chairman of Warner Music UK, had become more involved in the band's career. Dickins had the first available Terry mixes but didn't believe they were quite right for the charts. He contacted John Hughes and asked him whether he would be happy for 'Dreams' to be released as a remix. Hughes, supportive of efforts to attain a British hit, was enthusiastic.

Dickins got hold of some other versions of the mixes from New York, one of which was 'T's radio edit', which became the British and subsequent world hit. But that still didn't solve the problem of getting more exposure in Britain. The crucial element of the solution devised by Hughes centred on St Patrick's Day. Hughes rightly believed that on March 17 the band stood the best chance of getting on British television. They needed a show broadcast from London screened on the BBC on St Patrick's Day to ensure that they would be watched by millions of British viewers.

The Royal Albert Hall was booked. It was bigger than what Hughes was originally thinking of, but it was grand enough to convince the BBC to screen The Corrs showpiece. The show sold out in three weeks. Mark Cooper, Executive Producer of Music Entertainment of the BBC, was then asked whether he would film it. 'The truth is,' Cooper explains, 'the BBC commissioned that broadcast because it was St Patrick's Day, it was in the Albert Hall and it was The Corrs.' *In that order of importance.*

Chapter 1 explained what impact the concert had on the careers of The Corrs. It was a defining night, the magic of joining forces with Fleetwood, combined with a band that looked as though it had come of age.

The success of the televised concert was immediately shown in British sales. In the second week of March *Talk on Corners* was in the fifties, but eight days after the concert it was up to thirteen. The performance at the Royal Albert Hall had started The Corrs' sales momentum in Britain. What the concert also did was prove to Atlantic that The Corrs could achieve the type of success in Britain that they craved. At Warners, the then chairman, Rob Dickins began looking for new angles.

About six weeks after the concert the new version of 'Dreams' was given to Radio One, who immediately put it on the playlist. To this day nobody knows, including Radio One when asked in 2001, exactly why 'Dreams' made it onto the air while other Corrs' songs had not. The remixing, which had made it more accessible, obviously helped, as did the concert at the Royal Albert Hall. But Andy Murray does not think that the TV performance made as big a difference as is often suggested:

> At that stage we had worked seven singles to Radio One and they hadn't played any of them. The album had been in the charts; *Talk on Corners* had charted at number seven in the UK. This was not a group from nowhere. The idea that people see them on the telly and suddenly go that's who they are. I just don't believe that. We had showcases around them, they had been on various programmes, television and radio, and they had had play on Radio Two. People knew who they were. In my opinion they (Radio One) were looking for something they could play. It was the right thing at the right time.

'Dreams' did what other Corr's singles had failed to do — it went into the top ten and onto Radio One's A-list as well as Capitol Radio's and gave The Corrs the injection that had been missing in their efforts in Britain.

Now realising what the public and the radio stations wanted, Warners knew the formula and were only too willing to serve it up. 'What Can I Do?', the remix, followed and once again it was a success in the charts. The Corrs were now perceived as being accessible in Britain. Buoyed by what they were seeing, the band started to promote themselves more in Britain, their efforts leading to greater exposure and more sales.

Being in the right place at the right time was vital, as Andrea explained to *Q Magazine*:

> The first album came out when it was all Britpop and techno and we didn't fit into either. Perhaps we were too nice and melodic and that really wasn't what it was all about at the time. But we are not blaming anyone else we [were] just determined to write even better songs.

'The Corrs' success in Britain probably did come at a good time for them,' agrees Kevin Courtney. 'The style of music that they were doing, mainly middle of the road with a bit new agey, a bit poppy, was generally popular in 1998. I think there were a lot of adults looking for something that wasn't too on the edge, which covered the middle ground.'

'I think their penetration of the British market reflected the conservative tastes in the British market. It also reflected that tastes were running between young and old. People like Cher were making a big comeback. Her record was being bought by all ages. The Corrs fitted nicely into that. They could sell to Dad rockers and they could sell to kids who weren't interested in alternative music and who wanted something that was nice and mainstream that they could sing along to.'

*   *   *   *

Everyone in Ireland kept telling me that the real Ireland was the one situated in the west, in the Galway region. The mystic beauty of the landscape, I was told, was reflected in the culture. Understand that and you start to understand the rich traditions in Ireland. I was hooked and one weekend in September I headed across from Belfast. 'Make sure you enjoy yourself in Galway,' was the first thing that I was told when I arrived. It is a pretty town, populated by 50,000 who regularly say they 'live in heaven on earth'. Galway is like that — a beautiful spot, the gateway to the Wild West. I stayed there three days. Coming from New Zealand (the most beautiful nation on earth), I wasn't overwhelmed by the beauty of Galway, but there was a Celtic mysticism about the place. I couldn't find much Irish music in the bars that seemed to be chock-a-block with tourists, but I could almost feel it on the streets. As if the music was a sign, a symbol that this was the real Ireland. Yes there was something special about Galway and the West of Ireland. The landscape was part of it, as was the culture. But more and more I began to reflect that it was the people. I was beginning to understand more and more about myself and the world.

*   *   *   *

Remixing was, however, the key ingredient in The Corrs' success in Britain. Remixing had developed out of the club world in London and flowed through into pop music. It became a badge of accessibility to young people, proof that the music was modern. A remix proved easier to dance to and many DJs believed that remixing was fresh and that it was fashionable. It became a new style and form of music.

Radio remixes are also a constant way of keeping a musical act on the playlist with essentially the same product. In the modern world there is a much bigger market and if a band wants to service that market then they have to provide something that is new and, in the eyes of the public, fresh. One way of doing that is by changing the music a bit and remixing a song. 'If you made a single in 1995 and you were signed with EMI the first thing your manager would say is "who is going to do the remixes?"' says a music insider. 'It's a way for them to sell their song.'

Jim says that a remix takes a song in a direction that you wouldn't perhaps expect. He says The Corrs weren't sure about it at first, but the remix took each song in a fresh direction. 'There were one or two versions that we didn't think would work. Nine times out of ten we really liked the remixes.' Given his background in the technical side of the music industry, Jim naturally had more understanding of the significance of remixes than the girls had.

'Like any other band in the world, The Corrs want to be modern,' says Andy Murray. 'This does not mean that The Corrs will just accept anything. I mean, they loved the remix of "What Can I Do?" No changes were made to that. K-Klass did "So Young" and there were a lot of changes to that because the band felt the fiddle part should have been louder and they changed the rhythm part a couple of times. They loved the remix of "Runaway" and only made small changes.'

The reality is that the use of remixes to get the band radio play in Britain hasn't been translated into sales. At the time of writing around 2.2 million copies of *Talk on Corners Special Edition* (i.e. the remixed album) had been sold, about a quarter of the overall sales of *Talk on Corners*.

'Everything has to be new for retailers. A record is old after a week,' says a record insider. 'Replaced with something else and put in the bargain bin. The *Special Edition* was a way of keeping the music in the market. What the retailers want is a bigger slice of the pie, what record companies want is a bigger pie.'

Fan opinion was divided about the remixes. 'The general opinion about Corrs remixing among fans is now fairly neutral,' says *Corrsonline.com* coordinator Daniel Lindberg. 'There are more people who dislike the remixing than people who actually like it though. When the band first started to remix ["Dreams"] people were a bit shocked, and pissed off at the British music scene. Many heated discussions followed.

'The general understanding came a bit afterwards — that it was an attempt to get the band on British radio. So even though a lot of fans hated the remix of "Dreams", most understood it. What created chaos among fans was the remix marathon. With remix after remix being released in Britain, one worse than the other, many lost faith in the band. The remixes did well in Britain, but they didn't seem to do much elsewhere. Within a year the Internet fanbase had been almost replaced, not many "old veterans" left, and the average age of Internet Corrs' fans had obviously decreased. According to polls and endless discussion, Internet fans much prefer the original recordings, even those who got to know the band because of a remix.

'Very few prefer the remixes but many admit that they like one or two of them,' says Lindberg. 'I have to say that the release of *Unplugged* restored the faith of many, proved that The Corrs were still a 'real band' who could live without computerised music. One of the most recurring arguments against the remixes (apart from the one that many think they're downright awful) is that they make the band look like they can't make it without help from some DJ.'

*   *   *   *

I almost cried when I heard Bono, that inspirational leader of U2, recall the first time he heard Clannad's 'Theme From Harry's Game'. He said he was so moved he almost crashed the car. I was touring Dublin's Musical Hall of Fame, having come down from Belfast one Friday, needing to get my Dublin fix.

As I walked around the hall of fame, looking at everything, taking it all in, I was moved. I revelled in the names, the bands, the trends and the passion of it all. U2 deserved special mention and they got it. But near the end of the tour, hearing Bono, The Edge and The Corrs all speak about what inspired them moved me the most. I knew how Bono felt. Clannad had moved me when I was back in New Zealand. Their sound was, and remains, Ireland. Their haunting spirit and mystical values had got me through many hard times. Bono's own duet with Clannad, 'In a Lifetime', made me cry every time I heard it. Another Clannad song, 'Something to Believe In', had been a theme song for me back in 1992. So hearing Bono's honesty and the influence that Clannad had had on him made me reflect on the influence that Irish music had had on me. It was in many respects the inspiration to write these words, this book.

*   *   *   *

Regardless of the artistic integrity of the remixes, The Corrs were successful with them and were now the hottest band in Britain. Companies wanted to be associated with them, Pepsi signed the band to a £500,000 one-year promotional contract. It was a triumph for The Corrs that their music could be popular in this most difficult of territories.

CHAPTER 11

Success and its Trappings

The music industry, like every other industry, has always encouraged mass-market blandness. The Corrs may be a particularly purified expression of that, but they're no different from a million other mass-market conveniences.

Journalist Michael Ross

Once they had achieved success in the British market, making a major impact on the American charts became the goal for The Corrs. To help promote *Talk on Corners: Special Edition* in the US, the band started to spend more time there. To make the kind of major impact they wanted required months, not just a few days, in America.

Jim Corr told *Q Magazine* that The Corrs had a real challenge in breaking the US. 'Taste [in the US] is slightly different, that's for sure,' he says. 'But we intend to overcome all the hurdles that come our way.'

Getting The Corrs' music on American radio was obviously part of the strategy, but Pat Creed, senior director for product development at Atlantic Records at the time and now a senior marketing manager for Warners in Ireland, says that seeing the band is usually what wins people over. 'With The Corrs, radio [support] has tended to follow everything else,' he says. 'They get by more on the force of personality and the force of their very singular musicianship. People see them, and they just get it.'

Still, the limited time The Corrs had in the US on their various promotional trips was well spent. Opening for the Rolling Stones on their 'No Security Tour' in both Europe and then the US was an especially good move. They made an impression wherever they went and even the Stones are said to have liked what they saw and heard.

'It might have sounded a funny connection, The Corrs and The Stones,' Anto Drennan told *Hot Press*, 'but it worked. The backing musicians in their band said that it was the first time they had ever seen all the Stones go and have a look at the support act. One of our crew, Decky, was standing behind the stage and he saw Ronnie [Wood] and Keith [Richards] come up and Ronnie said, "Hey, Keith, look at the violin player". And all Keith said was "Nice ass". But they stayed for the whole gig.'

Larry King, buyer at Tower Records in West Hollywood, agrees that opening for the Stones was important for The Corrs' reputation in the US:

> I think the Rolling Stones' tour helped sales for The Corrs. There's an extensive Rolling Stones' fan population on the Internet, and I noticed that the [online] fans who've been following the tour haven't really been talking about the opening acts, except for The Corrs. People online have been raving about The Corrs.

All their hard work in the US paid off to some degree. In March *Talk On Corners* entered the Billboard top 200 at 177. It was The Corrs' first time ever in the American album charts and it suggested that, although they still had someway to go before making the same sort of impact that they had made in Britain, they were developing some sort of following.

As well as supporting The Rolling Stones, it made sense for The Corrs to try to start the same sort of momentum that they had established in Britain with a similar-styled St Patrick's Day concert in the US. They duly played a solo concert in front of 2,000 people at the Roseland Ballroom in New York. However, although the concert got wide exposure on television channels, it did not achieve the breakthrough that The Corrs had been looking for.

One thing for sure was that no one could say that The Corrs did not work hard during their time in the US. For the rest of the month of March 1999 they criss-crossed the US playing Boston, Pittsburgh, Washington, Chicago, San Francisco and Los Angeles. 'It's kind of difficult out here,' Sharon told *Q Magazine*, 'because we're starting from scratch again. We've been out here so many times promoting but it didn't get us very far. This time it's been a lot better.'

If The Corrs' lack of a breakthrough in the US was getting them down, there was always Britain to fall back on. In February 1999 they reached another milestone in their ever-expanding career. On the back of an outstanding 1998 in Britain they were nominated for and won 'Best International Act' at the annual Brit Awards.

Dressed mostly in white for the awards, they took the occasion to reflect on just what a year it had been. The biggest selling album in Britain was the icing on the cake. But what was the nicest sensation was that for all their hard work and dedication they had finally made it in a market that they knew was special. The Brit Awards was the realisation of this and The Corrs celebrated accordingly by attending a party in London thrown by Eurythmics's Dave Stewart and Annie Lennox.

Before they could troop off to the party, however, they found themselves the star guests at an impromptu celebration in their own dressing room backstage at the awards ceremony. It appeared that the world stopped by to congratulate them, including Tony Blair's wife Cherie Blair, Northern Ireland Secretary Mo Mowlam, Bono, Stevie Wonder and Muhammad Ali.

Also joining The Corrs in celebration were Gerry and Jean Corr; John Hughes and his wife Marie; former head of Warner UK, Rob Dickins, who was instrumental in breaking The Corrs in Britain; Andy Murray; Fran Lichtman, senior vice-president of Warner International; and Brian Avnett of 143 Records, the band's Los Angeles label.

Dundalk journalist Ian Coognan, who was invited to England for the event, remembers the significance of it all:

> There was this feeling with them that they knew they had really made it big in Britain and that this was the night when it was going to hit them between their ears.
>
> Coming from Dundalk it was just great to see. They were on cloud nine and I don't think there is much doubt that it was professionally one of their finest occasions. There were of course many musicians there on the night, but The Corrs stole the show. It felt to me that it was their coming of age.

* * * *

Belfast as a city is a complete contradiction. A city at the hub of terrorism and nationalistic warfare, it has some of the friendliest people on earth. You could feel the sectarianism though: it was in the faces of the people, the smell of the streets almost. You were either with them, or you were with us. I would cry myself to sleep wondering what to make of all of this. Alternatively I found some of the friendliest people in the capital of Northern Ireland. I remember travelling to a story when I saw one of these countless acts of goodwill. The photographer, who was driving, had something wrong with the back tyre of his car. A lady, driving in the lane beside us, motioned to us that something was wrong. We waved realising that we had a loose hubcap and moved over to the side of the road and stopped the car. We were surprised to find that another car had stopped in front of us. A smart looking gentleman got out and then proceeded to tell us why the lady was signalling to us. We knew what had happened but you had to admire the community spirit. That was something that was perhaps unique to Belfast. I just couldn't get my head around the place.

* * * *

The Corrs would have been inhuman not to have been affected by their success in Britain. It was, after all, what they had been striving to achieve since their parents toured County Louth singing cover versions of the latest hits that they had seen on *Top of the Pops*. Looking at their styles and mannerisms during 1998–99, it was clear that The Corrs had changed. Their dress sense became more elaborate; their jewellery more obvious; and their personalities more used to the glare of attention.

Still, in the early months of 1999, with the success of *Talk on Corners* still fresh, it was hard not to notice The Corrs, even though they were starting to work on their third studio album, *In Blue*. Such had been their success and the momentum that they had established, that a period out of the public limelight could not reduce their profile. Although mostly based in Dublin for the recording of *In Blue*, the band could not stop the tabloids showing an interest in their affairs, or lack of them.

In April 1999, Robbie Williams, at the time the biggest and most popular pop star in Britain, paid a visit to Dublin. The exact reason for his visit to Ireland has never been made clear. On his visit list was Andrea Corr, who was the focus of much media attention as, not only was she the lead singer of The Corrs, but she was a beautiful young women who did not have a boyfriend.

Andrea and Williams met at Johnny Fox's pub in the Dublin Mountains. On April 9, the *Irish Sun* screamed 'Robbie S-Corrs' on the front page. The story went as follows: 'Corr what a ladies' man! Pop sensation Robbie Williams looks smitten on a romantic date with singer Andrea Corr. Robbie and Corrs star Andrea spent an hour and a half over a seafood meal at Johnny Fox's pub in Dublin.' The article went on to say that the pair was kissing and 'they were very much the couple'.

This all came about, according to the tabloids, after Williams had sent Andrea numerous flowers with the question 'What can I do to make you love me?' It sounds tacky, but that doesn't mean Williams wouldn't have done it.

Both camps were quick to distance themselves from any liaison. 'Robbie and Andrea were discussing a duet, which Robbie wants to do with her. Realistically if you were going to have a romantic date, you wouldn't go to a pub high in the Dublin mountains that was full of American tourists,' a friend of Williams said.

A spokesperson for The Corrs went along with the view that it was a meeting of musicians and not lovers: 'He's one of the biggest male artists at the moment and The Corrs have two albums at the top of the charts, so it would make sense to do something together. But I can confirm there is definitely no romance.'

Andrea herself reflected on the incident around a month later when she told Dublin's *Sunday Independent*:

> Myself and Robbie were just friends. I don't think that because you might get pressure like that from the media that you should close the door on friendship.
>
> It was a totally ridiculous situation. We were coming out of Johnny Fox's and the driver, seeing the photographer there, started walking me away. I was suddenly in a toilet. People were, like, washing their hands. I remember thinking: 'This is the real world. What am I doing here?'
>
> If you walk out of somewhere and someone is pointing something at you, it's like a gun in your way. You immediately become defensive. You have a look like you've just been caught and you've done nothing wrong. It proves that reaction, which drove me nuts.
>
> So I went back outside to the driver and there had been some kind of scuffle. I said 'I'm not hiding — I'm getting out of the car.' And I walked up to the guy. I said, 'Look into my eyes. You know this isn't right. What are you doing this for?' And he couldn't look at me. He was 'Er ... I can't sing and I can't play!' So I felt I had appealed to him morally. I shook his hand and then the next day, there it was in the papers. Oh well.

What actually happened between the pair is less interesting than the way Andrea responded. It is almost naive that she should be surprised that a tabloid photographer would want to take shots of the hottest pop star in Britain with the lead singer of the biggest band in Britain at that time. For most of their careers The Corrs have had positive media. Reporters have not seriously invaded their private lives or written scandalous stories about them. The Robbie Williams incident was one of only a handful of incidents where The Corrs have faced serious bother or criticism from the media. One other obvious example was Michael Ross's attack on their efforts in *Talk on Corners*. On both these occasions their response was quick and, to say the least, very defensive.

Perhaps The Corrs were so negative about these two particular attacks because they happened on their home turf? Michael Ross is a Dublin-based journalist, while the *Irish Sun* photographs were taken when Andrea was off duty and close to home. Was this incident with the *Irish Star* an invasion of privacy? Perhaps. Should it have been expected? Most definitely. It is ironic that, for all her efforts to actively seek success and fame, Andrea was just not used to her space being invaded.

In another case of media-created romance, Andrea has repeatedly denied constant rumours that she is dating U2's Bono.

*   *   *   *

I was lucky that when I arrived in Belfast I got a job with the Irish News, *the nationalist newspaper in Northern Ireland. I started in sport, but ended up writing news features about one of the most interesting places in the world. I saw more than I had seen in any other job. I saw poverty, racial hatred, paramilitary funerals and too many dog shows. I wrote stories about interesting members of the community and blocked drains. I interviewed Maverick Unionist MP Jeffrey Donaldson. For any aspiring news journalist Belfast is an ideal place to learn your trade. News and stories almost seep from the streets. As in Dublin, I prospered career-wise and individually. Sometimes we learn the most by seeing how the other half live.*

*   *   *   *

Whereas for most of his musical career Jim has struggled to make ends meet — at one time spending time on unemployment benefit as he pursued his musical career — he ensured he made up for it when he achieved the success he had always craved. Close friends of his say his legendary reputation for women is accurate and they describe him as being 'like a child in a sweet shop'. Recently he has dated former Miss Ireland Andrea Roche on-and-off. It is ironic that Roche looks a lot like Caroline Corr and that, if she and Jim were to marry, Roche would become a second 'Andrea Corr'.

However, some in the music industry are quick to stick up for Jim. Says Andy Murray:

> If Jim chooses to go to night clubs and have drinks, or if he chooses to consort with attractive women outside the bounds of marriage I don't think that that's such a bad thing and I don't think it's something that any press person should have an opinion about. He's a bloke!

Success, of course, did not just affect the lives of Jim, Sharon, Caroline and Andrea, but those close to them as well. Jean and Gerry Corr also had their lives altered. They would often have people coming to their door, asking questions or just wanting to say they had been to the Corr household. Part of the reason that Gerry and Jean have been able to handle the pressure and the attention is that they are both described as being 'steady' people, well in control of it all. In that respect they are very similar to their children. If a problem did arise they would deal with it and get on with it.

One thing that has not changed has been the respect that Jim, Sharon, Caroline and Andrea feel towards their father Gerry and felt towards Jean. One of the main reasons why The Corrs give so little away in press interviews has been the reverence that they hold their parents in.

*   *   *   *

It is very hard not to like true blue fans of The Corrs. Like their musical tastes, they are pretty much middle-of-the-road people, inoffensive to most. Perhaps one of the most interesting was Mark Szachara, who lives in New York and runs a message board, www.corrboard.com, dedicated to The Corrs. The two unique qualities that Mark possesses which made him different from most hardcore Corr fans was that he is older than most of the others and he lives in the US. I emailed him, wanting to find out a little more about him and why he liked The Corrs. He emailed me back and slowly over the forthcoming weeks I got to know him. There was no doubt about it: he was very fond of The Corrs, going as far to say that he thought Andrea's voice was the best ever! Strong stuff. But I still found it interesting that a man over the age of 30, who lived in the US with his wife and children, had fallen prey to the charms of The Corrs and dedicated so much time to them.

*   *   *   *

With the success of *Talk on Corners* now behind them, The Corrs could start to think about a third album. Their achievements gave them a massive confidence boost as they began to write, compose and produce *In Blue*. With such commercial success, the band were now much freer to establish their own sounds and not worry about whether they had a hit on their hands.

Therefore, the success or otherwise of *In Blue* would rest very much with the band themselves. Now they had the freedom to dictate the direction they wanted their music to head in. This could have led to two reactions from the band. First of all, there was the potential for the band to take the confidence and success they had achieved with *Talk on Corners* and build on it to produce a third original album that was their best set of songs ever. Secondly, their success had the possibility of making them complacent. They had already sold enough albums to be regarded as being one of the most successful Irish acts of all time. They already had one of the biggest selling albums in Britain ever, while financially they need not have worked again had they so wished. All in all their place in history was secure.

Just as The Corrs hadn't been able to rest until they had achieved commercial success in Britain, the US remained a great frontier waiting to be conquered. In a number of interviews, Hughes has appeared a man possessed about breaking the US market. It is as if his past disappointments there had made him even more determined to reach what he considered his ultimate destiny.

Until The Corrs had achieved substantial success in the US and done what they knew they had the potential to do, they would not rest. *In Blue* would always be another opportunity. Additionally, the work ethic that The Corrs had developed and maintained for almost the entire previous decade ensured that there was no question of them slowing down. Their success in Britain had made them realise that, if they kept pushing, sooner or later the American market would respond. All that was required, they believed, was the right sound, the right break and, above all else, more hard work.

The challenge for The Corrs was to make a third album that was as successful as their first two. Although they had established themselves as a band that would guarantee a respectable number of sales whatever they produced, they needed to maintain the musical standards that they had set. Yet, such a pressure has not been handled well by all bands. For example, Oasis struggled with their third album, suffering, some suggested, from an identity crisis.

With *In Blue*, The Corrs had to maintain the sound that they had established with *Talk on Corners*, but at the same time try to do something different that would keep the British audience entertained. 'The problem The Corrs had was providing a distinct sound, and yet not repeating what they had done before,' said a Dublin music journalist who did not wish to be named. 'There was a real risk that the British would hear the tin whistles and the violins and say "ah, we've heard that before". Because of its novelty value, some of this music wears off a lot quicker than something with a bit more longevity. They needed to move with the times.

'With their third album The Corrs had to go from being a contemporary Irish pop band, to being a contemporary world pop band. It stood and fell on whether they could be a contemporary British band, a contemporary American band, as opposed to being just a contemporary Irish band.' Still, that was all in the months ahead. In July 1999 the time was right for The Corrs to celebrate their success to date with a giant homecoming party. On the guest list would be over 40,000 Irish fans.

CHAPTER 12

The Homecoming

The life that we have and the places that we've been together are wonderful — but Lansdowne has been the best of them all!

Sharon Corr

On July 17 1999 at Lansdowne Road in Dublin, The Corrs came home. Given that they had had so much success worldwide, playing Dublin was always going to be a big occasion for them. The band had never forgotten where they had come from and Ireland had never forgotten that The Corrs were Irish.

The open-air rugby stadium could host over 40,000 people, making it easily the biggest crowd that the band had ever played to in Ireland. It was also a special gig as it was one of the last concerts from the *Talk on Corners* era. Both the media and the promoters built this concert up to be one of the main occasions in the summer of 1999 in Dublin. Super band REM playing the night before at the same venue also helped to ensure that this was not just a concert, but an event.

While The Corrs had played at The Point in Dublin at the start of 1999, demand for tickets was still high. Over half the tickets for the Lansdowne Road gig were sold within the space of the first two weeks, while the last tickets were sold a day or two before the concert. This demand reinforced the view of John Hughes, who had talked the concert up to be one of the occasions of the summer in Dublin.

* * * *

You know you are somewhere different when you take a walk down the Shankill Road in Belfast. At the start it looks like a perfectly average street, if not a little desolate. Then you are hit with Union Jacks on street posts and the odd policeman looking particularly menacing with a machine gun in his hand. Before you know it you have hit gangland. In this area there is a bevy of flags, UFF murals, sectarian graffiti and more than a sniff of trouble. Look to your right as you walk slowly down the road and you will see the main reason why there is sectarian violence in Northern Ireland: this housing estate reeks of poverty, yet there could not be an area in Northern Ireland more passionately Loyalist. To me, sectarianism was as much about economics and poverty as it was about tribal identification. Walk a little further and the street takes on a more normal appearance. There is even some economic prosperity. Trouble, however, is almost always around the corner. This is backstreet New York without being backstreet New York. It is gangland with a capital G. All carried out in the name of the Queen and loyalty. I am sure she would be delighted.

*   *   *   *

As with many Corrs concerts, the media was not always as enthusiastic as the fans. *The Irish Times* had a business arrangement with the band's promoters that saw the concert advertised in the newspaper for a number of months beforehand, but it criticised the organisation of the pre-concert press conference on the Thursday before the gig.

At this particular press conference The Corrs said they were 'absolutely delighted' with the response to ticket sales and looked forward to performing in front of their home crowd. 'For us to sell out a gig like that, it's really amazing and an endorsement I think, of how much the Irish have taken to our music,' said Sharon, the week before she was named as the third most eligible woman in Ireland by *Ireland on Sunday*. 'Just to play to Ireland ... I suppose sometimes you feel it could be your most critical audience. But we've always been welcomed with open arms and with the mixture of traditional Irish music and pop music you would think that could be a bit unacceptable. So far, people have just loved it,' she continued.

As well as attending the press conference Sharon also took time out that week to see her lawyer boyfriend (and soon to be fiancé), Gavin Bonner, who had just been called to the bar in Dublin. So there was a double reason for her celebratory mood.

A combination of sunshine and cloudy skies meant that the weather for the concert itself was humid and almost ideal for these celebratory few hours for the band and their fans. The crowd, some of whom had started lining up about seven hours beforehand, was mostly young and good-natured — at least until the gates opened and the race was on to see who could get the best standing positions! They need not have raced, as it was only the hard-core fans that had lined up so early. The fans then waited for over two hours before support band Picture House made its appearance. During the rest period some of the fans went off and bought Corr T-shirts and programmes while others watched with beady eyes for the merest hint of something happening on stage.

In the second row back were two of the band's biggest fans — teenager Daniel Lindberg from Sweden and Mikko Hanninen, a Finn in his mid-20s, who had joined his Swedish friend to travel over for the concert. They were ready for a big night. They had their feathers to toss, their signs stating their devotion and asking for drumsticks and, perhaps most importantly, they were in 'Corrs mode'.

Between them they had been to around fifteen Corrs concerts, the last in Sweden a week before. These were serious fans and to them this was like going to church. Although they were not as hard-minded as some of the fans of other rock bands, they were no less passionate about their support.

*   *   *   *

Northern Ireland is full of contradictions and sadness. For 30 years the people of this troubled land have endured more than they ever should have. Religion is at the root of all evils, it is said, and it was at the root of all contradictions. While I was in Belfast I attended an Alpha course. Designed to encourage people to become Christians in a non-offensive and non-intrusive way, it is fantastic idea and, in my view, a very worthwhile concept. An introductory meeting was held at the Waterfront Centre, a magnificent new complex, and while I waited outside to go in I noticed some protesters. Confused, I went and had a look. Protesting were the Free Presbyterians, the religious cult headed by the Reverend Ian Paisley — a man of God. They were protesting that Alpha leaders and course co-ordinator Nicky Gumbel were not preaching the true word of God. I shook my head and wondered whether Northern Ireland could ever progress and become a normal and settled society with people like this in their community.

*   *   *   *

Also in the crowd of 44,000 this warm July night, were a great many friends of the Corr family. Barry Henry, his girlfriend and some of the friends of the Corr girls from Dundalk were waiting patiently to see their pals. Two months later, Henry recalled the concert with great emotion. He talked about the pride and passion that he and his friends felt, the feeling of 'yeah, take it to them' that led them all to tears when the band came on stage:

> When you see your friends, your best friends on this massive stage like we saw for U2, and for them to be associated with REM ... you know that they have sold so many million copies, but when you see them up there on stage, you think 'My God' they have arrived. It was almost completely surreal.

Picture House were the right band to open for The Corrs. Themselves a class act, they were upbeat and appeared to enjoy what they were doing. Their music was also good and they did what they were supposed to do — warm-up the audience. Their set was simple, enjoyable and fulfilling and yet left the crowd wanting more.

At about 8:30 p.m. The Corrs came home. The build-up to their arrival on stage was immense, passionate and highly emotional for everyone concerned. The large TV screens highlighted a scene from the *Runaway* video where The Corrs walked together, as if they were going to war. It gave the impression that they were walking on stage. Then the 'boom' of the first massive drum beat from 'Only When I Sleep' signalled their real arrival. The large black curtain opened and The Corrs were introduced to the 44,000 people who had come to see them play. The colour of the girls' outfits first struck the eye. Gone were the Dundalk and early fame days of mere black and instead a raft of bright colours separated Andrea, Sharon and Caroline from the night. Jim was still in black, although he also looked the part with a dark suit and academic glasses.

They were no major surprises in the concert. The Corrs gave their audience what they wanted with a range of hits from their two albums. Appropriately, they also played a good number of their traditional Irish numbers, including 'Joy of Life' and 'Erin Shore'. In many ways the Irish numbers were the highlight of the night. The Corrs appeared not to have forgotten where they had come from.

Naturally enough the Dublin crowd loved them. The Corrs responded to their reaction with a high-energy performance. There were also a number of celebrities present including Robbie Williams and motor racing driver Eddie Irvine who were sitting alongside Jean and Gerry Corr in the VIP area. Andrea had said that it was wonderful for The Corrs to headline their own act in Ireland. The Corrs had come home and it was obvious that they knew that this was a special night in their career. Throughout the concert she herself was often maternal, spending time with Sharon, Caroline and Jim during songs, as if celebrating their success.

Nevertheless, there were also some small glitches in the performance that night: Andrea was too early with the tin whistle on an Irish number, while there were also minor sound problems. There were also touches of nerves in the band's performance, which was perfectly understandable given the nature of the occasion. At times Sharon, especially, and Caroline looked overwhelmed with the reaction, seeming shy and reserved. As Sharon explained later, to be extroverted before your home crowd would see you get brought down to earth very quickly. Despite their fears, that was never likely to happen and they gave a performance that was special to both them and the crowd privileged enough to see it.

The reaction from the media was naturally mixed, given the often more extreme tastes of music critics. Edward Power in *The Irish Times* did himself no favours with a complicated and jumbled review, which included the following: 'The Corrs try very hard at seeming fazed by the scale of their surroundings. After all, mammy might be watching — wouldn't do to come over like Celine Dion in a strop.'

He also wrote:

> It's all perfectly lovely no matter how some of us loathe them for their mildness and unremitting chirpiness we have to admit that The Corrs can play — only, let's be honest, everybody has come to hear the hits and can only imbibe so much vacuum-packed pseudo-Celtic schlock. Sure, this stuff probably goes down a riot in Buenos Aires or Tokyo or wherever but it just won't cut it this close to home.

The crowd, however, appeared to love the concert and could not have had any regrets. It was a super show. Standing to one side was the man who had played the most significant role in making this happen — John Hughes. He deserved to smile. It was his night as much as it was anyone's.

But on such occasions, it isn't all just about music — it's about power. As an Atlantic Records insider reveals:

> Interesting story between [The Corrs'] management and Warner Music Ireland. They hate each other apparently, management feels that Warners doesn't do anything for the band, all the success comes from the office in London. Warner Ireland is hosting a party for REM Friday night after the gig and isn't doing anything for The Corrs.
>
> Warner, on the other hand, feel that any time they've ever approached the management with things to do, they never have time and always say no. They figured that the management would throw their own party, so they left it to them. Funny how one's truth isn't the other's truth. I guess on the outside of it, I can see both sides' points. It's all a battle of the egos and no one wants to even approach the other any more. So stupid.

*   *   *   *

Dressed casually but looking as though he was in a business mode, Sinn Féin leader Gerry Adams looked at me and I saw 30 years of history in his eyes.

I was interviewing Adams for the Irish News *and found him gracious, inspirational and good-natured. He was also bigger than I thought he would be — when I stood beside him he swamped me. Like most interviews, there was a reserved air about his answers early on. As if he had heard the question many times before and he was taking his time finding the answer from his memory. Slowly but surely, we connected as people. Like him or hate what he stands for, you have to admire his dedication to his cause. I admired the man and his struggles (if not the means themselves) and the longer I interviewed him the more I connected with him. This was what I had travelled for: I was such a long way from New Zealand but gaining invaluable life experience. Being totally unprofessional, I got him to sign his book for me and I got my photograph taken with him. I didn't really care if it wasn't what journalists should do. I left Adams's office on a high. They all laughed back at the office when I said what a cool experience I had had.*

*   *   *   *

It was around the time of the Lansdowne Road concert that an idea was put to the band and their management to release an unplugged, acoustic album. The idea came from Andy Murray and MTV and it was to officially produce a Corrs' album that was both pure and raw. After the remixes of the previous year, it was 180 degrees removed from their recent work.

John Hughes's initial wishful thinking was that he could get *In Blue* out before Christmas, but Warner's new idea was to quickly produce an album of Christmas songs. The general feeling was that it would be hard to sell and that an unplugged album would go down better, especially with one or two new songs on it. 'The difficulty was persuading the group that it wasn't going to kill their careers,' Murray says. 'It could have been a terrible idea, too much of a good thing.'

Insiders say *Unplugged* was an attempt by The Corrs to prove, especially to the British audience, that they really could play and that they were more than just remixed pop stars. Jim, in particular, felt that The Corrs had to show that musically they could play live and were more than able musicians. An unplugged album was a convenient way of doing this. Warners were also aware that many old fans of The Corrs didn't approve of the remixing: 'There was this view that *Talk on Corners* wasn't as flattering to their artistic ability as it might have been,' says a music insider. 'The view was that The Corrs were nothing but pop puppets. *Unplugged* was partially a way of dealing with these critics.'

There was talk of getting a big name, such as Paul McCartney or Eric Clapton, to play with The Corrs, although nothing came of it. As it turned out, just having The Corrs play with an orchestra was probably a blessing in disguise. 'It's not something that we planned,'

Hughes told *Hot Press* after the album's release. 'We were asked to do it and agreed. But it had to be done quickly and so, where most people prepare to do something like this for months, we just had four days to rehearse. And we've left it raw because that's the way we wanted it. There's no fixes. No safety nets. This is the real thing.'

On the face of it, The Corrs going back to musical basics and recording some of their popular songs acoustically, with the addition of REM's classic 'Everybody Hurts' and Philip Lynott's 'Old Town', as well as a couple of the new songs off the then unreleased third studio album, was a fine idea.

The addition of 'Old Town' was a spur of the moment thing. MTV were adamant that two new songs and at least three covers were needed for *Unplugged*. This was necessary to attract those buyers who had perhaps purchased a Corrs' album before but who needed some incentive to buy something that was noticeably different. 'We wanted to include another cover version and there was talk about doing a Beatles' song,' John Hughes said. 'But everyone does The Beatles and so I suggested doing a Thin Lizzy song, thinking Irish. But it was Andrea who came up with "Old Town"'.

With the lack of time in preparation terms and an orchestra waiting to record, The Corrs found that they only had two covers, 'Little Wing' and 'No Frontiers'. (The new songs were 'Radio' (taken from the Leo Pearson sessions in Dublin during 1997) and 'At Your Side'.) 'So they finish the session on Saturday with the recording set for Tuesday and they are one song short,' says Andy Murray. 'By the end of Saturday producer Mitchell Froom was starting to pull his hair out. I was keen for them to do "The Girls are Back in Town" or the "Cowboy Song" (which shows how much I know). Andrea then says "I know the one!" and starts humming "Old Town" and Jim then starts playing. The song had been a massive hit for Phil Lynott and not Thin Lizzy. The only reason I knew it was because I was the product manager in Britain of the original version in 1982. It had got massive amount of airplay in Britain, but it wasn't a hit. Luckily it was a song that I knew and it was a great song. So we sent the road crew out to buy the record but they couldn't find it. So on the Sunday I myself went out at noon to look, with the recording starting early in the afternoon. I go to every record store on Grafton Street. Finally at the back of one store I find this compilation. I go back to my hotel room and although it's almost unheard of, there is a CD player there. I write out the lyrics, photocopy them up and take them down to rehearsal. Jim isn't there. So the band learns the song without Jim. Jim arrives and then changes it.'

The song was also notable for the piccolo trumpet that gave it a decidedly orchestral feel. Although Mitchel Froom did not believe there was enough time to introduce the trumpet into the song, Andrea was firm in her belief that it had to go on the record. And so it did. John Hughes was another fan of the song. Fiachra Trench, who did the original brass piece, was around and so he rehearsed it with the band — and 'It was magic, hearing that music from twenty years ago come to life again,' he says. 'I knew Philip Lynott and I can tell you, I know he'd have loved it.'

The album was produced by Mitchel Froom and mixed by Bob Clearmountain, two of the best in their respective trades, and it was produced and sent into the shops in a period of weeks to catch the Christmas market.

Despite the speed in which *Unplugged* was produced, most critics loved it. Colm O'Hare, writing in Ireland's musical magazine *Hot Press*, was one of a number of critics who were very complementary, stating that on the whole the band did a good job. O'Hare was particularly praiseworthy of 'Radio':

> The acoustic guitar intro faintly recalls the Isley Brothers' 'Harvest For The World' (also a hit for The Christians) but that's where any similarities end. With an instantly memorable verse and chorus, it's one of their strongest and most mature songs to date. A sure-fire hit, given the right exposure.

Unplugged provided a boost for territories late in catching up with The Corrs, the album going to number one in Belgium and Austria. As well as being number one in Ireland it was number three in Switzerland and Singapore, number four in Norway, number five in France, number six in Denmark and Germany, number seven in Britain and number eight in Spain.

The album is certainly pleasant to listen to. 'Radio' went down extremely well with the public, while some of the Irish numbers, such as 'Lough Erin's Shore', lost nothing in the acoustic translation. Other numbers, such as 'Forgiven Not Forgotten', needed the electric guitar and were not a patch on the original. The album, however, is easy listening and was highly popular with the fans.

The album also had a direct benefit in that it provided instant access to 'Radio' and consequently the third album. The video for 'Radio' was taken from the unplugged album, while the song was playlisted by Radio One. It had been a commercial success for The Corrs and a return to their roots.

By the middle of 1999 The Corrs had developed into a brand throughout most of the western music world and were now not just a musical group. With their place in Irish music history firmly established and huge success in Britain achieved, they had met most of the goals they had set for themselves in John Hughes's now legendary ten-year plan, written when he first came on board with the siblings. But also written into that plan was the goal of being the biggest band in the world. Until they achieved widespread American success, that goal would elude them. *In Blue* was perhaps their best opportunity to stake their claim.

CHAPTER 13

In Nothing But Blue

There's an assumption that if you're in this business and
you're very successful that you're going to change in some
way. They haven't.

They're working at something that they're good at
and they want to make it better. Maybe the third album
will be the best of The Corrs.

Gerry Corr

In a year that was more home-based than the previous five years, The
Corrs had to deal with the illness and subsequent death in late 1999
of their mother, Jean. *The Irish Times* reported on Friday November 26
1999:

> The funeral of Mrs Jean Corr, mother of the pop group
> The Corrs, will take place in her native Dundalk
> tomorrow. Mrs Corr (57) died in hospital in England on
> Wednesday following a short illness.
>
> There will be a private funeral for family and close
> friends in the Church of the Redeemer, Ard Easmuinn, at
> 2 p.m.
>
> Mrs Corr and her husband, Gerry, had sung in the
> choir and had been instrumental in establishing a
> children's choir in the church in the 1970s. At the same
> time they played the local cabaret circuit as a duo, The
> Sound Affair.
>
> A spokesman for The Corrs' management has
> appealed to fans to respect the family's wishes and allow
> them time and space to grieve in private. This is
> obviously a very difficult time for Gerry, Andrea,
> Caroline, Sharon and Jim.

Jean Corr had been waiting for a lung transplant operation that would
have saved her life. She'd been taken to England for tests after a recent
bout of illness in the hope that a suitable donor would be found. Her
death was, to the public at least, unexpected. The family had been

well aware of their mother's perilous condition for several months but even close friends were unaware of how gravely ill Jean was and were shocked at the news.

The Corrs' Business Manager Barry Gaster issued the following statement:

> They are all terribly upset by this tragic turn of events. They don't want to say anything at the moment because they are just too upset. Jean had been at the hospital for a couple of days and was due to have a lung transplant. But unfortunately she took a turn for the worse and died on Wednesday.

In such a close family, the death of the matriarch was undoubtedly a huge blow. She had been part of the backbone that had given the four siblings their character and had enormously shaped their personalities. The loss of Jean Corr was also deeply felt in Dundalk. It was a shock to most, a loss to many.

*   *   *   *

There were times when writing this book that I struggled for motivation, struggled for reasons why I should give up nights and weekends. Then something would happen that would indirectly provide inspiration and give me understanding. On one cold and dark Friday night in late January 2001 I hopped off the train in Dundalk and was met by local journalist Anne Campbell. She worked for the Dundalk Democrat and I had contacted her about getting some photos for the book. She was perhaps younger than I was, had this big smile, was full of life and energy and had an infectious laugh. She felt it was her job to promote Dundalk to me despite the fact that I had been there a dozen times before. She took me for a drink and dinner in a swanky pub (she paid) and seemed to know everyone like a good community reporter should. I began to see the reasons why I was writing this book. She was bubbly, enthusiastic and the four hours that I spent drinking and talking inspired me, and once again showed me the beauty of Dundalk and the reasons why I could live there. The Corrs may feel as though they have outgrown Dundalk, but there was a strength amongst the people there that I admired. This was the Ireland that I fell in love with, an Ireland that had character and passion. I will remember evenings like that long after I have forgotten about The Corrs.

*   *   *   *

Without success in the US both The Corrs and John Hughes would still not have achieved what they had set out to do. In many respects this ruthless enthusiasm was much the same force that had driven them in Britain and, in the early days, in Australia and Ireland.

However, according to music journalist Kevin Courtney:

> With regards to the US, there are a whole lot of different problems. [The Americans] are obsessed with R and B, and if it's not geared towards R and B, it's geared towards this kind of very bland, kind of down home rock which is a different kind of thing to what The Corrs do.
>
> The Corrs don't do a blues-based rock like Hootie and the Blowfish. The other end of the scale is the hard core stuff, like hard core rap, hard music like Marilyn Manson. I think the market in the US is a little bit harder to penetrate for what The Corrs do is very middle-of-the road and in the US middle-of-the-road really doesn't do anything.
>
> The Corrs broke the British market by remaking Fleetwood Mac's 'Dreams'. They were giving a dance version of a familiar song to the British and this gave them an opening. The British music buying public were saying, 'We know this song, that has a dance beat, we'll go and buy that … okay, they're quite pretty and they're Irish, we'll have that'. Unless they do something that gives them an 'in' into the American market then they will find it difficult.

Making it in the US was never going to be easy. Or perhaps it was. According to Jeff Cohen, vice president of *Playboy*, the route was simple. His advice to the girls was to pose for his magazine, but there is no evidence to suggest that the offer was seriously considered.

The Cranberries' Dolores O'Riordan has been one of the greatest critics of The Corrs. O'Riordan claimed that the Americans would laugh at The Corrs because their sound was not hard enough or 'sufficiently raw'.

Despite John Hughes claiming that his own family considered it to be 'female jealousy', O'Riordan may not be totally off the mark with her criticism. The sound of The Corrs was, at that stage, certainly not raw and the Americans perhaps preferred their music with a greater degree of rhythm and blues than The Corrs had provided on *Talk on Corners*.

It could also have been the case that for all their pleasantness and ideal family image, The Corrs lacked personality in a marketing sense. Although Andrea had the personality and charisma to lead a band to

American success, she was still the baby sister and, for all her wholesomeness, was still not ideal copy for an American media enthusiastic to find bands with — in their opinion — personality and distinctiveness.

The Corrs' Celtic angle was also an issue. John Hughes suggested to *Hot Press* that part of the problem with The Corrs breaking the US has been the band's Irishness:

> On paper we were due to break the States first, but they actually had a problem with the whole Irish angle. Despite the fact that everyone thinks the Americans go wild for anything Irish, it's wishful thinking to imagine it's as simple as that. Our heritage is one thing — but if you're not what the market requires then it ain't going to happen.'

* * * *

I had been a fan of the Kennedy family for years. The political and personal charisma of John F. Kennedy had inspired me like it had millions of others around the world. When I visited Boston I spent two days at the Kennedy Library, while I had around 70 books on the Kennedy family. Thus, when I got Jean Kennedy Smith out of the shower one Friday morning in her Dublin hotel I was a little angry with myself. 'You were on my list of things to do,' she said, annoyed that I had disrupted her morning routine. But we started to talk and I couldn't stop gushing about my love for her family. She seemed a nice woman, down-to-earth and like me, was in love with Ireland. I interviewed her and she was so easy to talk to. Naturally we spoke about The Corrs — her fondness for the band was obvious. I put the phone down after talking with her and wondered to myself. I had spoken with one of the old generation Kennedys. This book had taken me to some wild places and I had met some incredible people.

* * * *

Atlantic Records had begun plotting The Corrs' American breakthrough in the middle of 1999, just as the group was conquering Britain. 'We decided what really broke The Corrs around the world was television, and then radio followed,' says Ron Shapiro, executive vice president and general manager of Atlantic Records, indirectly suggesting that appearance is almost as important as the music when it comes to marketing.

He then went on to say:

> We spent literally from last August to this March planning that, for the two weeks surrounding St Patrick's

Day, we would get as much TV as we could, by hook or by crook — based on favours, on tapes of what they look like on TV, on their success in Europe. There was also an emphasis on touring, with The Corrs opening dates for The Rolling Stones in the US and Europe — a famously tough gig, but one that the group handled with aplomb, eliciting ovations from fans who had ignored Fiona Apple and jeered Prince.

Atlantic applied a similar strategy in breaking the talented Jewel, who toured relentlessly and secured several high-profile TV spots before her album finally produced a hit single — about a year and a half after its release.

But despite the continued desire to break the American market, the general consensus was that for all its success elsewhere, *Talk on Corners* was not the album to do it. Their third album would be the one, John Hughes kept telling the media. A more rounded, a more mature sound would take The Corrs to a place where perhaps only U2, Van Morrison and The Cranberries had been before — wide success in the US for an Irish act.

Having started in May 1999, work resumed late that year on the third studio album. *In Blue* was written mostly by The Corrs, with three tracks co-written with Mutt Lange, husband and producer of Shania Twain. After the success they had achieved with *Talk on Corners*, The Corrs were now creatively freer from the shackles of record company executives and could produce the album that they wanted. Thus, The Corrs took more responsibility for *In Blue* than for *Talk on Corners* and had a greater level of input into its production.

The album started without The Corrs really knowing it. Andrea and Caroline wrote a song and when John Hughes said that 'there was a movie looking for a song' Andrea told him what she and Caroline had been doing. They immediately played the tune on the piano, impressing Hughes. He suggested that they go right away into the studio and record it, and before they had expected it, the seeds of *In Blue* had been sown.

Each time one of The Corrs wrote a song they would go into the studio and record it. Andrea has described the process of creating *In Blue* as 'liberating'. Although The Corrs were freer from the pressures that had so marked, in different ways, their first two albums, The Corrs and Hughes were still wary of producing an album that would go down well in the US. Perhaps the best way of doing this, they felt, was to write and record music that they were happy with and not write to any set formula as was the case with *Talk on Corners*. They now had the confidence to believe in their music and its quality and be content that the public would also like what they produced.

Given the illness and untimely death of Jean Corr, the music being produced on *In Blue* was heavily influenced by what The Corrs were experiencing, both individually and collectively. Not only was 'No More Cry' reflective of the pain the family was feeling, but there was a general emotional atmosphere about *In Blue*.

'The album was half done when that happened,' Anto Drennan told *Hot Press* of Jean Corr's death. 'I think her illness affected them throughout because their emotions were definitely more sensitised while she was sick. And "No More Cry" was a direct result of that. But it was very difficult for them.'

Recording took place in Dublin, except for 'Breathless', 'Irresistible' and 'All the Love in the World', which were done in tandem with Lange and composed and produced in Switzerland. Although The Corrs should have been used to working with such high-quality producers, they were still surprised by what they found in Lange. 'I've never worked like it in my life,' says Jim. 'He puts in sixteen-hour days in the studio. He's a total perfectionist.'

The Corrs had met Lange before through David Foster and, according to them, he liked their music. Lange suggested that they should write a song together. Andrea, willing to work with one of the best producers in the business, went to Switzerland and together the pair wrote 'Breathless'.

Foster says that although many people have taken credit for putting The Corrs and Lange together, it was his idea: 'Mutt knows what he is doing and he's had huge success with Shania (Twain), Britney and a whole lot of other acts. I knew that he would be good for The Corrs.'

The Corrs, along with live guitarist Anto Drennan, longstanding engineer Tim Martin, and Dublin-based producer/programmer Billy Farrell, plus John Hughes, handled the production of most of the album. They were concerned that, although they might have written, in their view, the best songs of their lives, outside producers brought in when the production process was almost finished would not be as enthusiastic. Additional assistance therefore came from Mitchell Froom, who had assisted with the *Unplugged* album.

Froom, a Woody Allen-like figure, was introduced for an intensive twelve-day period near the end to tidy things up and add his professional touch. There were some songs that he didn't touch; that he believed were good enough, although Froom's talent generally made sure that The Corrs had not missed the boat.

An Atlantic Records insider had stated before the release of *In Blue* that Mutt Lange was not the only opportunity The Corrs had to collaborate with a well-known producer:

> They did three songs with Mutt Lange and the rest are supposed to be all them. They got an offer to write and record with Max Martin (Britney, Backstreet), but they declined saying they didn't want to collaborate any more.
>
> Hughes said Andrea never wanted to play the tin whistle again. She wants to be pure pop. Then she said she thought the album was too pop, thinks the songs are meant to be 'darker' and wants to take off the Mutt Lange tracks. I always thought they were just a bit 'too perfect' and a bit 'cold'.

*   *   *   *

I went to busy, bright and inspiring London one weekend in February to carry out interviews for the book. To those not used to the pace and fury of England's capital city, travelling there is quite an experience: the people, the smells of the underground, the culture of Leicester Square, the overwhelming sense of opportunity. The visit both scared and inspired me. Just looking at the people lining up for theatre tickets in the middle of London made me understand why The Corrs were so keen to make their mark here. As if culture was right at your doorstep and that this was the ultimate judging ground. After a lengthy journey across London I finally met my contact. We lunched in a swanky suburban London café and talked about The Corrs. It was an enjoyable few hours as I saw another perspective on the world of The Corrs and the trials and tribulations they had gone through to make it to where they are now. I travelled across London that night excited by what I had heard, inspired by the city and reflecting that this was a very long way away from Dundalk.

*   *   *   *

In Blue is a mixture. Parts of it have the distinctive sound that made *Forgiven Not Forgotten* such an original and proud album. Other tracks are just lollypop music, repeating well-worn themes that, although done with more maturity, still leave the listener feeling empty and wanting more.

The first release, 'Breathless', opens the album in a bright and breezy way. Written in conjunction with Matt Lange, this track moves at a brisk pace and almost sounds like a Stock, Aitken and Waterman produced single. Anto Brennan's guitar gives the track rhythm, while the vocals are again strong. This is a catchy song and in many respects an ideal first release. To some degree it sounds much like 'Only When I Sleep' and does the same job of opening up the album at a brisk pace.

The pace then slows with 'Give Me A Reason'. This is one of the strongest tracks on the album: again Andrea's vocals lead the way and complement the pleasant sounds of Sharon's violin. This is more like The Corrs' sound of old, the pace of the track a throwback perhaps to an old Irish jig. The Corrs, however, still appear reluctant to write anything not involving love. Still, this is a much stronger song than the majority of tracks on *Talk on Corners*.

After a relatively strong start, the momentum that *In Blue* has established is lost and the album goes all soppy with 'Somebody for Someone'. This is weak. The track fails to have any real sense of emotion and is simply a song without any passion. On this occasion even Sharon's violin playing cannot save it from being nothing short of mediocre.

The next track, 'Say', again deals with the same topic — love and lost love. Yet this is a pleasant tune with Andrea again starring. Her voice is particularly pleasant, while the music score rides nicely. Despite being similar to many of the tracks on *Talk on Corners*, 'Say' suggests that The Corrs had to some degree matured. Love it or hate it, there is a maturity to this track that was missing on the previous album. The themes are still the same, yet the performance, the lyrics and the music are all more mature.

Just when the listener starts to think that The Corrs are making progress, we hear 'All The Love in The World', which sounds surprisingly like a Carpenters' song. This really is an awful track and again could have been written by a thirteen-year-old schoolgirl. There is no depth to it, while the melodies are just dreadful. When it comes to lyrics there is plenty to improve on. The chorus says it all:

> Don't wanna wake up alone anymore.
> Still believing you'll walk through my door
> All I need to know it's for sure
> Then I'll give all the love in the world.

A remixed 'Radio', which was first released on the *Unplugged* album, is up next and this is a real high point of the album. This version is even better and never loses the listener in pointless and repetitive sentiment. Once more Andrea gives a faultless vocal performance.

Mutt Lange also produced the next track, 'Irresistible', and the song moves at a brisk pace. Although not by any means a classic, The Corrs show what they can do when they put their foot down and up the tempo. But despite the pleasant sounding nature of 'Irresistible', this track has a manufactured feel about it, much the same way as 'Intimacy' did on *Talk on Corners*.

'One Night' is one of the better slow songs on *In Blue*. It is a more mature track than many of the slower songs on *Talk on Corners*. Andrea leads the way with soft sounding and decidedly pleasant vocals. Although it again fails to have the depth and passion of the best love songs, it is easy listening and flows nicely.

'All in A Day' is standard Corrs' fare: weepy lyrics, a touch of romanticism and Sharon's violin adding a nice interlude. This is a sound song, which includes a resounding portion of Irish mysticism that made *Forgiven Not Forgotten* such a special album. This track does not set the world on fire, but it is one of the better songs on *In Blue*.

'At Your Side' was one of the weaker tracks on the *Unplugged* album and the listener gets a second helping of it in this album. There is a cheeriness about this song, although there is no passion. It fails to get off the ground at any point and leaves the listener rather bored after about 30 seconds.

Given the death of Jean Corr in late 1999, it was inevitable that there would be some mention of it musically on *In Blue*. But somewhat surprisingly, The Corrs decided to write and sing about their father's lament at the passing of his wife with a raunchy, upbeat number that has a definite Blondie feel to it. Although 'No More Cry' is not the best track on the album, it is cleverly written and produced and a surprise given what could have been expected about such a sad topic.

This growing sense of maturity within The Corrs' work is also a feature of 'Rain', a smooth, relaxing and mellow track that almost sends the listener to a different world. Whereas on other tracks of *In Blue* the immaturity of the lyrics are noticeable, here The Corrs show a coming of age of sorts:

> Going crazy in the middle of the night
> Slipping, sliding into heavenly bliss
> Fallen angel spinning from the light
> Slipping, sliding into heavenly lace
> But it's all, it's alright now
> 'Cos we are living for this night for so long now
> Yes, it's all, it's alright.

The words say it all: this is a track full of emotion, passion and a daring insight into human emotion. If the critics were looking for something more mature from The Corrs with *In Blue*, well finally there were some examples of it.

There is a groovy feel about 'Give It All Up' and just for a moment the listener thinks they are back listening to *Forgiven Not Forgotten*.

Yet there is a distance about this track. It's as if The Corrs have greater confidence about their song writing and performing talents.

'Hurt Before' has the same sound as 'No Good For Me' on *Talk on Corners*. It has the inner workings of Andrea written all over it and it largely works because of it. This is about a girl finding herself, her independence and striving for some sort of guidance. There is obviously a hint of romance about it, but the theme is universal, the story real. There is no doubt that Andrea can tell a story and there is no question also that she can perform with the passion of the truly great front singers.

Sharon, as she does on so many Corrs' tracks, shows how vital her violin playing is to the Corrs' sound with a magical piece of playing on 'Rebel Heart', a passionate and moving piece of musical storytelling. This is quality. It never loses its momentum and in just over three minutes accurately reflects the issue of Irish independence in the last 80 years. This maybe is as close as The Corrs will ever get to performing a track that has the strength of message that so reflects U2's work.

In Blue is, on the whole, an encouraging, more developed and mature album than *Talk on Corners*. It is also a much better production. It does not have the freshness of *Forgiven Not Forgotten*, but then it couldn't be expected to given the musical and personal changes that The Corrs had gone through. Although *In Blue* is far from being a classic album, there is no question that for The Corrs it constituted development.

*   *   *   *

Just when I thought that the pathways of John Hughes and myself would not cross again, fate put forward another lifeline. It was suggested to me that I again contact The Corrs' office to see whether Hughes would talk to me this time. With about six weeks left in the writing process, I wasn't as enthusiastic as I had been before. I mean I had about 200 questions for him and I somehow doubted whether he or I had the two weeks that would be needed to answer them. Besides, I thought I had a profile of Hughes that was accurate. It was also suggested to me that The Corrs' main man had originally found me too polite and too obliging and that he had been wary of me because of that. I had to read the email more than once. I had been too polite? That's what I did wrong: I should have been abusive and demanded a meeting with him! I laughed, wondered what to make of the music business. I didn't think there was any logic in what I had just read, so I put it all down to experience.

*   *   *   *

Despite The Corrs being proud of *In Blue*, the critics were waiting. Michael Ross wrote about them again in the middle of 2000. Ross, perhaps the journalist most critical of The Corrs, went one step further this time, suggesting that 'despite their appearance, [The Corrs] are a colder and darker entity'. But this time he not only criticised the band's music but also their personal morals, choosing to tell a salacious but short-on-details story about one of the Corr family:

> Some time ago, an acquaintance of mine had a one-night stand with one of The Corrs. They met at a party, it was lust at first sight and before long they were in the hotel room. At one point Corr asked my acquaintance, whom for the sake of brevity we will call A, what line of work A was in. A works for a newspaper. Corr asked if A knew me.
>
> Cue exploding Corr. I had written something mildly snotty about the group some time previously and they have nursed the grievance ever since, abusing me intercontinentally, which naturally was pleasurable but only for a time. Next morning, as A got ready to leave, Corr stirred in the bed. Corr did not express appreciation for their night of intimacy, nor even proffer a telephone number, an invitation to meet again. 'Tell Michael Ross I know all about him,' was all that Corr said as A departed the room, feeling more than a little used.

This episode proved that given their success, The Corrs were now under a different sort of pressure. Some people in Ireland and Britain were now quick to knock them down for any reason possible. They were almost at the top of their industry and had produced albums that they could be proud of. But still some critics persisted with attacks on them. They were never going to be popular with everyone, but it appeared that in Ireland they were now almost operating in a glass bowl. To some degree The Corrs had out grown Ireland. They were ready to make a major attempt at gaining major success in the US.

CHAPTER 14

Trying to Leave the US Breathless

We're under a different kind of pressure now. The expectations may be a bit unreal. 'Hey can you sell another eight million albums?' No one wants to face into that. It's like can you win the cup again? Can you win the fight again? Can you win the war again? But when you're forced to face it, then you have to accept the challenge. Now we've got to outdo ourselves just to stay where we were. And that is a pressure.

John Hughes

John Hughes sunk his teeth into a chocolate muffin. His legal papers were spread out in a vast corner office on the 27th floor of Atlantic Records in New York and he was in form. It was just after 6:00 p.m. and the sun was setting romantically over Manhattan.

It was March 1999 and The Corrs were on yet another promotional push in the US. Hughes had been hard at work for the last two days and had not slept. He looked tired, but was encouraged by the fact that The Corrs' promotional push had seen their sales in New York jump from 3,000 to 7,000. With him was journalist Andy Pemberton, who was there to do a large feature on The Corrs for the English magazine Q. Perhaps encouraged by the grand setting that would make any man with any sense of ego feel like the King of the World, Hughes was riding the adrenaline. It could be that that made him say some interesting things:

I'm a man on a mission. I have something to do and it's gonna work. As an artist I got my ass kicked, I had a young family and I had to provide for them for years. I understand the kind of doors that are open for The Corrs, because I was there when those doors closed on me. I'm damn well not going to let it happen a second time.

You know something, I can't do anything about my own career, but by proxy I wear little frocks and dance around the stage and sing my heart out.

As Pemberton tells the story, Hughes then got up, walked over to one of the huge corner windows and stared out at New York. Quietly he said to himself, 'This will be done. To whatever end.' Such was the determination of Hughes and The Corrs to reach their lofty goals in the US. *In Blue* was yet another opportunity.

After the success of *Talk on Corners* there was huge expectation both in Ireland and throughout the world as to what musical direction The Corrs would take with their third original album. Some fans longed for a return to the early days of their careers, when they wrote music from their hearts and, almost, the streets of Dundalk.

Other fans hankered for more of the same weepy songs that had catapulted The Corrs to pop stardom in Britain in 1998. Most just wanted The Corrs to be true to themselves and their obvious musical talent. Realistically, *In Blue* could only be a progression for The Corrs. They had been through too much — both professionally and personally — in the previous two years for it to be anything else.

However, it was apparent before the launch of *In Blue* that The Corrs were experimenting with a tougher, more rugged image. Their music had not changed dramatically, but the image was stronger, more determined and certainly more American.

Irish fans were able to get one of the first looks at The Corrs' new, tougher image in early 2000 on the *Late Late Show*, when the band played 'Breathless' live. The band has obviously gone for a harder image: Caroline was hitting the drums with reckless abandon, Andrea was dressed in leather and looked particularly seductive, while Jim's new pimp look suited this whole new style. Apparently it was even difficult to get Jim to remove his glasses for the photo shoot for the cover. 'Jim is *in love* with his Prada shades and won't take them off very often, although he was begged by the stylist,' says an Atlantic Records insider.

The Corrs needed to impress with *In Blue*. With *Talk on Corners* being such a success in Ireland and abroad, many in the record industry believed sales of less than eight million would be, in relative terms, a failure. As John Hughes has suggested, starting out with the same sort of sales goals was never going to be easy.

Still, *In Blue* had plenty of advantages that the previous two Corr studio albums did not have. Whereas in the past The Corrs had had to fight to get their singles played in Britain, their popularity in the marketplace now ensured that the first single from *In Blue* was going to get substantial airplay and perhaps even give The Corrs their first British number one.

*   *   *   *

It didn't matter how many articles I read about The Corrs, how many times I saw them promote their albums on television or how many times I listened to their music, I could not forget that they were from Dundalk. Perhaps this was due to the fact that although The Corrs as a band and as individuals had gone through significant changes down the years, they were a family band and it has been virtually impossible for them to escape their past. It was as if their backgrounds were carried around with them each time they spoke to one another. It seemed that The Corrs did not wish to dwell on where they had come from, or the environment in which they had grown up. But to me they could not avoid it; it came shining through each time they spoke, sang and performed.

*   *   *   *

The Corrs launched *In Blue* at a star-studded reception at London's designer Saville Row store, Joop!, in the middle of 2000. Along with Gerry Corr, various celebrities from the music and movie industries were present including Spice Girl Emma Bunton, MTV's Cat Deeley, Kate Moss, Natalie Appleton of All Saints and film director Alan Parker, an old friend of the band.

Such a swanky occasion was proof of how far The Corrs had come in the last ten years. Proof within the industry that The Corrs now had firm brand recognition and were again capable of moving large quantities of albums. The fact that so many celebrities had turned up also suggested that The Corrs were popular outside the bounds of music. They were now celebrities as much as musicians, personalities as much as performers.

Regardless of the merits of *In Blue*, the Irish and the British loved it. The album went to number one in Britain the first week it was released, while 'Breathless' did what no other Corrs single had done before — going to number one in July before being knocked off the top spot by Ronan Keating's 'Life is a Rollarcoaster'. Before that the closest The Corrs had come to having a number one hit in Britain was when 'Runaway' entered the British charts at number two eighteen months before, only being prevented from reaching the top spot by Britney Spears.

Ireland's love for The Corrs was ongoing and proof of this came a few weeks after *In Blue* was released. During this week, all their released albums were in the Irish top 30, something few, if any, acts had done before. *In Blue* stayed steadily at number one while *Talk on Corners*, *Unplugged* and *Forgiven Not Forgotten* positioned themselves at numbers eight, twelve and 29 respectively.

But for The Corrs, Ireland had long since become almost irrelevant in their quest to sell as many records as they could. Popularity in Ireland would always mean a lot to The Corrs, but *In Blue* was all about another opportunity to make an impact in the US. The US had always been the ultimate prize, from both a music and financial point of view. The band would never be in the same league as some of the biggest acts in the world if they had not broken the world's biggest market. As John Hughes himself has said many times, 'why sell twenty million albums when you can sell 30 or 35 million?'

The American market had remained the bane of The Corrs' existence since they had made it big in Britain with *Talk on Corners*. The peculiarities there had long tested their patience. Despite selling respectable numbers of copies in the US with their first two albums, it had largely been an impregnable market. It certainly wasn't for want of trying. Not only was *Talk on Corners* given its own release date in the US, but The Corrs had themselves made countless promotional trips to the US.

It hadn't been just a trying experience for The Corrs themselves but also for what fans they did have in the US. New Yorker Mark Szachara is one of the most enthusiastic fans of The Corrs in that country. He runs a highly informative Internet message board in their honour, spending hours communicating with other fans of the band as well as Atlantic Records in New York. He has followed The Corrs in the US through their ups and downs and has a number of theories as to why they have taken time to make their mark there. He says that the success of 'Breathless' and *In Blue* has been more about providing the American market with what they want.

'Songs like "Breathless" and "Irresistible" are closer to what young Americans are embracing, but The Corrs still lack the big-time flash and dazzle that young Americans crave,' he says. 'They want a total entertainment package, not just solid musical talent. To be fair, it's been that way for some time, with doo-wop groups of the 1950s being put together by record companies in much the same way as they are today.

'But what's different is the complete absence of musicians with awe-inspiring musical talent,' argues Szachara. 'There are no Jimi Hendrixes or Eric Claptons or Neil Pearts any more. And the reason is that Americans don't care if the people entertaining them have talent or not. As long as there's a spectacle to behold, it doesn't matter who's putting it on. And the truth is, The Corrs have thus far never provided the spectacle.'

It doesn't help matters that The Corrs appear to be a down-to-earth, wholesome family. While Andrea could be marketed along the lines of Britney Spears, she's always photographed as part of the band. Szachara feels that the rest of the family 'don't all have that special Andrea mystique. They're beautiful, but never in a "dirty" way. They don't try to pass themselves across as whores, and ironically, it hurts their marketability. And when you throw big brother Jim into the picture, you can forget about it.'

As they are today, The Corrs are unlikely to be a US number one act, because they don't appeal to the group that spends the most money on music: teenagers. 'Teenagers are simply not going to go for music on the basis of its own merit,' says Szachara. 'They need high-energy glitz, which is not what The Corrs are about. The adult contemporary crowd is a lot different. They still have a problem allowing "new" acts into their tight little circle, but at least they seem to *listen* to what's being played. It's more than just a beat.'

Szachara suggests *In Blue* comes closest to providing music that is accessible to the average American. Nevertheless, The Corrs' sound is much more appropriate for what Americans were listening to in the 1980s — strong melodies, rich production and skilled instrumentals:

> But it's the year 2001 now, and I think Americans get scared if they hear a hint of a genuine musical instrument on a studio album. They want rap, hip-hop and dance. And fortunately for Corrs' fans everywhere, *In Blue* still isn't in that category. But unfortunately, that means it's not going to be their breakthrough album. Shania Twain and Faith Hill and the like have had success with music like The Corrs, but they reached that success through other charts, such as country. The Corrs are trying to take the short path to that success, and I'm not sure it's possible.

*   *   *   *

It's often a funny experience ringing the US from Northern Ireland. You get one of two reactions: on the one hand the Americans will think it cute that you are ringing from a place where they themselves might have ancestors. On other hand other Americans will speak to you as if you are from another planet. The people I was trying to contact knew of The Corrs and yet I could have been speaking about someone from the middle of Africa for all they cared. The funniest conversation I had was with a woman at a radio station in New York. 'I think The Corrs are great people,' she told me in a rich New York accent. We got to talking and I asked her what it was like working for the man I was trying to get an interview with. 'I love it,' she said proudly. 'It's a privilege as he's just a wonderful person.' Everybody seemed wonderful there. 'Can I have your direct number?' I asked, not

wishing to go through hundreds of departments again to reach my new friend.
'That's not the kind of thing I do,' she laughed, making me wonder whether
I had instead just asked her for her home phone number. Ah yes, the radio
industry in the US is a long way from journalism in Northern Ireland.

*   *   *   *

Part of the reason why The Corrs were not vogue and fashionable in the US was that, despite their regular promotional appearances, they did not spend considerable time there. When they *did* market themselves in the US on a regular basis, sales increased significantly. For example, in one week in March 2001, after a series of promotional appearances, *In Blue* made an 81 per cent increase over the previous week's sales and it moved up from number 79 to 42 on the Billboard charts.

Yet, The Corrs did work hard when they were in the US. In August 2000, they flew to the US, for their first round of promotion for *In Blue*. Among the various appearances was a spot on the popular morning show, *Good Morning America*. It was yet another concerted attempt to spread the message through the mainstream American media. But the key was getting played on the radio so the American public could hear what The Corrs sounded like.

In Blue was finally released in the US in September 2000. The album debuted at a highly respectable 21 on the charts and was fourth on the US Internet-only sales chart.

Within four weeks, it officially went gold (sales of 500,000 copies). It took *Forgiven Not Forgotten* five years to reach the same status: *In Blue* was making its mark in the US.

The Corrs sold more copies in the US than they previously had because their name recognition had improved. Slots on a host of television and radio shows, playing before The Rolling Stones, and all the previous promotional visits they had made to the US were all having an effect.

In October 2000 The Corrs took a break from their promotions in the US and returned to Ireland to take part in Amnesty International's third annual campaign against torture. They were showing that they were maturing both as individuals and as a band and were now prepared to voice their opinions on issues that they cared strongly about. They had done that after the Omagh bomb in 1998, but that was a one-off that had stirred the emotions of everyone in Ireland. They had also been made 'Ambassadors of Pop' to the European Union to convince Members of the European Parliament to fight Internet piracy, but that was also about protecting the rights of musicians in general. The connection with Amnesty was the first real sign that The

Corrs were developing their own social voice in the Irish community.

The purpose of the campaign was not only to protest against torture, but also to help individuals who Amnesty International feared were at risk. After spending most of their career being non-political it was enlightening to see The Corrs publicly care about something other than chart success and the amount of travelling they did each year.

The band then returned to the US on their second and by far most successful wave of promotion with *In Blue*. They won their first American music award, in the 'Best Kept Secret' category, thanks to the fans that voted online in the VH1 'My Music Awards'.

On December 1, The Corrs performed at the World Aids Day 2000 concert on MTV and on December 10 they performed with various other artists at the 19th annual *Christmas in Washington*, aired by TNT on December 17. On the guest list were President Clinton and the First Lady.

In that same month President Clinton visited Ireland for three days in what was effectively a goodbye tour. Visiting Dublin and Belfast was almost routine for Clinton, but for the first time on his travels Dundalk was scheduled as a stop. The Corrs were asked to play for the President in Market Square, although they could not find the time to return home to play. With virtually the whole of Dundalk turning out to see the American President, including thousands from outside the town, the fact that The Corrs could not break into their tour to return home and play did not impress many townsfolk.

As 2000 ended, the band continued to be at the cutting edge of technology. The Corrs' December 21 concert at London's Wembley Arena was broadcast live on digital TV throughout Britain, making it the world's first interactive concert. Different camera angles were available to fans with digital TV, allowing them different vantage points of the group as a whole and the band member of their choice. It was yet another sign that although their focus was on the US, The Corrs remained outstandingly popular in Britain and Europe.

The year 2000 had been traumatic for The Corrs, who have said that the loss of their mother in 1999 continued to affect them significantly and that this was very much the backdrop to the writing and production of *In Blue*. As Sharon told *Hot Press* in 2000: 'What I find particularly difficult is — I'm always surrounded by a lot of people, so you generally have to stifle your tears and hide your feelings and try and find a corner where you can be alone.'

In memory of their mother, The Corrs decided to hold a benefit concert for the Freeman Hospital in Newcastle. The concert was held on January 8 2001 and its aim was to raise money for a new hospital wing, which would give the hospital the facilities to carry on its work in deciphering the mysterious disease that claimed their mother's life. The Corrs raised over £100,000 for the hospital in a terrific gesture that was appreciated by everyone there. It turned out to be an emotional night for the band.

Also present on the night was Gavin Geddes, co-ordinator of The Corrs' Fans Freeman Appeal on the Internet. He presented a £4,000 cheque to the band themselves, in front of the press and staff members from the Freeman Hospital. 'Unfortunately, it was a pretty quick presentation but Andrea, Caroline, Sharon and Jim have asked me to pass on their sincere thanks to all those who donated to the appeal,' said Geddes at the time.

The fans' donations were recognised by Andrea during the concert. 'We'd also like to thank the fans that have also been donating through the Internet,' she said. 'This really does mean a lot to us. Not only to us but also to those and their loved ones who suffer from lung disorders.'

Back on the charts, not everything was going well for The Corrs. 'Irresistible', The Corrs' second single from *In Blue*, was proving to be anything but, landing at number twenty in the British charts after the first week of sales. Ever since The Corrs had achieved widespread success with 'Dreams' in March 1998, their singles had been in the top ten, so this was a disappointment.

When it came to sales The Corrs had always been more of an album band than a singles band, but the fact that 'Irresistible' was not universally popular suggests that it was the wrong option as a second single. 'Give Me A Reason' — which was originally intended to be the second release — would have been the better option.

Interestingly for those following the band's success with, and fans' criticism of, remixes, the inevitable *In Blue: Special Edition* contained new tracks only on a bonus disc, rather than a wholesale remix of the original album.

*   *   *   *

I don't know how many times people have asked me which of the Corr girls I fancied most. My standard reply was 'I've sort of lived with them for the last two years, I'm bloody sick of them and want to divorce all three!'

To be honest, I did become sick of The Corrs and everything they did or did not stand for. It wasn't necessarily them that I was sick of, more the fact that I was spending so much time on one subject. Most journalists are used to covering something and then moving on after a short time. With this book it was for more than two years on and off. Then again, the fact that the Corr girls were so attractive made it a more pleasant experience than what writing a book on Alice Cooper may have been!

Apart from that inspiring performance in Italy back in 1998, I can't say that I got excited about the Corr girls. The Corrs ended up feeling more like brothers and sisters than anything else.

* * * *

While 'Irresistible' was not doing as well as The Corrs would have liked, they were making progress in the US. *In Blue* was selling effortlessly in comparison with earlier Corrs albums, and The Corrs were also developing an active following. For example, they scored the number one spot on Billboard's Internet sales chart.

The success of 'Breathless' and *In Blue* was largely twofold. It was first of all about the Americans seeing how big The Corrs were around the world and secondly it was about the band at last getting the formula right with 'Breathless'. The Mutt Lange produced song had strong lyrics, a catchy beat and a somewhat raunchy video that worked well in selling the song. The track had the harder edge that was so obviously lacking from their first two original albums. It was also a reflection of the work that The Corrs had put in while in the US.

'If you want to make it big in the US, just like any territory you have to spend six if not nine months there per year,' says Andy Murray. 'If you are big in Britain you have got to be there five months a year, so obviously you can't be in five places at once.'

While the rest of the world was preparing itself for the release of 'Give Me A Reason', the American public was still focused on 'Breathless'. Around 300 stations across the US added the song to their play list, making this the first time ever that The Corrs climbed the US radio airplay charts. VH1 had the video in large rotation, with MTV slowly following suit, opting to show an alternate version.

'Breathless' made its first appearance on VH1's Top Ten countdown at number ten, knocking off Faith Hill's 'The Way You Love Me'. It was the first time The Corrs had been on a US countdown. Total Request Live (TRL) listed the video as a 'Wannabe', meaning it was only a matter of time before The Corrs broke into the TRL Top Ten countdown. The show, popular with the younger generation, represents the most fashionable music trends of the moment.

The good news kept on coming for The Corrs in the US. 'Breathless', along with 'Rebel Heart', earned the band two Grammy nominations. Although The Corrs did not win either award, the American music industry was starting to take notice.

David Foster is wary about saying that The Corrs have achieved everything that they are going to achieve in America and believes there is still much work to be done there. He says their progress has been due to a number of factors.

> I think you have to give The Corrs credit for the work they did here and the fact that they worked so hard at get their name out there. They got plenty of TV and I think that made a huge difference.
>
> Spending plenty of time here has also been crucial. During their careers they have been so popular in so many places in the world that it has made it difficult for them to spend a lot of time here. But now that they are concentrating on America it has made it a lot easier for them to get exposure.
>
> I also believe that 'Breathless' was the right track at the right time and obviously the contribution of Mutt Lange was central to their success.
>
> But generally I believe it was just their time and after all their work they fully deserve what success that they have had here.

Just as their hard work was starting to pay off in the US, the momentum that The Corrs had established with *In Blue* all came to a grinding halt early in 2001. They had been fortunate that throughout their careers they had not been inflicted with major sickness or injury. Though there had been times when they had felt like crying due to exhaustion, their luck ran out on the *In Blue* tour.

In late January 2001 they were forced to reschedule six concerts and cancel a charity gala at the Royal Albert Hall on January 29, as well as later concerts in Asia and Australiasia, because Andrea was unable to perform, or indeed fly. She had developed a serious ear infection and was instructed by doctors not to perform. A complete rest was needed to prevent permanent damage. Jim commented: 'This is the first time in our career that we've had to pull shows. We are really sorry to disappoint the fans, and look forward to making it up to them.'

However, the *Daily Mirror* was not shy in suggesting that Andrea was faking her illness and reported her 'miraculous recovery' after she'd been pictured jogging around a park in Dublin. Andrea hit back at such claims, saying that her ears were still very sore and that she was still on antibiotics.

John Hughes said:

> She's out there struggling to get battle fit for the tour. She's been banned from flying for a month and doctors

are monitoring her progress every few days. She has a cyst in one ear and an infection in the other. She uses in-ear monitors onstage, so there was no way she could perform. Her hearing is badly impaired. She's now trying build up her immune system again and is following doctors' orders on how to recover. This includes getting plenty of rest, fresh air and exercise.

It seems unlikely that Andrea was faking the illness and nobody has suggested any good reason why she would cause such great disruption. In any case, it wasn't long before Andrea was able to return to work and join The Corrs' next push in the US. On March 16 2001, The Corrs headlined New York City's Radio City Music Hall after playing a similar sell-out show in Chicago a few days beforehand. The band's first concert in the prestigious venue also sold out quickly.

Brian Kennedy opened for The Corrs. An amazingly talented performer in his own right, the Irishman's lush lyrics and soothing sounds were worthy of a concert of his own, although it is questionable whether he was the right musician to ignite an audience on this occasion.

The Corrs came out after a half-hour intermission, playing 'Give Me a Reason' before 'Forgiven Not Forgotten'. Although their albums change, The Corrs don't. You can like or dislike the way the songs on the different albums are produced, but when it comes time to see them play live, their music and performance is much the same as it has always been.

An emotional rendition of 'No More Cry' and an upbeat performance of 'Breathless' were the highlights of the night. During the concert, the audience stayed seated for the most part. But from the opening notes of 'Breathless' they leapt to their feet.

The *Irish Voice* wrote:

> Riding the wave of their new-found US popularity, The Corrs rocked Radio City Music Hall the night before St Patrick's Day.
>
> It was a night to remember. The cold drizzle licked the pavement of the midtown sidewalks, making Manhattan feel more like Dublin. People clad in green scurried through the streets as their workday ended, and it seemed as though the city was powered by emerald electricity during the rush hour.
>
> When the girls appeared on the big screens with that as their backdrop, they took on an otherworldly

appearance that seemed to confirm their stature as video goddesses. Looking exquisite with her jet-black hair and glam makeup, Andrea Corr ... left the shoes in the dressing room, choosing instead to pace the stage in bare feet with a form-fitting designer dress that made her look like a panther. She was very aware of the camera that propelled her image on the big screen, and she used it to full advantage.

Contrary to popular belief, how they looked is only one part of what makes this band great. They sounded considerably more muscular in a live setting than the bland band that occasionally shows up on records with The Corrs' label on them. Free from the constraints of pop producers that try to homogenise their sound, the band was free to rock out on 'Give Me A Reason' and 'Forgiven Not Forgotten'. Jim Corr injected a wicked chunky guitar riff during 'Radio'.

It was at the Radio City Music Hall Concert that The Corrs announced that they would be opening for U2 in Miami at the start of their 'Elevation' tour and possibly combining with them sometime during their concert tour. Although on this tour U2 were not playing the large arenas (Ireland aside) it made sound business sense for The Corrs to align themselves with the biggest band in the world. The impact would further increase their profile in the US, while the two Irish bands had a closer fit than The Corrs had with The Rolling Stones.

The Corrs and John Hughes both knew that to make an impact in the US they would have to spend time there. But the reoccurring problem was that they were in demand in so many other parts of the world.

CHAPTER 15

Hard-Corr Fans

I think we are very lucky with the music we play, because
the type of fans we meet are so respectful, so special.

Jim Corr

On the Friday afternoon before The Corrs performed at Lansdowne
Road in the summer of 1999, a lunch was held at a traditional Irish
pub in downtown Dublin. The occasion was a pre-Corrs' concert bash
and there were about fifteen fans of the band in attendance. They
came from, amongst other parts of the world, Belfast, Sweden,
Finland, the US, England and Scotland. One girl had even come from
Singapore to see The Corrs play, though she was the only female
present. The average age would have been no more than 25.

About half of these 'hard-Corr' fans drank beer and a few had food.
There was an air of expectation present. It could have been about the
concert the following day, or perhaps about the dinner that had been
arranged for them all that evening. The talk was reserved, as much as
it is when any group of people get together for the first time. Despite
the natural reservations, there was this feeling that everyone was
keeping a secret from the other, but that each one knew individually
what that secret was. As if someone was too scared to say: 'Well they
are attractive aren't they?' or 'Who do you *really* fancy the most?'

Still, there were no crazed fans present, nobody who would boil
one of The Corrs' pet rabbits (or perhaps their dog Judy). They were
all nice people and were generally similar to the music of The Corrs:
wholesome, family orientated, non-offensive but a bit bland perhaps.

It was not a passionate meeting of fans, nor was the talk
particularly Corrs-related. But in the group there was still a general
appreciation of The Corrs and what they did. These were the people
who you would have been happy to meet on a dark night. These were
people who could have grown up with the Corr family in Dundalk.

*   *   *   *

*I met Belfast radio disk jockey Joe Ferguson one cold afternoon in winter in
perhaps Belfast's most luxurious café. At that time he was a big name in*

Belfast entertainment (he would move to Liverpool some weeks later). He worked for one of Northern Ireland's most well-known radio stations and he was one of those people who you should know. Among Ferguson's many claims to fame was the fact that he was one of the biggest fans of The Corrs. He even admitted to me that he was in love with Andrea in a very innocent sort of way. I thought this was kind of sweet, but as I interviewed him it was pretty obvious that his enthusiasm for the band was serious. His passion for The Corrs scared me a little bit and he seemed generally besotted with them. As we drank coffee I listened to the man tell me about his passion. He wasn't playing up his support of the band one little bit. Again I left the café amazed at the passions that The Corrs were able to provoke. It is nothing short of a frightening power.

*   *   *   *

The Corrs have sold over twenty million albums worldwide and have a firm fanbase. Most fans of the band, in the wider sense of the word, are content with buying their albums, watching their concerts on TV now and again, buying tickets when they play in person in their city, and generally enjoying their music for what it is: a harmless, good-natured sound that offends few. But it is natural, given the success of The Corrs, that there are some that will take their enjoyment a few steps further.

The fact that the band contains three attractive and reasonably young women further adds to their appeal. But, apart from a few cases of worrying behaviour, The Corrs have generally not been followed by groupies normally associated with a band of their popularity. They do not have, for example, legions of teenage girls running through hotel corridors.

The rarity of obsessive fans of The Corrs is undoubtedly due to two main factors. First, because the middle-of-the-road music of The Corrs appeals largely to the mainstream and not to the extremes, they get a fairly restrained audience. Secondly, as many of the hardcore fans of The Corrs are male, there might be plenty of ogling at concerts, but there is little outward show of emotion in comparison to what you get at a Westlife, Five or Boyzone concert. On the whole, true blue fans of The Corrs — those that are seriously moved by their music, fame and image and go to huge lengths to prove it — tend to be young and come from all over the world.

The lengths that fans of The Corrs go to get close to the band varies. Some are happy just going to as many concerts as they can, while others will pester the band with letters and shower them with presents on their birthdays. Some will listen to the music of The Corrs religiously, while others will go through phases of listening to it. Even though they are not as extreme as fans of other bands, hardcore fans of The Corrs are just as passionate. Here are three examples which illustrate this point.

Cormac Fox (22) is a Dubliner and describes himself as 'the band's original fan'. Having followed The Corrs since 1995, he admits that no one has applied themselves to the band quite the way he has.

A musician in his own right, he would travel the length and breadth of Ireland to watch The Corrs play and hold up signs with the message 'Give Us a Wave'. After that he became known to the band as 'Give Us a Wave Cormac!' Naturally enough he became well known to the Corr family and to this day he keeps in contact with Gerry Corr. As Cormac says:

> Music is very important in my own personal life and in my social circle. Every day I am in contact with music, whether it be through one of my jobs or through dancing the night away. I am a member of my local nightclub, Scruples, which I frequent about three times a week. I really love music and I know the words of nearly all the songs there. Music/dancing is a great way to impress the ladies, you know! I teach the piano to a couple of people and I also play the piano in Dobbins Bistro in Dublin at least once a week, which I thoroughly enjoy. So, music does play a key role in my social (and economic!) life.

Finn Mikko Hanninen (27) is also a dedicated fan. Having travelled constantly around Europe in the last three years to see the band play, he says there is nothing quite like the thrill of seeing The Corrs perform live. He says, however, that he was not raised in a particularly musical environment:

> I wouldn't say it's very important, at least it's less important than in other cultures such as the Irish. Still music is everywhere where there are people, and this is true of Finland too. Also Finland does have its own traditional songs and music style (which is not really that far from traditional Irish music). The modern musical environment is very strongly influenced by the international music scene though.

Mikko says he discovered The Corrs virtually by accident:

> I used IRC (Internet Relay Chat, a real-time international chat system) quite a lot around 1996–97, so made many friends through that. One of those people was

from Australia, and so when we were chatting one night in early 1997 she mentioned this Irish band, The Corrs, that she was going to see in a concert. So, I said I didn't know them, but I was curious because I've always more or less liked Celtic or Celtic-influenced music. She offered to send me a tape of them. So, about a week or two later I got that tape, it had the *Forgiven Not Forgotten* album on it. I listened to that tape for a week in my car, before I went to a music store and bought the CD.

Despite that, I didn't become a major fan right then and there, even if I did listen to the album quite a bit. Sometime in October 1997 I think, I was browsing the selection in a music store and noticed the *Talk on Corners* CD. I didn't know that there would be a new album out, so it was half an accident. I bought that on the spot.

I actually still remember that night I went to see a movie or for some other reason got home rather late, so I decided to use headphones for listening to the new CD. I was in a good mood and the music from the headphones sounded perfect — the guitars in 'Only When I Sleep', the catchy choruses of 'I Never Loved You Anyway' and 'So Young', and Andrea's incredible voice on 'Queen Of Hollywood'. That's when I think I became a fan, though still not a 'hard-Corr' fan.

Since Mikko was using his computer while listening to the album, he decided to see if there were any websites about the band: 'I hadn't done that before. I found out The Corrs were doing a mini-tour of Europe and playing in Dublin in December. I went to the concert as planned, and I was blown away by the performance and that was when I became a true convert.'

Such were his impressions of the band that Mikko wanted to get involved in promoting The Corrs in some way:

This concert was also what sparked off the idea to set up (an Internet) mailing list for the band. When I had looked at the websites earlier, I had noticed that there apparently was no mailing list dedicated to them yet, and there probably would be demand for something like that since there were quite a few web pages already ... And after a bit of a slow start, the mailing list was set up on the January 8 1998.

*   *   *   *

*In the early days of their careers especially, The Corrs would often talk in
the media about missing home and their families. I kind of knew how they
felt. For the first year I was away I didn't miss New Zealand that much at
all. I had no desire to see other Kiwis, nor did I have any hankering to go
home. I missed my family and friends, but I was still developing my own
identity, my own sense of goals and objectives. And Britain and Ireland
presented so much opportunity and excitement. I realised now why so many
artists and writers from New Zealand and Australia had come to England
or Ireland in search of the Holy Grail. Still, there were times when I missed
New Zealand. I would see Russell Crowe, Sam Neill or Anna Paquin on
the big screen, or go to see Neil Finn play in Belfast and be genuinely
moved. Proud that New Zealanders were taking it to the world and
achieving so much. There could not be a more proud New Zealander than
I. Yet, I wasn't necessarily sure that I wanted to go back home just yet.*

*   *   *   *

Coming from Dublin, Cormac learnt about The Corrs in the early
days of their career. He says it was almost love at first listen and sight:

> The first time I heard them was when I was cycling to
> school one day in the pelting rain with an icy breeze
> whipping around my poor shrivelled body. I was listening
> to the radio (FM104's *Strawberry Alarm Clock*) on that
> Monday morning and 'Runaway' was their 'Strawberry
> Pick of the Week'. I remember the two male DJs
> commenting on the rather favourable appearance of the
> girls!

Cormac says he originally liked The Corrs for a variety of reasons:
'Their heaving, voluptuous brea ... Mmm, I guess it was a combination
of their music and the girls' good looks, combined with the general
party atmosphere at that time. Actually, to be honest, the latter two
probably were much greater influences on me at the start than the
music.'

Of the three fans profiled in this chapter, Swede Daniel Lindberg
(nineteen) has at stages been the most committed. The webmaster of
Corrsonline.com, he says he spends at least three, and often five, hours
each day on Corrs-related tasks. Logical and highly organised by
nature, his desire to get close to The Corrs has seen him travel
regularly around Europe, as well as travelling to Dublin in 1999 to see
the band play at Lansdowne Road.

Daniel says he likes The Corrs for a variety of reasons: 'It was a new
fresh and original sound, with the violin and all. I've always liked

traditional Irish music,' he says. He believes his interest in The Corrs has changed in the last couple of years:

> A couple of years ago I worked hard on Corrs' stuff because I really liked the band, nowadays I do it because: (1) fans have nowhere else to go, (2) I'm hired to do the job. It's a big project and I'm not really doing it for the band any longer, I'm doing it for myself and for the fans. The band haven't given me anything back, but the fans have.
>
> Like many old fans I'm deeply disappointed about the band's new musical direction, and change of image as a whole. I will never doubt their talent but I will not like the music they make just because it's them. The Corrs came along with an original and fresh sound — *Forgiven Not Forgotten* will always be the best album to be released in the 1990s, and *Talk On Corners* will always be a worthy sequel.
>
> The Corrs can still put on great live shows. With a standing audience at a medium-size venues they are still really special. Forget seated UK gigs, you fall asleep at those. I'll sure do more concert trips around Europe. When I work on the site today I don't even think about The Corrs. It's just mechanical and effective work. Think too much about what you're doing and you lose focus.

Like most male fans of The Corrs, the looks of the girls stand out for these three fans, almost, perhaps, as much as the music. Cormac believes that their appearance is an inherent part of what and who The Corrs are:

> If the group were ugly, they wouldn't be The Corrs. If the group were four Jimmys, I would never have liked them. It's all down to sex appeal and the way that Andrea can croon to you, ... 'make love to me through the night' ... That hooks you in a way nothing else can and you follow it like a sheep. Yes, we're all sheep, Andrea's the shepherd, and the pastures are the albums — like that!

Mikko appears less obviously affected by the looks of the girls. Yet he too believes that looks are part of their general appeal: 'How important? Not very important. To borrow someone else's words, it's an added bonus. I won't claim that it's insignificant, just that it's not a major factor.'

Like any three fans, the goals of Cormac, Daniel and Mikko differ. They all agree on one thing, however: The Corrs have given them enormous satisfaction and pleasure. Cormac says he enjoys following The Corrs not for only their music, but for the opportunity to try to meet them:

> I think I get a kick out of it. I mean, perhaps, it's as shallow as I'm trying to impress other people, whether it is other fans or The Corrs themselves. The hours I spend on The Corrs are, if I'm to be honest about it, to impress them and perhaps they will appreciate me more and think of me more as a *friend* whatever that is.
>
> But the hours and money I put into it all have wasted a lot of time. No, the word isn't wasted as I enjoyed it all so much and got so much out of it, but I don't have the time to do all of that now unlike other fans who seem to spend hours on the Internet, updating their pages. Now, I gotta get on with my own life.

For his part, Mikko says there are a host of reasons why he likes The Corrs:

> First of course, is the band and especially their music, it's so good that it deserves to be promoted. What I do as the mailing list administrator is promotion in a very indirect way.
>
> Secondly, and more important, the mailing list is a discussion place for the fans, and I see myself as working on something that helps the fans. I like to help people and I enjoy using my skills in creating and maintaining something that people will find useful and enjoyable. Every time someone mentions that they've made friends on the mailing list, or have found it to be a useful source of information, I feel rewarded. Of course, if someone gives me some direct recognition of what I do, that feels good too.

Cormac says having grown up and now getting on with his life, he would still reluctantly (if she asked nicely) go out with Andrea: 'I don't think I would go out with Andrea! Ok, I didn't believe me either … But, in a way, it's true as her life is too weird for me … '

*   *   *   *

In March 2001 over 80,000 tickets were sold for a U2 concert to be held in August that year in Slane, Ireland. All the tickets were sold in just 45 minutes. There were scenes of Beatles proportions in Dublin as fans rushed to get their tickets for what was sure to be a remarkable concert. U2 hadn't played Slane since 1981 and this was likely to be their only concert in Ireland that year. Everyone in the Republic and in Northern Ireland was talking about this concert, which was certain to be special for a number of reasons. I also tried to ring up for tickets, only an hour and a half after the phone lines opened. I was one of thousands of people to miss out. But what the demand showed was that U2 was still wildly popular in Ireland twenty years since they began, and that ability and impact on Irish society appeared as great as ever. But would The Corrs be able to sell out Lansdowne Road again in ten years time?

*   *   *   *

Andrea seems to be the fans' favourite Corr. Cormac says:

> It would be Jim or Andrea. Andrea — obvious reasons, also she seems to have a bit of spice in her which she'd need to mix with my sweetness (sugar and spice and all things nice). She also always recognises me and chats, unlike the other two girls. Jim is the friendliest to me though and always has a kind word and handshake for his family's greatest fan. He seems always real nice and he likes a good party.

Mikko agrees:

> I'd be lying if I didn't say Andrea, but I have to admit it's not an easy choice. All of the girls are exceptionally talented, have a very nice personality and are beautiful. Maybe I favour Andrea because I'm very close to her in age. She's just such a talented, beautiful, sweet and nice person. Of course the other girls are talented and beautiful too, but Andrea's the one who's captured my heart.

The three fans' friends know how much The Corrs mean to them. Cormac says:

> They all think I'm a bit mad but they realise that I've calmed down a bit on them. Saying that though, sometimes I'll be talking (ok, chatting up) a girl and we'll be discussing musical tastes and one of my friends will butt over and tell her that I'm Andrea Corr's stalker, which isn't really what I need. Actually, at the New Year's Eve gig at The Point when I went backstage with my friend, the latter found Jim and brought him over to me saying, 'Jim! This is your greatest stalker, Cormac'.

> But, I know my friends know that it is a 'healthy' obsession and not one that really affects my life too much (anymore). It did for a while when I'd be too busy doing something 'Corrish' to come out but I'm much more *normal* now.

Mikko says although his friends are understanding he does not really care what they think:

> I think it's mostly passed as a quirk. Some have more understanding about it than others do. And no, I don't really care much if I'm seen to be odd, we all are weird in some way or another. But I think my friends are very good in that way, they might not understand it but they also don't tell me to 'become normal' or anything like that.

Cormac says his family has finally realised that his support of the band is healthy — now:

> They don't mind at all. They know it's fine and not affecting me. Perhaps, they were worried a few years ago, but they know I'm intelligent now and have everything in perspective; unlike many fans who are going through the early stages — I wonder if a psychologist could do a report on this?!?

Like any common interest, enjoyment of The Corrs has led to the development of many friendships. The more enthusiastic of the fans tend to know each other and go to huge lengths to fuel their passion for the band, just like the fans of any other group. Mikko says he has developed many close friends from his support of The Corrs:

> Generally, I like them. It's nice to find some kindred spirits and talk about our favourite band. There are a lot of Corrs' fans, and in any large group of people there are going to be some people who you don't like or can't get along with, but overall I've had mostly positive experiences when corresponding with other fans. Because of the mailing list I get to get quite a lot of emails from new people all the time, asking for help or information or something like that.
>
> Sometimes there follows a full discussion over email from the initial emails, and those are very nice. I've made quite a few Net-friends that way. I know several who are very, very enthusiastic, even more so than I am in my view, but I'm not sure how to rate obsessiveness.

Compared to me, there are people who have larger Corrs' collections, or have seen more concerts, or know more about the band. I don't think that I can name any single person as being the most obsessed. Especially since I've not personally met many of the people who appear to be that way, and so I can't know whether my perception of them (based on just emails and other forms of digital communication) is accurate.

Daniel agrees with Mikko on this point. As co-ordinator of *Corrsonline*, he is in a great position to examine the impact that being a fan of The Corr involves:

There are a lot of good people out there and I have a lot of friends all over the world. It's really fun meeting and talking to other fans in real life. There are also a lot of nutcases and teenage fanatics with whom you can't have a proper conversation about anything. We shouldn't forget all the jealous trolls and flamers whose only joy in life is to piss people off.

But for Daniel being a fan of The Corrs has ultimately meant developing new skills and co-ordinating a team of fans. It has also meant making money out of the band:

I co-ordinate ten people and everything around that has got to work in order for the site to run smoothly. It has become a job. This has dramatically changed how I look at The Corrs. I've had nothing but Corrs around me day after day for years now. To me they are just ordinary people, nothing special. For the website this is good, I can work far more professionally but still with passion since I have a goal — to make *Corrsonline* the biggest unofficial band and artist site on the Internet.

We are one of the biggest now, and we just keep growing. I set my goals high from the start — to make the best Corrs' website. It was still just a hobby project by a fan though, I never thought it would go this far. Today I know that it can go further. Running *Corrsonline* has given me more friends than most people manage to gather in a lifetime. It has given me working experience within several fields (apart from the obvious, web design) — finance, marketing strategy, management, research etc. It's great to see what you can achieve through hard work. To see your website, along with yourself, grow more famous and popular by the day is a great feeling.

Even though the thrill of receiving massive positive feedback day after day is long gone it's still something that makes it more worthwhile to carry on. I try to provide the best service for the fans, giving them what they want. I've done a lot trying to get the band's management and record company on my side, a band management who are uninterested in the Internet, and a record company which, apparently, knows very little.

Perhaps the ultimate test of their devotion to The Corrs is to ask whether these three fans could walk away from their passion. Could they choose to support another band, get a new hobby, move on to another obsession?

'I don't think I'm obsessed anymore,' reflects Cormac. 'Could I walk away? Would I want to? They don't really harm me and I get a lot of enjoyment out of it and meet some really nice people so why would I want to walk away? But, if I had to, I guess I could. I'd have to say goodbye first though!'

Mikko agrees, but would not necessarily move away from the experiences that he has had:

I do think that I could just walk away from a lot of things. I don't think I'd want to let go of the friends I've made through sharing the same enthusiasm. I may eventually lose interest in being quite this enthusiastic, but I don't think I will ever stop liking their music. If I find that I don't like the sound of their future albums, which is always a possibility, then that would probably lead me away.

Daniel suggests that he too, could walk away, although The Corrs would always be special to him:

At their best they perform great music and I just love watching them in concert. Sure, there have been times when I haven't agreed with the musical direction they have taken, but for me part of the enjoyment is spending so much time communicating with fans of the band and hearing what they think.

For me the website has been very special and I am sure in future I will look back and have only good

memories of The Corrs. The site and travelling around
Europe to see them play has been fun and I have made
many quality friendships as a result.

Still, even though these fans love The Corrs and what they stand for,
they want something in return. To be rejected by the band in any way
hurts and if they do not respond to their fans in the way they want,
there is generally a feeling of helplessness.

Daniel was a dedicated fan some time ago, but he is now changing
his tune, due mainly to being ignored by the management of the band:
'I'm far from obsessed and I would have walked away ages ago if it
wasn't for the website. I don't listen to them very often nowadays; if I
do it's some bootleg. *In Blue* is a sh*** album anyway.'

Despite spending up to five hours a day working on Corrs-related
work, Daniel has become disillusioned with The Corrs in the last
eighteen months: 'I am sick of The Corrs, live gigs is all they can really
give me at the moment,' he says. 'I still love *Forgiven Not Forgotten*,
Talk On Corners (original edition) and *Unplugged* but re-mixes
combined with *In Blue* and all the frustration around the site (being
ignored and pushed away) has been too much.'

*　　*　　*　　*

*Ian Coognan looked at me and laughed. 'How ya doing Todd?' he cried,
offering a hand and welcoming me into his shop one Saturday morning.
Coognan was the first Dundalk journalist I had spoken to about The Corrs
and he was as Dundalk as The Corrs themselves. An entertainment writer
with the* Argus *in Dundalk, he also worked at his brother's picture framing
shop by day. A unique individual with short hair, a ring in one ear and a
ready smile for anyone, he was useful to my research as he appeared to
know everyone in Dundalk, including friends of the Corr family. Over a
period of months he gave me numerous contacts and recommendations and
actually took me to McManus' to arrange an interview there. But my
lasting impression of Ian Coognan will not be of how he helped me, but of
the man himself. His manner, his Irishness, his understanding of the world
and his love of life contrasted greatly with the pressure that I had put myself
under. He could have been described as a 'great character'. I was pleased to
have met him and, without knowing it, he taught me a great deal.*

*　　*　　*　　*

Despite the odd frustration, if these three 'hard-Corr' fans are
anything to go by, The Corrs have loyal supporters who have, in many
respects, grown up with the band. They might not necessarily agree
with the direction The Corrs have moved in musically, but generally

they still support what they are doing. How else could you explain the hours that Daniel Lindberg spends working on his website? Or the extent and cost Cormac Fox went to in travelling around Ireland to see The Corrs play in the early days of their careers?

The Corrs may have made many lasting impacts, but perhaps their biggest is in bringing happiness to so many people. Should that be the ultimate test? Should the fact that Cormac Fox will, to some degree, always remember the phone call he got from Andrea or biking in the rain to school and hearing 'Runaway' on the radio for the first time, be as important as any of the countless awards The Corrs have won?

Is having a number one hit any more important than Daniel Lindberg looking dazed and emotionally drained on the DART (urban railway) going back into Dublin after the Corrs' concert in 1999, clearly moved by what he had seen?

Or what about Mikko Hanninen running like Brian O'Driscoll to the front of the stage at Lansdowne Road that same night to get the best position so he could toss his feathers, swing with the best of the fans and try and make eye contact with Andrea? Is that any more important than selling a million albums?

The Corrs have inspired people from around the world with their blend of non-offensive, optimistic melodies and harmonies. In the process they have made millions and gained the recognition that they once craved. But when you see the reaction they can provoke all the media hype seems rather irrelevant. When an artist can communicate with an individual, when they can move them in the best possible way, enrich their life and provide them with motivation, well then, that is real success and worth more than all the money and awards in the world. And in that sense The Corrs have achieved more than what they ever dreamed possible.

CHAPTER 16

The Price of Success — Art Versus Commerce?

'Corrs' is an Irish word for 'babe'.

American TV host David Letterman

In 1999 The Corrs were in London rehearsing for yet another *Top of the Pops* appearance. This time they were performing 'Runaway', a single that was being re-released in order to cash in on their new-found success in the British market. The rehearsal went smoothly, especially since all the band had to do was mime and look both pretty and dreamy at the same time. The Corrs had done this sort of TV show numerous times before and by now it was almost second nature. After all, nobody can look pretty and dreamy quite like The Corrs can.

Although they give a faultless preview performance, impressing most of those in the studio watching the dry run, it did not enthuse everyone watching. A lawyer sidled up to a journalist from the magazine *Q* and gave his opinion. 'Overrated,' he huffed and walked off.

It was perhaps an inevitable price of success that people would start to question the artistic and long-term merits of what The Corrs do. That the more popular they got the more people would start to look beneath the surface and evaluate the long-term consequences of what The Corrs have produced. Not only that, but the reasons why they have been successful.

Given that The Corrs have sold over twenty million units around the world it is natural that there has been some criticism about their music and their impact on the world. It seems inevitable in this modern age that anyone who is successful is regarded as having 'sold out'. This criticism has tended to come in three general directions: first of all, that The Corrs are more about good looks than substance; secondly, that The Corrs, for all their musical ability, have not really said anything; and thirdly, perhaps the most common criticism, that they have sold their musical souls to the highest bidder in search of musical glory.

Perhaps the most obvious criticism has been that The Corrs are nothing more than pretty faces. There can be no denying that on the whole The Corrs are a good-looking band. Most would suggest that Sharon, Caroline and Andrea are attractive women, while — perhaps to a lesser degree — Jim is a good-looking man. The Irish press has been particularly quick to pass comment on the looks of The Corrs, one article going so far to suggest that no one who looks as good as The Corrs comes from unfashionable Dundalk.

In their July 11 1999 edition, *Ireland on Sunday* named what they considered to be Ireland's 50 most eligible women. The only criterion for making what was essentially a pointless (but nonetheless fascinating) list was that the woman could not be married. Sharon Corr was placed third. The newspaper waxed: 'Vampish Sharon looks stunning with her new lighter hair colouring. Has been called "angsty" and an "ice-maiden", which she denies. In fact she is the most talkative of the three sisters.'

Andrea was in seventh place. The newspaper didn't hold anything back on its comments: 'Like the rest of The Corrs, Andrea has undergone a total transformation in style in the past two years. She was once what could be called "frumpy", but now flaunts a pouting, waifish, radiant image.'

Coming in lowly at number 23 was Caroline. It said of her: 'Svelte and gorgeous, Caroline is often mistaken for Andrea as they look alike, although Caroline is somewhat taller.'

Andrea has also been described as 'the most beautiful woman in the world' and the 'sexiest woman in Ireland'. All rather flattering and it is reflected in the number of designer products that The Corrs have been inundated with since they achieved commercial success.

Sharon believes that suggestions that The Corrs are nothing more than a good-looking band and can't play, have well and truly vanished:

> I think because of the way we've broken countries like England through live performances, it's acknowledged that we're considered for our abilities as musicians who can pull off shows in front of thousands of people.
>
> It only frustrates me if I'm talking to someone and all I am is, y' know, 'aesthetically pleasing'; as if that's all we are.

Caroline also gets angry, occasionally, with those who think that The Corrs are nothing but three pretty faces. As she told one magazine:

> It's a mistake to say we have no conviction in what we do. There are people who say, three good-looking girls and

their brother, nice family, writing nice songs, it's not serious. But if we all had torn jeans and greasy hair the expectations would be different, and perhaps we would be different people. We can only be what we are.

*   *   *   *

If you want to know what Northern Ireland could be like it is necessary only to travel to Glasgow. Central Belfast is similar to central Glasgow. They both have the same sort of Victorian architecture in the middle of the city, while in both the people are warm and inviting. But where there appears on the surface little religious sectarianism in Glasgow, it is hard to escape it in Belfast. One weekend I travelled over to Scotland and was impressed with what I saw in Glasgow. Funnily enough, it gave me a greater understanding of Northern Ireland in the sense that it was possible to see the Scottish influence that is such a big part of Northern Ireland's culture and history. I had now seen Dublin, Glasgow and where the two cultures merged — Northern Ireland. By going to Scotland it proved to me that there was no right and wrong in Northern Ireland, just shades of grey that constantly saddened me and made me grateful to come from a place where all of the branches of Christianity could live together in reasonable harmony.

*   *   *   *

Hate it as they might, it is hard to ignore the impact that being attractive has on both The Corrs' careers and their appeal. What the band appears to object to is the assumption that, because they are good-looking, there is nothing behind the good looks, whether musically or personality-wise.

Journalist Michael Ross suggests that the looks of The Corrs cannot be underestimated in explaining why they have been successful, but he believes there is more to them than just the way they look: '[Looks are] important. But Andrea's voice is good, and that's more important than her looks. You don't see a band when you hear their song on the radio, after all. If The Corrs were just pretty faces, they wouldn't have succeeded.'

'There is nothing new about the marketing of The Corrs,' says Kevin Courtney. 'What else would you do? Would you put a paper bag over their heads? Everybody loves beautiful pop stars. All the current British and American teen queens, they're marketed on their looks as much as anything else.'

Andy Murray says that it's an easy way out for people to say The Corrs are gorgeous: 'They were gorgeous when they didn't sell a lot of records, they are gorgeous now. So what's happened in between? The fact is that they have had a lot more airplay and a lot more coverage.'

David Foster agrees. Putting on his producer hat, he says that if The Corrs were just pretty faces then they would soon be found out:

> There is no question that the band's good looks have had a mostly positive impact on their careers. But there is far more to them than that. There is intelligence and genuine musical talent. As a producer, it was my job to peel back the layers and see what was there.
>
> And with The Corrs there was plenty — perhaps mostly obviously a love for music. If they couldn't have played I would have found out immediately. But I was so impressed with what they could do.
>
> When you look beneath the surface you will see just how good The Corrs are. Obviously the average sixteen-year-old buying a record will not do that and instead may be motivated by the looks of the girls, but anyone who buys their music and truly loves music will understand and experience The Corrs' talents.

Good looks are one thing, but charisma is another factor in the group's success. To be specific, Andrea's charisma. Quite simply, The Corrs only have one true star. Four talented musicians, but only one natural performer. Only one member who possesses that rare 'X factor', the charisma that only the most popular and talented performers possess. Robbie Williams has it in the extreme, as does Mick Jagger, and Madonna. When Andrea comes on stage she has the ability to move the crowd and take them to another level, another world perhaps. She has a presence that the other Corrs do not possess. She can excite crowds, thrill them and tap into their deepest emotions.

Barry Egan, from the *Irish Independent*, has written plenty about Andrea Corr. His fascination borders on being over the top, although in his writing he has given a glimpse of her personality, her sense of intellectual curiosity, her social conscience. He writes:

> Examined closely, Andrea's lyrics chronicle a woman of morality and sensuality, navigating an emotional journey for which there are no maps. She has unmasked love's illusions along with her own fears and desires. The 25-year-old has broken stride with her peers and pitched into the riskier plateaus of singing straight from the heart, however unpleasant. The weight of sadness that seeps out around the edges is fascinating.

This view that Andrea is the band member with star quality is not to say that the other members of The Corrs are not important. Jim's production ability and his efforts on the keyboards contribute enormously to the sound of The Corrs, as does Sharon's violin playing. But as Andrea continued to grow and mature, so did The Corrs' success. She herself has said that she personally would not have been ready for the changes that would have had to be made if The Corrs had achieved huge success with *Forgiven Not Forgotten* in the US.

There is something deeper to The Corrs than three pretty faces, something much larger than just mere good looks. If that were the case, they would have had no musical background, no sense of ultimate destiny. They would be hollow eggs who would not have lasted.

The girls' good looks have had both positive and negative effects. The 'appearance factor' has obviously resulted in more copy, more media attention and more public recognition. It has seen The Corrs get into places that they wouldn't have got into had they not been as 'aesthetically pleasing'. It is arguable whether they would even have got into David Foster's office had they been less attractive. It has also naturally had a large impact on their appeal in an industry where good looks are almost as important as the music being created.

The negative side of this is that The Corrs have at times struggled to be taken seriously as musicians. The media stereotypes place them in the mild, but not substantial, category. They have had to go to extra lengths to stress their music and, to a degree, downplay their looks. Record executives suggest that in the eyes of many they have become too closely associated with fashion and glamour.

After the success of the remixed *Talk on Corners* especially, The Corrs became personalities rather than just musicians. The result was that they were more likely to pop up on the society pages as they were the arts and music pages. Therefore, questions were obviously going to be raised about their place in the industry and whether they had in fact been manufactured. The *Unplugged* album was a way of addressing this concern.

*   *   *   *

Spend all the time you want in Belfast these days and you are regularly told, whether directly or indirectly, that to understand this confusing place you need to have lived through the Troubles. That somehow unless you have seen people you know killed, and have had your life disrupted by soldiers on the streets and sometimes in your own backyard, that you could not understand the mentality of the people here. I had lived in Northern Ireland for a year and through my job believed that I had some idea about the culture, the problems, the way the people thought. Then, in a rather subtle way, I realised that I knew virtually nothing. One Saturday I was working with a talented young photographer called Niall Carson (whose photos appear in this book). That week I had interviewed Gerry Adams and was feeling pretty excited about the whole thing. I told Niall and asked him whether he knew Adams. 'Well actually I do,' he said rather innocently. I asked him how and he replied: 'Well actually my father spent some time in jail with him during the Troubles. He's a friend of the family, so he is.' Wherever you were in Northern Ireland you probably heard the thud of me coming back down to earth. I had learned my lesson about how little I knew about Northern Ireland. I just wish the Americans would.

*   *   *   *

The second major criticism of The Corrs is that for all their talent they produce harmless but essentially worthless pop music that should not be treated seriously or get the same sort of attention as other forms of music. *Irish Times'* journalist Kevin Courtney outlines this argument:

> I still don't think The Corrs have much substance as far as the style of their music is concerned. It is very broad-based mainstream music ... there is always this argument about what is mainstream? What's the point in playing something that only ten people want to listen to when you can play something that 10,000 people want to listen to?
>
> I don't think it's just a question of taste. I think music has progressed on its left field, on the stuff that goes against the mainstream. The underground stuff, the alternative music, has always been what has driven good rock music and I think The Corrs will always be middle-of-the-road, far more than say U2 ever were. That's just the way they play. That said, they are a lot better than The Cranberries, whose music is a terrible lie. They [The Cranberries] are trying to be an alternative rock band. What they are is this very bland, mainstream parody of a rock band. I think The Corrs are a much better band, have a much more focused sound and have a much greater vision about what they want to achieve.

But surely pop music is, by its very nature, less important than other forms of musical expression? No. Great pop can move the listener as readily as any other form, creating emotion with strong lyrics and overriding melodies. The fact that it is conveyed in a more accessible manner should not make it any less important. For example, Stevie Nicks sitting down in front of a piano in the middle of the night in

1976 and composing 'Dreams' is perhaps as beautiful as anything The Rolling Stones have produced. Pop music at its finest is therefore one of the strongest and most emotive mediums available. And it is even questionable whether The Corrs are even a pure pop band. At its best, the sound of The Corrs is a combination of pop, traditional and rock.

There are two common ways of judging the importance of art. First of all, the test could be that whatever gives artistic pleasure should be respected and appreciated for what it is, regardless of whether it has any artistic merit or not. Under this criteria artists such as Britney Spears and Westlife would be deemed important because they have given satisfaction to millions.

The second, and most popular, method of criticism is to question whether an artistic endeavour has pushed the boundaries of mankind. The Beatles initially wrote and performed pure pop, some of their early lyrics as shallow as Andrea on her sappiest day ('She loves you, yeah, yeah, yeah'), but eventually changed the musical landscape by creating music that was fundamentally different than what had been produced before. In an Irish context, U2 went further than any other band or musical act from Ireland and crossed boundaries that few dreamt possible.

The importance of The Corrs' music is completely subjective. Take the opinion of Irish journalist Michael Ross:

> What The Corrs do is not music. It's marketing; it's radio, commercially alluring. It's utterly soulless; it belongs to a tradition of commercially successful soulless noise but not to the Irish tradition of music.
>
> At its best, Irish traditional music is radical and beautiful and daring. What The Corrs produce has none of these qualities. There is a conservatism within the Irish tradition, certainly, and there is a conservatism to what The Corrs do. But it's a different kind of conservatism. Irish traditional music is conservative in the sense that many involved in it are wary of innovation and experimentation.

Ross believes this is understandable in an art form in which so few people are involved, which is constantly exposed to what the conservatives would see as a dilution by the dominant culture. 'However, even within Irish traditional music there is extraordinary radicalism,' he argues. 'The fiddle player Tommy Potts, for example, was one of the most inventive and radical traditional Irish musicians of the 20th century — "the Paganini of the fiddle" as Paddy Moloney of the Chieftains calls him — and though he was to an extent marginalised within the tradition, he still belonged to it and created something new within it.'

Ross believes there is nothing radical about The Corrs, other than their hunger for commercial success. He suggests there is nothing innovative about them beyond 'the perfection of their marketing'. While he is obviously very much anti-Corr, the criteria for judging Irish artists as espoused by Ross is a useful one. The issue is perhaps whether the music of The Corrs is 'radical, beautiful and daring'.

It's hard to pin down exactly what The Corrs' music is, because their styles have changed (or been changed for them) with each album. *Forgiven Not Forgotten* is full of originality, passion and, given the amount of traditional Irish music in it, daring. A strong case could be put that *Forgiven Not Forgotten* does have some of the attributes that Michael Ross was talking about.

For all its commercial success, *Talk on Corners* has never been regarded as a landmark album on the music scene. Given the number of producers involved and the extent to which the band tried to produce a hit and establish themselves in the British market, it would be difficult to suggest there was much passion involved outside the willowy parameters of Andrea's imagination. Some of the songs may sound beautiful, but *Talk on Corners* did not push the boundaries or challenge the frameworks that The Corrs had established with *Forgiven Not Forgotten*.

As most of the tracks on *Unplugged* had been released on the two earlier albums, or would be released on *In Blue*, or were cover versions, it would be unfair to judge the music on this album using these criteria.

In Blue perhaps falls somewhere in between *Forgiven Not Forgotten* and *Talk on Corners* applying Ross's criteria. While it was a progression over *Talk on Corners*, it was far from radical and though there were parts of the album that were beautiful, it would be an overstatement to call *In Blue* daring.

The Corrs get a cautious pass in the 'radical, beautiful and daring' test. They do not move any boundaries, nor do they question our existence. They may make us feel good about ourselves, our lives and the world in which we live, but they have not written themselves into the annals of music history.

But despite this, three things need to be remembered. For all the criticism, The Corrs are talented musicians who have been brought up on a stable diet of piano, guitar and violin from an early age. Furthermore, in Andrea they do have a truly natural performer who has the charisma of the very top acts. Finally, although they have not altered the musical boundaries, they have produced music that in some cases will be remembered longer than a good many other acts who are top of the pops at the current time. As Andy Murray suggests:

> Of course you have to have an understanding of an impact a band has had on society at large, and yes U2 are an influential band. But I don't think you could say that The Corrs are without influence in the sense that if they are a major group and played on the radio then they are going to have an impact. Without The Corrs, for example, you probably wouldn't have had B*Witched. They [B*Witched] are a celebration of the more flimsy aspect of what people like rather than the more solid aspect of The Corrs. This includes the song writing, the melody and the harmonies. In terms of harmonies The Corrs are absolute geniuses.

It would be too harsh a judgement to suggest that for all the success of The Corrs they have not produced music that is important. Although any music that stirs human emotion is valuable, songs such as 'Runaway', 'Toss the Feathers', 'Love to Love You', 'Only When I Sleep', 'One Night' and 'Give Me a Reason' do possess residual qualities that will ensure The Corrs are heard on our radios for several years to come.

*   *   *   *

The media's interest in The Corrs always intrigued me for its inaccuracy as much as its genuine information value. The Corrs themselves have often been critical of the stories written about them and the fact that journalists can get it so wrong. John Hughes has even said that one article on Andrea in an Irish national newspaper was a total fabrication and that the interview never took place. Although The Corrs appear overly sensitive about the way the media has reported on them, to some degree their criticism is valid. As the writing of this book was coming to an end, two stories on Andrea's love life appeared in British Sunday newspapers on the same day. One said that she was not dating Bono from U2 and that she was perfectly happy being single and dedicating herself to her career. The other story stated that she was supposedly smitten with a British record company executive! You can understand why The Corrs are cynical and dismissive. Still, given their profile and marketability there is no surprise that the media in Britain and Ireland will take every opportunity to write about them.

*   *   *   *

The third major criticism of The Corrs is that, especially since the start of the remixing, that they have sold their creative souls in order to achieve commercial success. These criticisms have come from varied sources, including the 'hard-Corr' fans.

But there is a more general level of criticism about this so-called selling out. The argument goes that The Corrs have changed dramatically in appearance since the *Forgiven Not Forgotten* days and the result has been that they are now more about image than music. Michael Ross suggests there is plenty of evidence to back up this theory:

> If you compare pictures of The Corrs early in their career with pictures of them later, you can see just how much image control has gone into them. The same thing has happened with their music. It's perfection of a sort, but artistically barren. I cannot see the point in spending one's life pursuing commercial success as they have done.
>
> One truly outstanding creative moment should, to any musician worth his or her salt, be worth more than just more and more commercial success, but whereas other commercially successful pop acts such as George Michael have used that success as the springboard for greater artistic experimentation and creativity, The Corrs have gone in the other direction. The more commercially successful they have become, the more bereft of imagination and adventurousness their music has become, not that it was particularly imaginative or daring in the first place.

Or as one Atlantic Records insider suggests:

> [The Corrs] are so talented and they did whatever they had to do to 'make it'. Their dream was music industry success and not necessarily growing as artists. I do think they are good people who try and steer clear of the 'fame' trap, and just want to play music for a living. But that's probably why they have such trouble in the US. No interesting story ... too boring ... not breaking any musical trends.

On the other side of the argument, John Hughes has, perhaps not surprisingly, suggested that the band is anything but manufactured. He believes that if he could manufacture a band like The Corrs he would do so every month. Ned Spoon, Minor Detail, Andrew Strong and

Robert Arkins are just some of the Irish acts that Hughes notes have come and gone in the big, bad music world. As he told *Hot Press*:

> First you have to have the talent. You have to have the natural ability for harmonies that they have. You have to be able to write songs the way they do. You have to have a sense of timing. The fact that they look good helps a lot. You need the windows of opportunity to be there — and to seize them. And then you've got to have the kind of disposition, which means that you're willing to work non-stop. And people call that manufactured?

Andrea has also commented on this supposed manufacturing of The Corrs. Her line is that it would have been virtually impossible to 'manufacture' The Corrs and that everything they do is 'honest'.

Few critics of the band believe that The Corrs have been manufactured in the sense that Andrea and John Hughes have defined the word. They're not the Spice Girls, not Boyzone. They're a family band who (mostly) write their own songs, rather than a bunch of strangers lumped together because they all look good and who are told to sing something someone else has written (to music played by other musicians).

There appears to be a difference between The Corrs' camp and their critics about what this term 'manufactured' actually means. What would appear to be a more accurate description of this criticism is that The Corrs have sold out their musical integrity for, some would suggest, 'the big buck'. In other words they have placed dollars and pounds above the desire to write creative, original music that marked *Forgiven Not Forgotten*.

On the face of it this argument has some substance. There was a major shift in musical direction from *Forgiven Not Forgotten* to *Talk on Corners*; with a move away from traditional Irish music to a more clearly defined pop sound that appeared specifically designed for radio airplay and universal sales. Again, *In Blue* was a shift from what had been produced before, although in another sense the greater direction employed by The Corrs suggests that it was an artistically more self-controlled album.

This debate about whether The Corrs sold out their art for commercial success is not unique to them. It has been going on for centuries in both philosophy and history. Dr Hugh Bredin, senior lecturer of philosophy at Queen's University in Belfast, does not see any dilemma in artists doing their best to make as much money as they can from their craft. According to him there is a clear distinction between art and commerce:

In a pure sense someone who sells sweets and tobacco at the corner shop is involved in commerce, while someone who performs, acts or sings is an artist even though some critics might not suggest what they are doing is art.

The general consensus in philosophical terms is that it does not really matter if the artist is trying to make money from their work, nor trying to reach a certain market with what they produce. From a philosophical point of view, it has no impact on the way the work is viewed artistically.

Dr Bredin maintains that throughout history artists, musicians and other persons of artistic ilk have attempted to sell their work and have had to do so out of necessity:

There would not have been many artists who would have been able to survive if all they were producing their art was for the mere enjoyment of it. Look at Mozart and what he produced. He wrote opera that was popular and he wrote it purposely in a way that was accessible to the masses. But there are few people today who say that his music wasn't great.

Much the same as musicians today, Dr Bredin says that he can think of few artists, writers or actors who performed their talent for anything other than money. 'Perhaps there were a few small poets who would write for the beauty of writing, but generally being an artist has been to most a way to make money and improve their standard of living.'

The common view in philosophy of art and aesthetics is that quality and popularity aren't necessarily the same thing. 'If you look at one of Ireland's great writers, W. B. Yeats, he also wrote detective studies, which weren't of artistic or literary value but for him an entertaining pastime,' says Dr Bredin.

Although a majority of philosophers suggest that the motives behind an artist performing aren't as important as the art that they produce, there are some limits. 'Ideally the motivation need not affect the art,' confirms Dr Bredin, 'but you could argue that if a band is artificially produced and comes together for the act of making money, well then perhaps motive is more relevant.'

Regardless of their motives, on a philosophical level The Corrs have not sold out. Like thousands of artists before them, from Shakespeare to Mozart to Van Morrison, they were able to pedal their art and make more than a comfortable living from it. Part of the reason why their critics have been quick to suggest that The Corrs sold out was over the issue of remixing. The facts suggest, however, that The Corrs have not remixed anywhere near the number of singles as other artists.

This criticism was given further credence by the fact that it was only when The Corrs started to release remixed singles that they achieved any sort of tangible commercial success in Britain. However, if anyone should take the blame for this it should be a music industry that often requires a single to be remixed before it is deemed accessible enough to be able to be played.

Furthermore, the facts suggest that the special edition of *Talk on Corners*, on which the remixed versions are contained, has sold around a quarter of the number of the standard version of the album outside Britain. Clearly people wanted the regular album, even though they might have heard the remixed version first.

This is not to say that The Corrs have always put their art before commerce. It could be argued that if The Corrs sold out it wasn't necessarily with the release of the remixes, but in the creation of the original *Talk on Corners* where well-known American producers were brought in to try and produce a sure-fire hit.

By taking a more hands-on approach with *In Blue,* and only bringing in professional producers when they couldn't go any further, The Corrs themselves acknowledged that, for all its worth, *Talk on Corners* was over-produced. Like it or loathe it, *In Blue* was certainly more about The Corrs and what they had to say than *Talk on Corners.*

It's difficult to judge if a band has 'sold out' when you remember that very few bands can elect to do things on their own terms and go against the record company. Sure, after the success of *Talk on Corners* The Corrs did have more power to chart their own direction, but in general they have performed and worked in an industry which has its own set of rules.

Remixing was, and is, central to gaining accessibility on radio stations. Pretty faces sell, as do wholesome images. People like to read about nice families. They want to know who stars of the pop world are going out with. They want to hear nice songs when they drive to and from work. They want to know (whether they like it or not) what Jim's favourite recipe is and for how long did he really go out with former Miss Ireland Andrea Roche?

If there is a culprit in The Corrs becoming more commercial it is not the band itself but the industry which demands a piece of everyone who enters into it. The Corrs have adapted to this in their desire to reach their potential. They have played by the rules, done the photo shoots, thousands of promotional appearances, shaken millions of hands, spoken to the right people and had their artistic ability shaped to cope with what the marketplace requires. In that sense they are no different to Mozart and the trials and tribulations that he went through.

Although they are not completely innocent victims in the big bad world of music, their careers have been marked by playing within the rules of the music industry. The result is that they have become both jaded and experienced. They have tried to reach their goals by adapting to what the unforgiving market wants. They have, in commercial terms, placed themselves in the marketplace as a product and asked, in the nicest possible fashion, for the consumer to purchase them.

Where this enters the debate about what is art and what is commerce is up to the individual. But what seems fairly certain is that the distinction has become blurred and has the critics scratching their heads and asking whether there is anything that can truly be regarded as artistic anymore? Art has perhaps been replaced by getting your face on *Top of the Pops*.

It is highly questionable whether The Corrs have sold out. What they would appear to have done, if anything, is adapt their music and style to an unrelenting industry that sees them act as puppets and market themselves like any other product. It would seem that this is a necessity to making it in the music industry in this time and place.

For all their talents and ambitions, The Corrs have fallen in the cracks between art and commerce. Natural musicians with a great passion for their craft, they have needed to adapt themselves and their image to suit the market-place. They have become to some degree, by their very involvement, victims of all that we despise in modern society.

Yet throughout it all The Corrs have largely tried to retain some musical integrity, some understanding of the passion that engulfed them all those years ago back in Dundalk. Amongst those traditions The Corrs fit. To say that they are merely stunners with nice voices would not be accurate. Nor would it be correct to suggest that they have nothing to say or that their music is necessarily worthless and has little intrinsic value.

CHAPTER 17

The Lasting Legacy of The Corrs

When you arrive in the English charts and you discover that all around you are Irish acts of different kinds and with different objectives, then that's gratifying. Coming from the 1960s, I know how unlikely that would have seemed then. If you had told anybody that Irish bands, regardless of format, were going to dominate the English charts, it would have been laughable. We were the joke of Europe. The butt-end of rock'n'roll. Now we dominate it and we get more criticism at home than we do abroad. I'm confused by that.

John Hughes (in Hot Press)

Diminutive and amazingly striking, Andrea Corr returns to the stage and looks at the 13,000-strong crowd at the *Manchester Evening News* arena with the gaze of a confident pop star. For over an hour and a half Andrea and her three siblings have rocked the arena, taking the crowd along for a ride that contains four albums, numerous hits, plenty of memories and for each of the Corrs, almost a biographical account of their lives.

It's Thursday April 5 2001 and The Corrs are in the middle of the *In Blue* tour, a series of concerts that have had to be rescheduled due to Andrea's health concerns. It's the second night in Manchester and the arena is again almost sold out. Fathers have brought their teenage daughters to the show, boyfriends have brought girlfriends, middle-aged women have come along with their friends and there is also a fair sprinkling of older people in the audience this evening. This is not a rock audience though. There are no passionate fans prepared to jump the stage to get just a touch of the band. There are no legions of teenage girls screaming their hearts out. This is an audience that is, if anything, civilised.

Two big screens at the side of the stage rain down images of Dundalk's finest exports and are essential for those at the back of the arena. Close up the girls look as though they are enjoying themselves, while their immaculate grooming is obvious. However, there are signs tonight that Andrea is not at her best and still recovering from her ear infections: the way she regularly looks at her sisters for support, the way she plays with her ear-piece. But she is still the effervescent, dynamic front person who has been so important in the success of The Corrs. She does not wear shoes, but that seems lost on an audience only too quick to praise her for what she is doing for them this evening: igniting, pulling, showing, flirting and yet never stopping to slow down.

Andrea stands in front of her crowd for the encore, the audience that she has captivated, cajoled, encouraged and almost pleaded to enjoy the music. Having performed a particularly energetic rendition of 'Breathless', the last song of the regular set, Andrea could be excused for also being out of breath. With that song The Corrs had lit the building with passion, dynamism and out-and-out energy. They had received their due reward with an overwhelming response from the crowd.

The performance had lifted the audience and demonstrated to any remaining doubters that The Corrs can play, entertain and be a world-class act.

*   *   *   *

I finished this book emotionally in Manchester one wet April evening. I had intended to bring over a photographer with me to photograph the band in concert and write the conclusion to two and a half years of effort. The mistake I made was that I was honest and said that the photos would be for this book. Naturally the management wasn't too happy with this and after around 30 phone calls, they finally declared that we would not be allowed to take photos. So my photographer and I decided to go to the concert anyway. It never fails to surprise me how popular The Corrs are with such a wide section of the population. There was everyone from school children to grannies going in to see The Corrs play ... what other band could do that? The telling impact of the band came when the friend I was with (who was not a great fan of The Corrs) said when 'Runaway' began 'that takes me back to when I sat my A levels'. Powerful.

*   *   *   *

As Andrea stands in front of the audience, perhaps for a moment reflecting on the often difficult year that she has had, she almost pauses for a moment. She looks to her right and finds Sharon Corr's eyes almost before she knows it. Sharon gives her a reassuring smile and then suddenly the band moves into 'So Young', one of the crowd's favourite songs and an instantly recognisable number that could only light the audience's fire.

The Corrs have sung this song hundreds of times before. But it still catches the imagination of the predominately middle-class audience.

They clap their hands, stamp their feet and join The Corrs in celebrating the fun of being alive.

In behind, Caroline Corr is almost literally thumping holes in her drum kit. Caroline, the most underrated of The Corrs, has had an amazing night and of the four, has probably given the most effort. She has set the pace of The Corrs' performance, energising the music and giving it emphasis and momentum.

At one point during 'So Young' Andrea turns to Caroline and you can almost feel the symmetry between the sisters. As if there is a telepathic bond, created not only by their closeness of age, but also by spending years sharing the same room.

Jim Corr has also had an impressive night, keeping the show running with ruthless professionalism and in his own way proving that once again he is the consummate professional musician. There are times during the show when his sound is almost too good, his timing too immaculate. He is not the star, but he is in control and helps provide reassurance for his sisters.

The pace rises as 'So Young' moves to its exciting and thrilling conclusion. The crowd is losing itself and instead of looking and admiring The Corrs, now they are fully involved in the concert. *They* are part of the entertainment. 'Clap your hands Manchester,' Jim says in the middle of the song, and his reaction is universally approved and greeted by a crowd only too willing to obey.

The song ends with Andrea giving the crowd everything she has got … and just for a moment she lets herself go and gets taken over by her passion. It is refreshing, pure and beautiful all at the same time. 'Go, go, go,' someone shouts near the back. The crowd has gone absolutely berserk, the smell of perspiration filling the arena and only being taken over by the screams and whistles of the audience.

The Corrs have won over Manchester with their natural talent, enthusiasm and passion for what they do. They are the ultimate package, the ultimate provider of good times. It was telling that 'So Young', a song about making the most of opportunities when you are young and free, was so popular.

Somewhere amongst the four Corrs on stage were three little girls and a little boy who grew up following their parents perform around a little area on the east of Ireland.

Somewhere amongst the glasses of beer, the over-inflated tour programmes, the touchy arena staff, the enthusiastic backing band, the million pound lighting and the big dressing-rooms, were a family band that thought they could get a gig in an Irish movie.

Somewhere amongst the limousines, the propositions from soap stars, the friendships with musical gods and the inevitable price of success that needed to be paid were four children who used to attend the Church of the Redeemer, who took piano lessons and who used to spend weekends playing with their friends on the streets of Dundalk.

Jim, the spotty kid who used to work at Tescos in Dundalk. Sharon, the naturally talented but somewhat lazy violin student. Caroline, the girl who could remember endless lists of drinks at McManus'. Andrea, the drama queen, the lead actor and the natural mimic who entertained her family from almost day one.

Up here on stage this evening they are The Corrs. They are musicians, entertainers and, to some degree, actors. They inspire, create, entertain and emotionally move. They are talented and they give pleasure to millions of people around the world. *However, what is their lasting legacy?*

In the first place, it can safely be concluded that The Corrs are clear examples of Modern Ireland in action. They represent everything that is good with Éire in the late 20th and early 21st centuries: the opportunity, the freedom to show expression, the desire and ability to make their mark not just in Ireland, but throughout the world.

They have prospered partly because of the time and place that they were brought up in. They have had opportunities that their parents did not, while they have embraced this freedom now being espoused in Ireland.

The Corrs have benefited from and grown alongside the success of a host of other Irish acts, such as U2. They have not felt burdened by being Irish in the global marketplace. They have put their product into the international arena and waited for it to be judged like everyone else's.

The Corrs are ambassadors for the new Irish enlightenment. They reflect the opportunity that hallmarks this new era. Ireland is almost as much a hero of this story as The Corrs themselves.

I asked at the beginning of this book whether The Corrs were talented musicians or whether they were just four pretty faces who got up and sang nice songs in harmony? Forgetting their appearances for a moment, the evidence is conclusive that The Corrs are all individually and collectively talented musicians.

Jim's musical ability was noted at secondary school. Even during his wilderness years as a session musician on the notoriously difficult Irish circuit, he somehow managed to survive financially. Not only that, but he made friends and gained respect from his peers as a talented professional. Like John Hughes, Jim's vision for what was possible and his determination to make something of himself and his family band makes it clear that the eldest Corr is not only a talented musician, but a fine leader.

The musical talents of Sharon and Caroline have also been well documented in this book. Although not a child prodigy as some media have portrayed her as being, Sharon possessed all the essential attributes of a fine violinist. She also had a tremendous voice that impressed all those who heard her.

Caroline was also musically talented. David Foster's comment that she was one of the 'few chicks' he had met that could hold a beat is testimony to her musical ability. The fact that she too had a beautiful voice suggests that, although not as extroverted as her sisters, from an early age she was as musically gifted.

The musical and general artistic background of Andrea suggests a performer with enormous ability. The comments of her former schoolteachers paint a picture of a girl with a true talent for anything musical or dramatic. The view of close friends also paints a picture of an extroverted young person who liked to be in the limelight. In short, Andrea has been a natural performer almost since she was born.

When you add the fact that the girls can harmonise better than almost any other band and have the advantage of having similar voices, it is impossible to suggest that they are not anything but musically talented.

*   *   *   *

Watching The Corrs in Manchester was an emotional experience for me as this chapter in my life was ending. The Corrs had been with me from my first days in Ireland and were symbolic of my time here. I watched them sing, play and dance and it was the strangest feeling. I felt emotional, delighted to be there and yet somehow distanced from the whole thing. As if it was all surreal. On several occasions tears came to my eyes. On more than one song I looked up and gave thanks for the opportunity to ask questions and have experiences that I could have only dreamed about before I left New Zealand. As The Corrs played their final song of the night, 'Toss the Feathers', I thought of Dundalk, shook with emotion and bawled my eyes out. I left the arena in a daze, proud of what I had done with this book and in some ways thrilled that I had seen The Corrs perform at the peak of their career.

*   *   *   *

Given that The Corrs are musically talented, the second question posed in this book was whether they sold out their music souls in their quest for commercial success? This question is difficult to answer. The changes that took place in their musical style from the outstanding *Forgiven Not Forgotten* album through *Talk on Corners* and *In Blue* suggest a band catering to a large extent for the supposed tastes of their market. The water is made murkier by the record company politics that went on in America to obtain sure-fit hits with *Talk on Corners*. The result was an album that The Corrs were not entirely happy with and that had too many weepy, immature songs on it.

Although *Talk on Corners* would sell more copies than the band themselves had realistically hoped for, the large input of outside producers and songwriters points to The Corrs compromising their musical style and, perhaps, their musical heritage in the process. The Corrs were not totally to blame for this. External pressure placed on them from their record company, and faceless executives who thought they knew best, saw The Corrs packaged like any other commodity.

To be successful in the music industry today you have to play the game, pay the paymaster and sell your natural talents to image consultants and mass marketing experts. The result of all this was that The Corrs started producing remixed songs, appearing on covers of magazines, talking to tabloid newspapers and becoming personalities almost as much as musicians.

Their collaboration with well-known producers and songwriters also saw questions raised about whether The Corrs were in danger of having their music taken over by professional hit-makers. Somewhere in all of this there was the risk of The Corrs forgetting why they had entered this industry in the first place.

However, they do deserve credit for realising what was happening to their careers and their image. The music and passion of spirit that had been instilled in them in Dundalk all those years ago was too strong, too ruthless to be ignored for too long. After their commercial success with *Talk on Corners*, their status enabled them to call the tune to a much larger degree with the writing, production and overall direction of *In Blue*. The Corrs were back to where they began: in control of their own work.

But The Corrs were now big business and everybody wanted a piece of them. They were fair game in the media. This, of course, lead to questions about their private lives and the substance of their work. They still had, to some degree, to feed the commercial tiger. And whether they liked it or not, they still had to play the promotional game if they wanted to sell albums.

To say that The Corrs have sold out would be wrong. If any criticism could be levelled at them it would be that they have been too hungry for success, too ambitious, too willing to run that extra mile. Although it is perfectly acceptable for an artist to sell their work to as many people as possible, to lose sight of the beauty of your art is an inherent danger.

To reach their goals The Corrs have had to become part of the ballgame. They have had to build their profile by doing the shows, putting in the hours and using whatever means possible to establish themselves as a brand. At times the music has appeared lost in this circus.

You have to feel for The Corrs and appreciate that, although success has changed them, they have remained relatively normal. The excesses of pop stardom have not passed them totally, but they appear to have remained well-grounded people who know that fame is fleeting. In that respect their parents deserve a lot of the credit for not only their success, but also the way the band has handled it.

While many of The Corrs' long-term fans pine for the days when only 2,000 people turned up for their gigs and when they almost knew the band on a first-name basis, their concerns for the band's direction have been unjustified. The Corrs have proven popular because they are fundamentally musically talented, because they can write catchy songs, because they look good and because in Andrea they have a natural performer who has the charisma to take the band's audience into another world.

When you add the above together, to expect The Corrs not to have developed and significantly increased their worldwide following would be naïve in the extreme.

Critics may also say that, although The Corrs are musically talented and may not necessarily have sold their artistic souls to the highest bidder, the music they have produced has little cultural significance. This argument has greater potential than the other propositions, as The Corrs are operating in the world of pop, even though their music at its heart is a combination of pop and traditional Irish music. It does not necessarily follow that good pop is not as important as other forms of music. At its best pop can move an audience more than any other form of music can.

Forgiven Not Forgotten changed the boundaries in the sense that it was another important example of an Irish band combining the traditional elements of their national music with an accessible pop sound. In short, the music appealed to many.

U2 proved that for Irish bands to be popular it was important to produce a universal sound and The Corrs tried to do that. Although they should not have felt tied to writing and performing traditional Irish songs, the trade-off was that in writing songs that were more universal they risked writing songs that said nothing and were similar to what many other bands were producing.

Overall, The Corrs should be widely respected as musicians, entertainers and performers, but they have decided not to set out and ultimately move the artistic boundaries of our very existence. As yet they have not pushed the boundaries of the environment they have created and played in. They have not asked universal questions, demanded answers to problems and, rather dramatically, not questioned in their own minds perhaps the one question that everyone asks at one stage and would like the answer from artists: *why are we here?*

This is not to say that what The Corrs do and have done is not important. It is. Their talents and art have brought satisfaction to millions of people around the world. We should appreciate The Corrs for what they do, their talents, their abilities to take their audiences to another world, but we should be realistic about their impact in a cultural sense. We should appreciate that they are fundamentally pop stars and not social commentators. They have not helped set the agenda nor embraced in their art the serious questions in the lives of their audiences.

While the medium of pop music does not necessarily always lend itself to serious contemplation, The Corrs have had the opportunity through their music to make some serious statements about the world around them. Some suggest that as The Corrs are a pop band they have been unable to write about serious topics, that it was outside their brief. That rather than Andrea writing and singing about the anguish of being 25, she could perhaps have taken a wider view and sung about serious topics.

Although a more mature album, *In Blue* was a lost opportunity for The Corrs to express themselves a little more forcefully with the subject matter of their music. While they made public comments that showed they did care about certain issues, they did not include this in their art. Part of the reason could be that because The Corrs have been so determined, so hungry for success and worked so hard that somewhere they have lost sight of the world around them. That they have become isolated within the family cocoon and at some stage lost touch with reality in an artistic sense. The situation is also made worse by the fact that the band's most prolific writer, Andrea, from the age of sixteen has had very little experience of living a normal life.

The Corrs are entertainers and musicians of the highest order, but for whatever reason they have decided not to push the boundaries of their art and culture. This is only important in quantifying what their lasting legacy will be. It should never disguise the enjoyment that they have given to so many millions of people.

The Corrs have made living on this planet a great deal more pleasant. They have made us feel good about life and ourselves in general. They have provided a ray of light and a beacon of hope. This is all very worthy but this should not be confused with cultural significance. The lasting legacy of The Corrs will be as entertainers and musicians of the highest order.

The story of The Corrs is romantic and should illustrate to anyone who has dreams that they are achievable if you work hard, believe in yourself and never forget the *real* reason why you are doing it.

*   *   *   *

On April 5 2001 a girl of about eleven lined up with her father to collect tickets to see The Corrs play that evening at the Manchester arena. Her eyes sparkled when asked whether she liked the band, what her favourite song was, which was her favourite member, what her favourite album was? Such was the expectation, she looked as if Father Christmas were coming that evening.

For just a second she showed that, whatever you think of The Corrs and their music, you couldn't question the enjoyment that they give to so many. Whether you think they push the boundaries or make a real difference to our way of life, you couldn't question their impact.

For some reason when I looked into that young girls' eyes and witnessed her big smile nothing else seemed important.

*   *   *   *

As I reflect on this book and an important time of life it is hard not to think fondly of The Corrs. Although I never did get to meet them, to me the people connected with the story that I met from around Ireland and overseas will always be what this book is about. The countless cups of coffee, the off the record conversations, the drafts, the emails with the editor of this book, Brian Hallinan, and the self-doubt. There were times when I questioned why I was writing this, times when I asked myself whether this was a professional task or whether it was personal. Was I just a fan who happened to write for a living? I can offer no explanation, only to say that from that Sunday night in September 1998 when I first saw The Corrs play on television, there have been more ups than downs. More pluses than minuses. It has been a journey about understanding both The Corrs and myself at the same time. I don't claim to know The Corrs, but hopefully in this book I have demonstrated the impact that The Corrs have had, both on me and the world at large. I hope that you have enjoyed both journeys.

Bibliography

BOOKS

Ardagh, John, *Ireland and the Irish, Portrait of a Changing Society*, 1995.

Barry, Frank, *Between Traditions and Modernity: Cultural Values and the Problems of Irish Society*, 1987.

Bishop, Patrick, *The Irish Empire*, 1999.

Branson, Richard, *Losing My Virginity — The Autobiography*, 1998.

Bredin, Hugh, Santoro-Brienza Liberato, *Philosophies of Art and Beauty — Introducing Aesthetics*, 1999.

Collinson, John, *Van Morrison: Inarticulate Speech of the Heart*, 1998.

Cornwell, Jane, *The Corrs*, 1999.

Cruikshank, Ben, *Van Morrison: Into the Sunset*, 1996.

Dunphy, Eamon, *The Unforgettable Fire: The Story of U2*, 1987.

Freeth, Mark, *The Corrs — 21st Century Celts*, 1998.

Gaster, Paul, *Corner to Corner — The Corrs: The Authorised Behind the Scenes Book*, 1999.

Glatt, John, *The Chieftains — The Authorised Biography*, 1998.

Hopstandter, Albenl and Kuhns, Richard, *Philosophies of Art and Beauty*, 1995.

Kenneally, Thomas, *The Great Shame — A Story of the Irish in the Old World and New*, 1999.

McArthur, Brian (Ed.), *The Penguin Book of Twentieth-Century Speeches*, 1999.

McCrum, Mark, *The Craic*, 1998.

O'Brien, Edna, *Mother Ireland*, 1991.

O'Connor, Nuala, *Bringing It All Back Home*, 1993.

O'Toole, Fintan, *The Irish Times Book of the Century*, 1999.

Rogan, Johnny, *Van Morrison — A Portrait of an Artist*, 1984.

Turner, Steve, *Van Morrison — Too Late to Stop Now*, 1993.

Waters, John, *Race of Angels — Ireland and the Genesis of U2*, 1994.

Waters, John, *Modern Ireland*, 1996.

FILMS/TELEVISION

The Commitments, 20th Century Fox, 1991.
The Corrs at the Ambassador's Residence (not screened), 1996.
The Corrs: Live At Lansdowne Road, Atlantic, 2000.
The Corrs — Live at The Royal Albert Hall, 1998.
The Corrs Unplugged, Warner Music and MTV, 1999.
Evita, Hollywood Pictures/Paramount, 1997.
The Gathering, A Celebration of Irish Culture and Tradition, Sony Music, 1997.
The Late Late Show (RTÉ), May 16 1997.
The Late Late Show (RTÉ), July 2000.
Pavarotti and Friends, 1998.
The Quest for Camelot, Atlantic, 1998.
The Right Time Video (Norwegian Television), 1998.

PRESS RELEASES

Warner Music Ireland — Talk on Corners Release, October 1997.

NEWSPAPERS AND MAGAZINE ARTICLES

Argus, (Dundalk) July 6 1996.
Argus, August 30 1996.
Argus, September 6 1996.
Argus, July 17 1998.
Argus, August 23 1998.
Argus, November 20 1998.
Australian Musician, autumn 97.
Baltimore Sun, March 5 1999.
Belfast News Letter, January 9 1999.
Belfast News Letter, January 14 1999.
Belfast News Letter, July 31 2000.
Belfast Telegraph, November 17 1997.
Belfast Telegraph, July 19 2000.
Billboard, July 9 1994.
Billboard, July 22 1995.
Billboard, October 17 1998.
Billboard, April 10 1999.
Boston Globe, October 28 1998.

Boston Globe, March 22 1999.
Christchurch Press, February 20 1998.
Christchurch Press, February 21 1998.
Christchurch Press, February 23 1998.
CLEO, June 1998.
Cosmopolitan, November 1998.
Daily Mail, January 1 1999.
Daily Mirror, June 10 1996.
Daly Mirror, August 25 2000.
Daily Record, September 1998.
dSide magazine, March 1999.
Daily Telegraph, January 21 1997.
Daily Telegraph, September 20 2000.
Daily Telegraph, March 9 2001.
Drum Media, July 16 1996.
Dundalk Democrat, April 4 1970.
Dundalk Democrat, March 6 1999.
Eres, October 16 1998.
Gazette, June 6 1998.
Guardian, December 6 1998.
Heat, January 1999.
Heat, April 2 1999.
Highlife (British Airways in-flight magazine), May 1999.
Hot Press, December 10 1997.
Hot Press, March 1999.
Hot Press, Christmas/New Year 1999–2001
Hot Press, September 2000.
Hot Press, 2001 Annual, Christmas/New Year, 2000–2001.
Hot Press, January 17 2001.
Independent (London), January 20 1999.
In Dublin, July 15–July 28 1999.
Ireland on Sunday, July 11 1999.
Ireland on Sunday, July 18 1999.
Ireland on Sunday, November 28 1999.
Ireland on Sunday, July 9 2000.
Irish Echo, January 30 1997.
Irish Independent, March 24 1999.
Irish Independent, April 9 1999.
Irish Independent, April 11 1999.
Irish Independent, July 13 1999.
Irish Independent, July 14 2000.
Irish Star, July 4 1998.

Irish Star, April 9 1999.
Irish Star, July 6 2000.
Irish Star, July 10 2000.
Irish Star, July 21 2000.
Irish Star, August 4 2000.
Irish Star, September 6 2000.
Irish Star, November 11 2000.
Irish Star, March 7 2001.
Irish Star, July 19 2001.
The Irish Times, December 22 1995.
The Irish Times, July 5 1996.
The Irish Times, December 24 1996.
The Irish Times, September 26 1998.
The Irish Times, November 26 1998.
The Irish Times, January 13 1999.
The Irish Times, January 16 1999.
The Irish Times, February 20 1999.
The Irish Times, March 12 1999.
The Irish Times, June 29 1999.
The Irish Times, August 3 1999.
The Irish Times, November 26 1999.
The Irish Times, December 30 1999.
The Irish Times, March 8 2000.
The Irish Times, July 16 2000.
The Irish Times, July 19 2000.
Irish Voice, March 17 2001.
MAN magazine, December 1998.
Mirror, January 11 1999.
Mirror, May 9 2000.
Mojo Magazine, May 1999.
New York Post, February 16 1999.
The New York Times, January 15 2001.
News of the World, September 22 1998.
Ottawa Sun, October 17 1998.
Philadelphia Daily News, March 11 1999.
Q Magazine, July 1995.
Q Magazine, September 1998.
Q Magazine, November 1998.
Q Magazine, February 1999.
Q Magazine, June 1999.
Q Magazine, July 1999.
Rhythm Magazine, May 1999.

RTÉ Guide, January 26 1996.
RTÉ Guide, March 13 1998.
Spectator, August 24 1991.
Straits Times, September 24 1998.
Straits Times, September 26 1998.
Sun, March 19 1999.
Sun, April 9 1999.
Sun, April 23 1999.
Sunday Independent, April 11 1999.
Sunday Independent, May 30 1999.
Sunday Independent, June 20 1999.
Sunday Independent, September 12 1999.
Sunday Independent, June 18 2000.
Sunday Independent, July 16 2000.
Sunday Independent, December 17 2000.
Sunday Life, February 4 1996.
Sunday Mirror, January 17 1999.
Sunday Morning Herald, January 21 1997.
Sunday Tribune, October 1997.
Sunday World, February 28 1999.
The Express, August 29 1998.
This Morning (television interview), May 29 1998.
The Sunday Times, November 19 2000.
The Times, October 31 1998.
The Times, December 7 1998.
The Times, December 18 1998.
Top of the Pops Magazine, October 1998.
Undercover (Australia), Issue 8, February 1998.
USA Today, April 2 1999.
VIP Magazine (Ireland), August 2000.
Washington Post, September 11 1991.
Washington Times, June 14 1998.

TOUR PROGRAMMES

The Corrs — Talk on Corners Programme, 1998.
The Corrs: Talk on Corners Tour, December 1998–March 1999.
The Corrs: Tour In Blue, October 2000–January 2001.
The Corrs — Tour Programme, May–July 1999.

WEBSITES

The author wishes to point out that more information on The Corrs can be obtained from *Hot Press'* website (www.hotpress.com).

www.corrsonline.com

http://www.olografix.org/krees/foster.htm- The Unofficial David Foster Home Page.